The Mandocello

by Mark E. Freemantle

Online Audio

To access the online audio recording go to:

WWW.MELBAY.COM/30770MEB

WWW.MELBAY.COM

The Mandocello

Foreword

It has been over 100 years since *The Bickford Method for Mando-cello* was published. Not only has it been out of print for a considerable period of time, the Bickford method book was written in treble, or "universal" clef, which is not the logical clef for a bass-range instrument. It is time for a new mandocello method book, written in bass clef. I hope that this book, ***The Mandocello***, will fill that need. Thank you for purchasing this copy.

I organized the method book to provide a basic introduction to the mandocello and offer playable tunes while progressively conveying the necessary theory and technique. Coincidentally, this is the same approach used by Myron A. Bickford.

Section 1: Introduction, the Basics, covers the essential elements of holding the instrument and pick, tuning, and some fundamental tenets of music theory. *Section 1* goes into great detail about proper technique and how playing the mandocello is unlike playing a guitar or mandolin. Try not to rush through this section; it includes a lot of the details a teacher would cover during approximately the first month of face-to-face lessons.

Section 2: Tunes, Techniques and Theory, contains tunes for solo mandocello, and mandocello parts from orchestral or ensemble arrangements. Most method books include duets for a student and teacher; the assumption is that the book will be used by a student taking formal lessons with a teacher, or that the reader has a partner available to play the second duet part. Formal instruction is very valuable and, by all means, take lessons if you can find a mandocello teacher. The premise of this book is that a teacher may not be readily available and you might have to learn by yourself.

Section 3: Becoming an Advanced Mandocellist, addresses the challenges of learning new tunes, becoming familiar with the fretboard further up the neck, the tenor clef, chords, and sight reading. Etudes and chords are introduced in a precursory fashion whereby the student can determine how to proceed.

The Mandocello is written for beginning mandocellists, which may include people who play other fretted instruments. Both guitarists and mandolinists will find comparisons of their instruments to the mandocello. Although *Section 1* is basic, or introductory, I strongly suggest that even experienced players work through it to gain the techniques and insights that make playing the mandocello both a joy and a challenge.

Special Thanks

I am deeply indebted to two special people: Norman Levine and Marilynn Mair. The late Norman Levine, the founder of the Classical Mandolin Society of America, sponsored a concert in Silver Spring, Maryland on March 4, 1995, featuring Marilynn Mair on mandolin. I studied with Marilynn at her summer camp, the American Mandolin and Guitar Summer School (AMGuSS). I attended the camp for several years and got to know her as both an accomplished performer and patient teacher. It was due in part to her encouragement that I wrote this book.

Table of Contents

Section 1 Introduction—The Basics

1.1 Types of Mandocellos

Modern mandocellos come in two general designs: a design similar to a mandolin and another modeled after modern guitars. The Gibson K1-style mandocello, illustrated below, has a teardrop or oval shape. The guitar-style models are similar to a flat-top, or archtop guitar, both illustrated below.

K-Style Mandocello

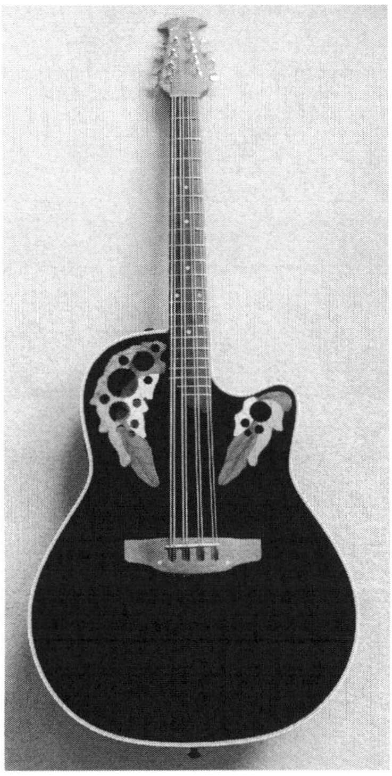

Flat-top mandocello

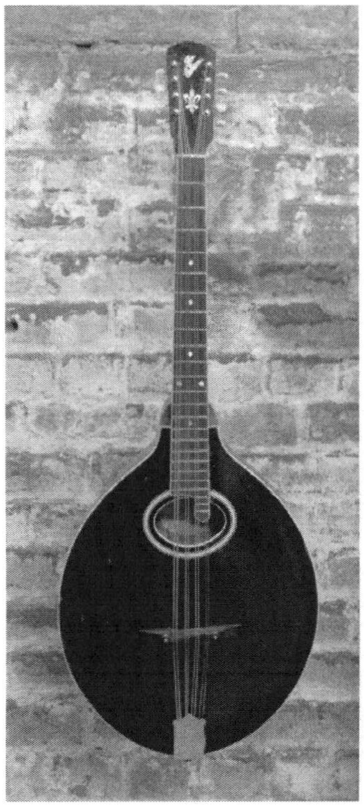

Archtop Mandocello

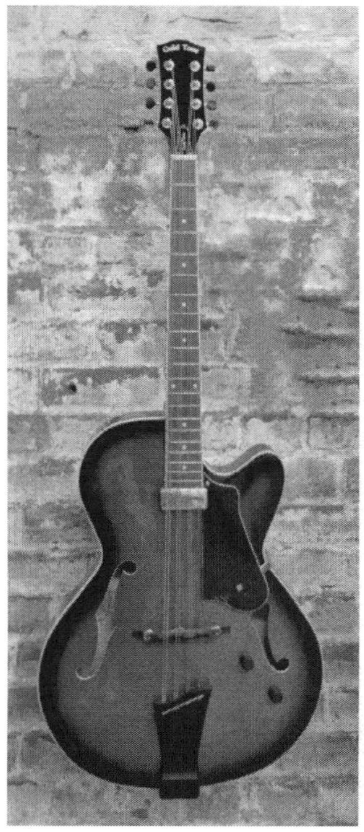

It is a matter of preference as to which model to choose. Scale lengths are similar to guitars and range from 24.75" to 25.5". More recent models include pickups that allow for amplification.

1.2 Holding the Mandocello

There are two basic approaches to holding the mandocello: 1) the classical guitar style, which uses either a footstool for the left leg, or a cushion and 2) the folk style which requires no footstool but places the instrument on the right leg. Playing with a strap and standing might be a third option, but it is not common to practice while standing. Try playing without a strap to facilitate learning the critical details related to sitting, holding the instrument, and arm placement.

The following pictures illustrate the two basic options.

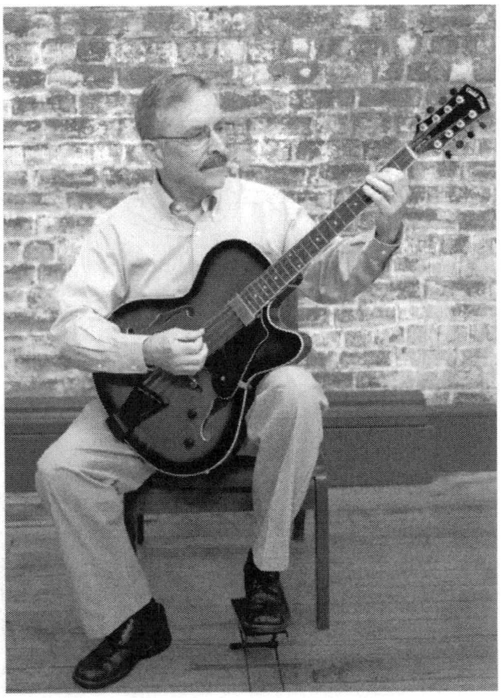

Figure 1: Raising the left leg with a footstool

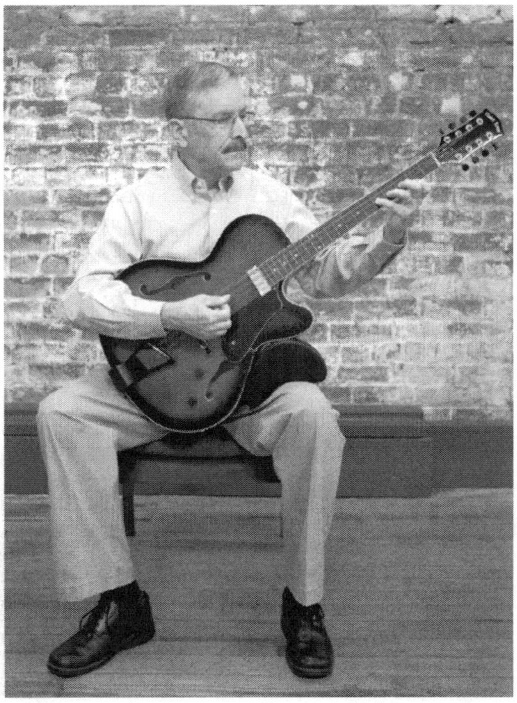

Figure 2: Using a support cushion

In the traditional classical position, the left foot rests on a footstool, adjusted as needed, and the right foot remains flat on the ground. While the left hand must extend outward from the body, notice that the right hand is comfortably in the middle of the instrument. The neck of the instrument is at an approximate 45-degree angle; the neck should not be parallel to the floor when using either a footstool or support cushion.

An alternate classical position uses a cushion or support device which raises the instrument and allows both feet to remain on the floor. For either position, it is important to use a chair that has a flat seat that is not sloping backwards. Try to sit in a way that allows 75% of the weight to be on the seat and 25% on the feet. Mandolinists may have a greater tendency to lean over the instrument; try to sit upright with a relaxed, but straight back.

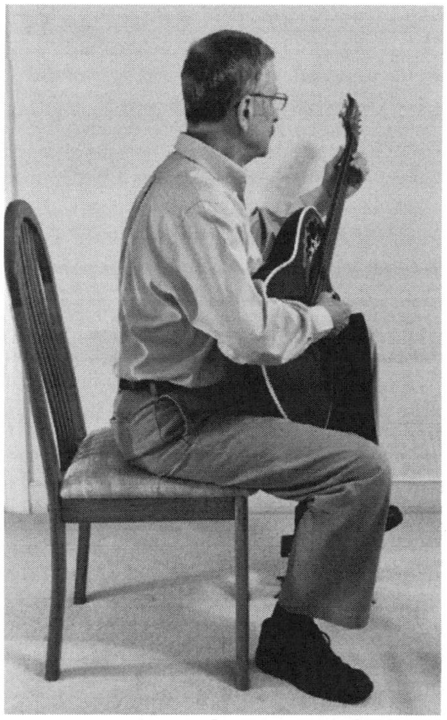

Figure 3: Seated in a straight-back chair and using a footstool

The classical position is often used for the oval-shaped mandocello. Some mandocellists may also use a strap or leather cloth to hold the instrument in place. The cloth can be used on either leg.

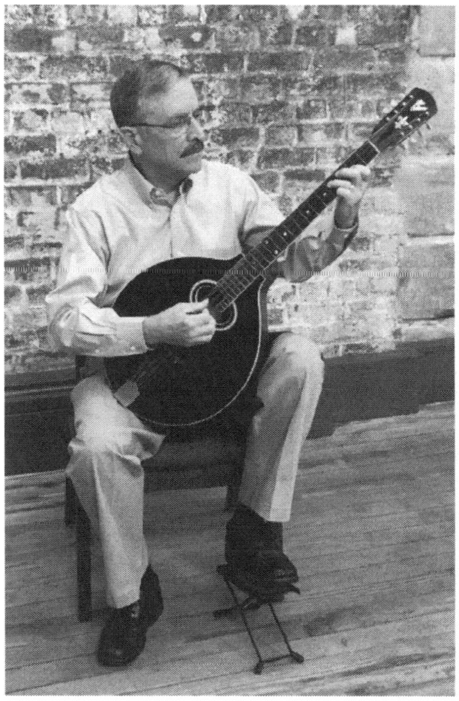

Figure 4: Classical position with cloth on left leg

The second approach is called the folk position; both feet are on the ground and the left arm remains closer to the body.

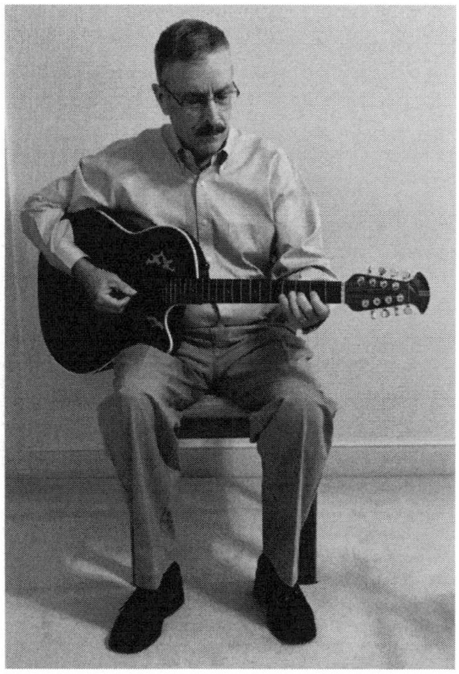

Figure 5: Folk position

Which method should you use? If you play classical guitar, the choice is obvious. What about transitioning from mandolin? I strongly recommend trying the classical style. The folk style, while appearing comfortable and almost natural, has two common pain points: 1) The right shoulder is typically "hiked-up" and can cause nerve-related issues because of the misalignment of the neck and shoulder. 2) The left arm extends outward from the body, causing challenges with fingering notes and general tiredness from excessive reaching. Whichever method you choose, if pain ensues, consider changing your position, or reducing your practice time. While a strap is unnecessary, it is often used to provide some assurance of safety and convenience.

1.3 The Left Hand

The position of the left-hand thumb is very important. Before placing your left hand on the neck raise your left arm as if you are about to grasp the neck. Now, close all four fingers until the thumb and fingers touch. Ideally, the thumb will touch both the index (first) and second finger. This is the "C-clamp" preparation for the left hand. See illustration below.

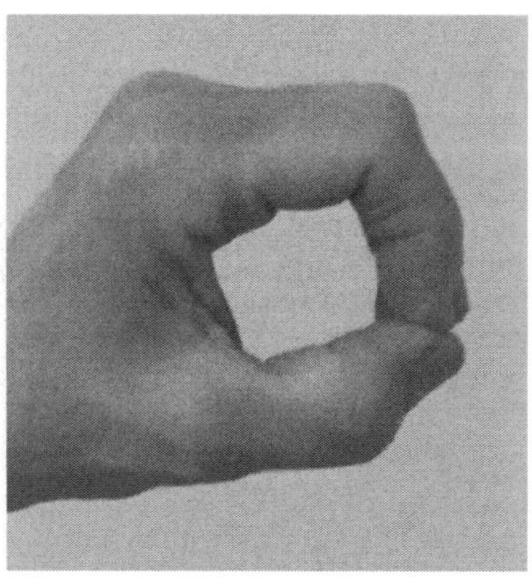

Figure 6: "C-clamp" grip

Notice that the thumb is primarily touching the tip of the two fingers in the illustration and the first knuckle of the thumb is slightly flexed. Adjust the hand slightly so the primary contact is with the second finger only. This is the preferred orientation and will allow the most flexibility in reaching the notes with all four fingers, as you will discover later. Practice opening the hand, with fingers spread wide, and then close it, touching the thumb and second finger, tip-to-tip. The hand will eventually default to this position. This will become second nature with practice and is commonly referred to as <u>muscle memory</u>.

Now change the C-clamp by touching all four finger tips together, and angling them so that the pinky extends past the ring finger (finger 3), finger 3 extends past the middle finger (finger 2), and the index finger (finger 1) is slightly behind finger 2. The thumb should now contact finger 1 on the tip and finger 2 on the side.

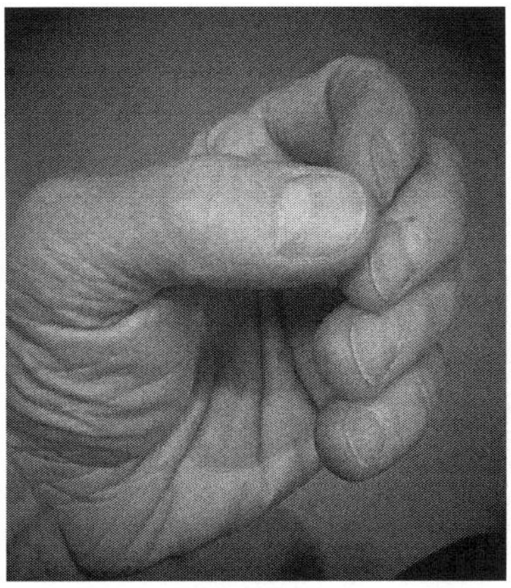

Figure 7: C-clamp extended

Place the thumb on the backside of the neck. The first knuckle should touch the neck near the middle. Do not allow the tip of the thumb to extend above the edge of the fretboard. Do not cradle the neck of the mandocello in your hand; there should be a gap between the neck and your palm. See illustrations.

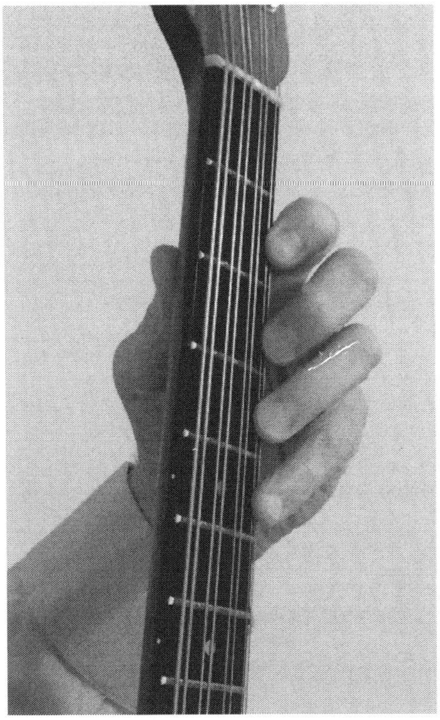

Figure 8: Fingers extended

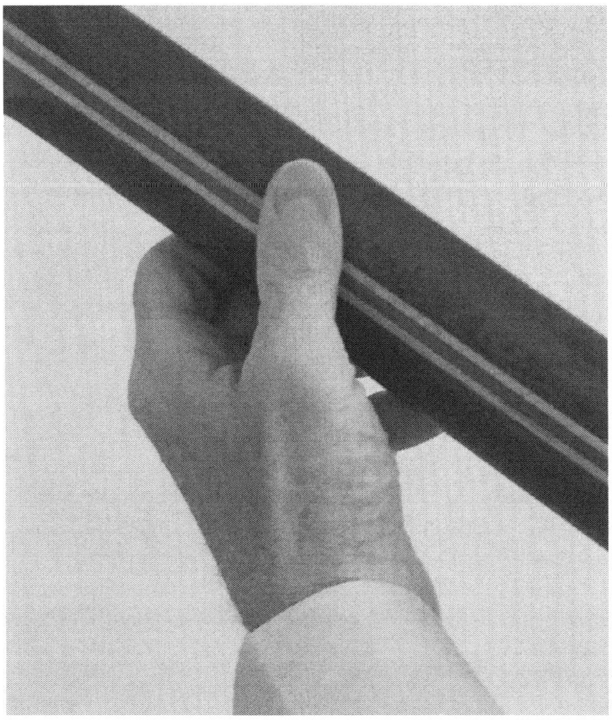

Figure 9: Proper thumb placement

The fingers of the left hand should curl over the fretboard and touch the strings as needed. Touch the four fingers on the first pair of strings; there is no need to press down. Align the thumb directly below the second fret. This should become your "home position" and is where your hand will default to when you first pick up the mandocello. Practice finding this position. Lower your left hand to the side. Relax, lift and place. This too will become second-nature muscle memory. Please note: At this point we are working on the proper hand placement on the neck. The fingers are likely touching each other and don't spread sufficiently to allow one-finger per fret coverage. The ability to separate the fingers will become essential. We will cover that later.

NOTE: Holding the instrument incorrectly can lead to a weak, arched left wrist. As a beginning mandocellist, you should constantly evaluate how you are sitting and holding the mandocello. The wrist should be straight and relaxed when positioned correctly.

1.4 Choosing and Holding the Pick

The size, shape and thickness of the pick is largely a matter of preference, do not assume, however, that the pick you normally use for guitar or mandolin should be the same pick you will use when playing the mandocello. Because of the thickness of the mandocello strings, it is often necessary to use a larger pick, both in size and thickness. Passages requiring a smooth, connected approach (*legato*), may sound better when using a pick with a more rounded point. Experimentation will determine which pick to use for the style of music played.

NOTE:If the mandocello is your first plectrum instrument, use a thinner pick initially. Try a medium guitar-style pick or one within the range of 0.46 mm and 0.73 mm. The increased flexibility of a thin pick will facilitate proper hand-wrist motion in the right hand; for a beginner, the tonality of the sound is of secondary concern.

The way you hold the pick is one of the key factors in determining the tone quality of the sound produced. There are two approaches: In the first, the pick is held parallel to the strings and contacts the strings equally on either side of the pick; in the second approach, the pick is held at an angle to the strings such that only one edge of the pick touches the strings on a downstroke and the opposite edge of the pick touches the strings on an upstroke. Learn both methods as they can serve different purposes regarding tone and its relationship to the style of music played. The two ways to hold the pick differ based on the orientation of the thumb: When the pick is parallel to the strings, we relax the thumb, or place it in **extension**, that is, there is no bending of the interphalangeal joint of the thumb (the knuckle closest to the thumbnail). See illustration.

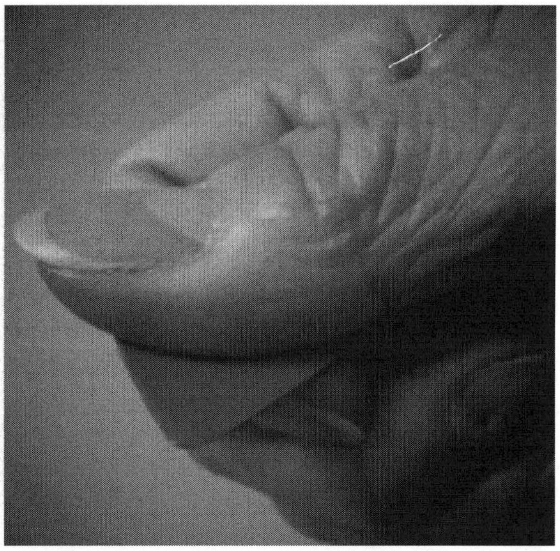

Figure 11: Pick hold with thumb in extension

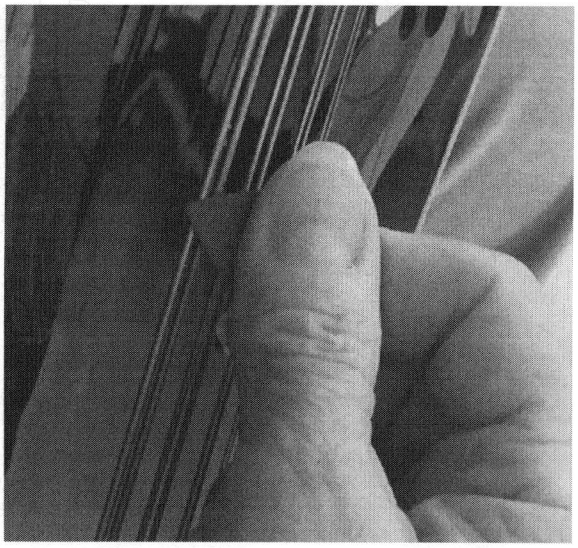

Figure 10: Thumb in extension with pick parallel to string

In the second approach, the thumb knuckle is elevated, or in **flexion**. The edge of the pick strikes the strings and can cause pick movement unless you apply a firm grip. I consider the resulting sound harsh, as compared to an extension-thumb approach, but this approach may be necessary for fast pick movement, or to achieve a desired tone quality.

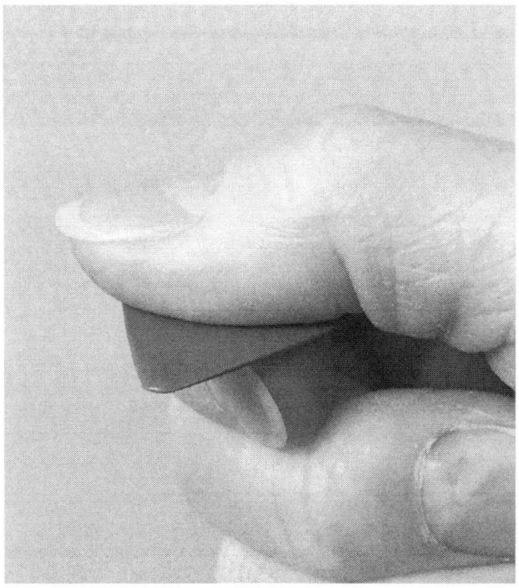

Figure 12: Notice angle of tip joint of thumb in flexion

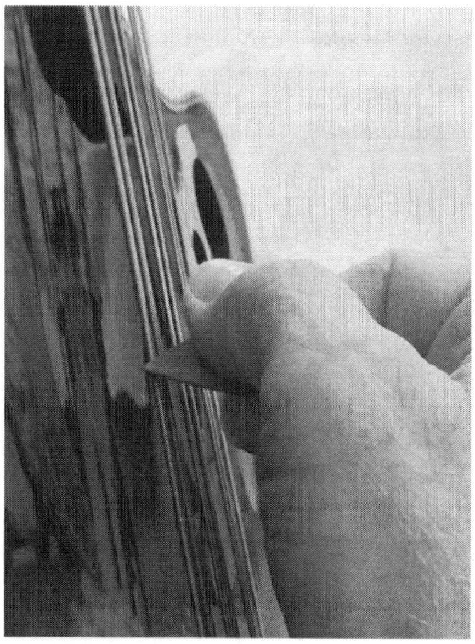

Figure 13: Leading edge of pick in contact with strings

In both examples, at no time does the wrist come in contact with the top of the instrument or the bridge of the instrument. Those who play bluegrass mandolin will find this challenging, since it is common to rest the heel of the hand or the wrist on the bridge. It is difficult to find the "sweet spot" [referring to tone quality] since it may be beyond the reach of a stationary wrist. You can find the sweet spot on any mandocello by playing between the end of the fretboard and the bridge. The location of the sweet spot can vary between different types of instruments. Experiment to identify its location on your mandocello.

1.5 The Right Arm, Wrist, and Hand

Since we have identified how to hold both the instrument and the pick we can bring the two elements together by considering: How do the right arm, wrist, and hand generate the sound we desire? Once again, we have two general approaches influenced, not by our preference, but by the design of the mandocello being played.

On the flat-top model, the right arm touches the edge of the instrument and the hand and wrist orientation are nearly parallel to the strings. This allows the wrist to the held in a relaxed, natural position, as illustrated below.

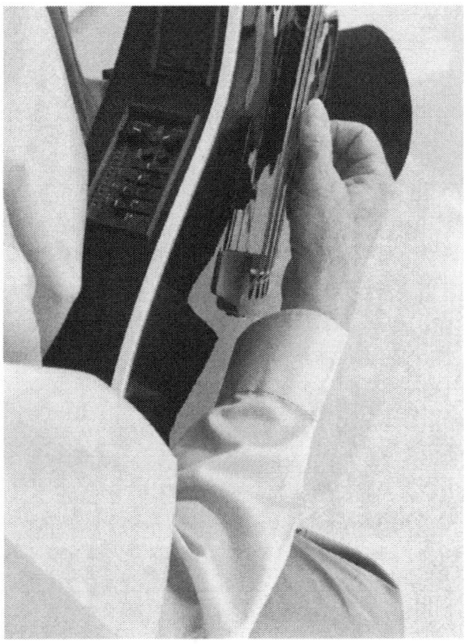

Figure 14: Hand, wrist and arm are in alignment

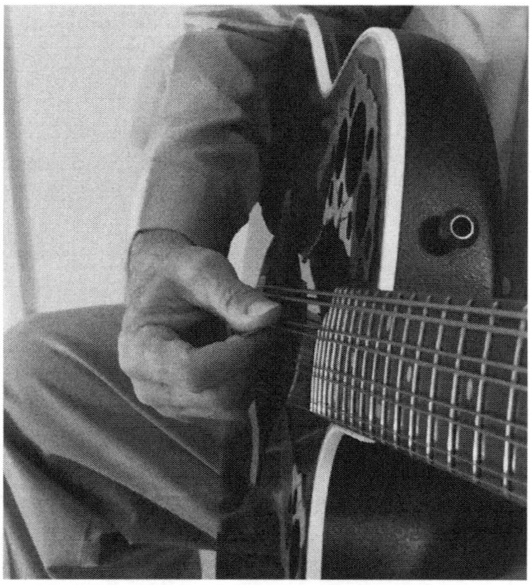

Figure 15: Hand, wrist and arm are nearly parallel to flat-top instrument

On the arch-top or oval-shaped mandocello the right arm still touches the side of the instrument because of the arch of the instrument and bridge; see images below. The wrist is bent slightly so the hand and pick can contact the strings. Note that in either mode, neither the heel of the hand nor the wrist rests on the bridge. Also note that the pick guard is never used as a "pinky-rest." Allow the hand to move freely.

1.6 Tuning the Mandocello

The pitches of the mandocello strings are the same as a classical cello: C, G, D, A from low to high. Each pair of strings is called a **course**, so the mandocello has four courses of strings.

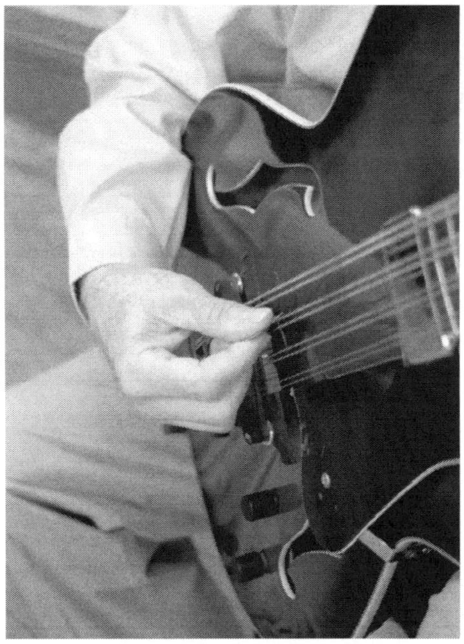

Figure 17: Arched wrist on archtop mandocello

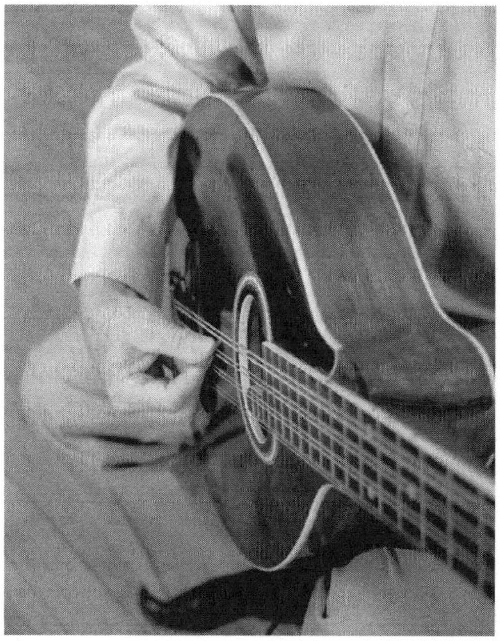

Figure 16: Arched wrist on oval-shaped mandocello

Before we define how to tune the mandocello, we need to define terminology that often confuses players. While the strings may come in pairs, we define the mandocello as having four-strings – C, G, D, A. The only time we identify all eight strings is while tuning. Other than that, we consider the mandocello a four-string instrument, since we play each pair of strings simultaneously. The string numbering convention follows that of guitar and mandolin—the highest-pitch string (the A course), closest to your leg, is string number ①. D is ②, G is ③ and C is ④. Notice that the string numbering convention is the inverse of the normal description of the open-string note names – C, G, D, A. The perfect-fifth tuning is common to all mandolin and string-family instruments, with the exception of the upright bass.

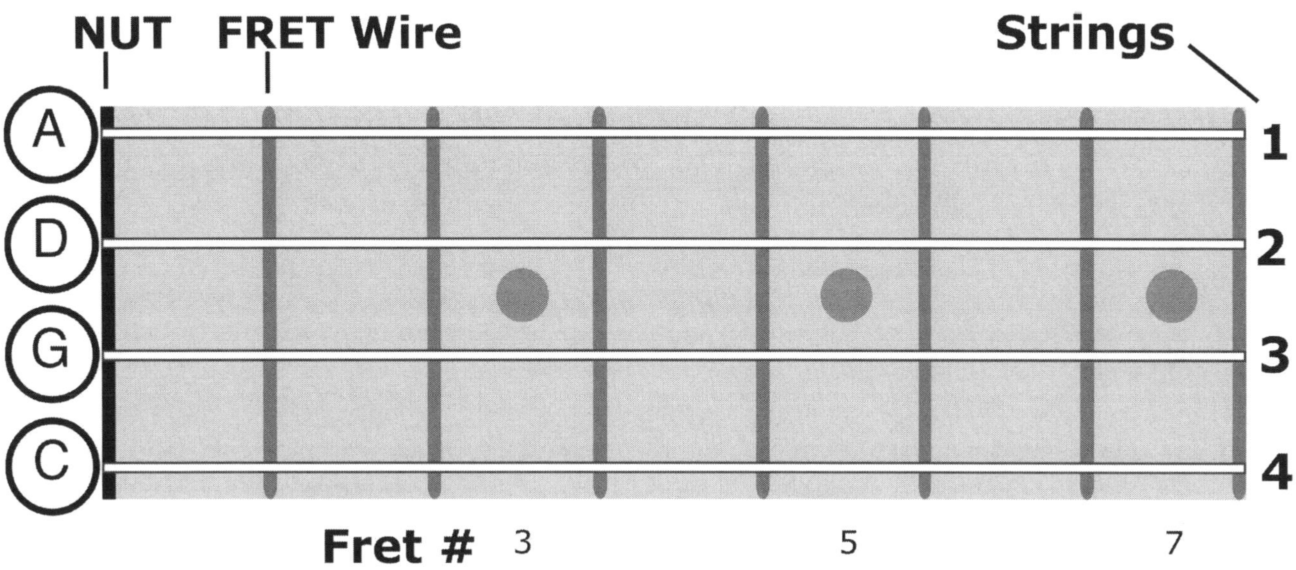

Figure 18: String Notes and Fret Marker Dots

Tuning with an Electronic Tuner

Most music instructors suggest using an electronic tuner. It is possible, with practice, to tune by ear, but don't spend all your practice time tuning. Make music instead! Cell phone tuning apps work well and are often free or inexpensive. The only drawback to a cell phone app is that you cannot use it in a group setting, as too many musicians will be trying to tune or play at the same time. If you do not own a tuner, bring the mandocello with you to a local music store and try several clip-on tuners. [Clip-on tuners are less susceptible to interference from other instruments being tuned at the same time.] In theory, any electronic tuner will work. In reality, it depends on the design of the tuner, where or how it attaches to your instrument, and how well it responds to the note-range of the mandocello.

The Tuning Process

The tuning process starts with an accurate C note. This can be established by an electronic tuner, a piano, or another instrument providing an accurate pitch. Most plectrum players tune from the low string, C in this case, to the high string, A. If you have never tuned an instrument with pairs of strings, you need to follow a precise approach:

Hold the mandocello in the normal position. Do not lay it on your lap. Play the top C string, the one closest to your chin. Do not play the pair of strings, just the top string. While this string is vibrating the lower C string must not vibrate. Use the pick to pluck both strings and immediately touch the pick to the **bottom** side of the lower string. This will stop the lower string from vibrating. To tune the lower string, rest the pick on the upper string to stop it from vibrating. If you tune past the desired pitch (making the note too high in pitch), tune down below the pitch and try again. Tuning Down-to-Pitch is rarely successful; **always tune Up-to-Pitch**. Repeat this process for strings ③, ②, and ①.

NOTE: because of the size of the strings, which under tension put a lot of pressure on the top of the instrument, it is often necessary to repeat the process across all 8 strings. As we tune each string to pitch it applies more pressure to the bridge and top, which can cause the previous strings to be too low in pitch and thus need re-tuning.

Tuning Utilizing the Fretboard

It is also possible to tune by ear by matching the note on one string at the 7th fret to the adjacent string, played open. If you are playing with a mandolinist or guitarist, ask them to provide a low G note. Tune the two G strings, upper and lower, as described previously. To tune the D string, play the D on the G string, at the 7th fret. This note occurs in the bass clef at only one location, but can be played on the mandocello on the open D string, or on the 7th fret of the G string. The notation is the same in sheet music, and the pitch is the same. The quality of the sound may change, because of the difference in string thickness between the D and G strings. Tune the A string in the same manner – play the A note at the 7th fret of the D string. But that only completes the tuning of three of the four strings. How do we tune the two low C strings? By the use of octaves. Play the C on the fifth fret of the G string. This pitch is one octave higher than the open C string. With practice, you can tune by ear, using the higher pitch to tune the lower string.

Tuning Harmonics

The last approach is to tune with harmonics. This principle is difficult to explain, but if you are already familiar with harmonics on another fretted instrument, you can use them with great success to tune the mandocello. The harmonic at the 12 fret is the same pitch as the harmonic on the adjacent lower string at the 7th fret. As with the above approach, you must start with a note set to the proper pitch.

One last point on tuning: Electronic tuners are often more precise when using harmonics. This is because there are fewer overtones in the harmonic note, and the electronic tuner may identify the harmonic more precisely. Experiment with your tuner to see which approach works best.

1.7 Picking the Open Strings

Even if you already play a plectrum instrument, review this section because we want to introduce a critical technique for playing the mandocello called the **drop-and-stop** method of picking.

The Drop-and-Stop Method

1. Start with the pick resting on the upper C string. The thumb should be in extension; the pick should be parallel to the strings, with the side of the pick in contact with the strings and not simply one edge of the pick.
2. Slowly raise the pick up by turning your forearm. Do not lift from the wrist; just rotate the forearm.
3. Now drop the pick and play *through* **both** C strings. The movement is like a pendulum in motion.
4. Stop on the string immediately below, i.e., the upper G string.

The pick now rests on the lower G string. You can think of this as a resting position, but it is not a *rest stroke*, as defined in classical guitar. [By comparison, a classical guitarist will start with the index finger on a string, play the string by collapsing the finger, moving the 3 main knuckles, and immediately rest on the next lower (in pitch) string which is closer to the chin.]

To play the same string again, return to the starting position, that is, move the pick and rest it on the upper C string. You can also think of this process as Start, Lift, Drop-and-Stop, Return. Practice this method slowly on just the C string. Don't rush the process. Upon returning to the Start position, the pick should stop (mute) the sound of the upper string only. Do not rest the right-hand fingers on the strings, nor plant the pinky in place on the pick guard or top of the instrument. The movement of the arm, wrist, and hand should be one fluid motion. Relax the left arm; do not touch the neck of the mandocello unless you feel it is necessary to hold the instrument. [We do not consider the left-hand position for learning the drop-and-stop method.]

Play this exercise slowly. There is no need to count; we will address counting later. Now move to the G string and repeat the process. If your pick hits the lower C string, you are likely lifting the arm and not merely rotating it. Think – small movements; you are not trying to strum the string like you would when playing a full four-note chord. Review the four steps above. Do the same exercise on the D string.

So, what happens when we get to the A string and we have no stopping point below it? Once again, we depend upon muscle memory. Having practiced this method repeatedly with the lower string stopping the pick, the hand expects the stopping motion and the pick stops on the "invisible string" below the A string. [This same principle applies to the classical guitarist playing a rest stroke on the lower E string.] Spend more time practicing the Drop-and-Stop on the C, G, and D strings than on the A string. This will facilitate muscle memory.

1.8 Introduction to the Bass Clef

The mandocello gained popularity during the early 20th century, and, in North America, all publishers of mandocello music used the treble clef. This was likely because most people learned how to play a mandolin or guitar first, and since those two instruments used the treble clef, it seemed logical to simplify the transition to the mandocello by using the same clef. The publishers called this *universal notation*, where the lowest note on the mandocello, the C string, is assigned the middle C position in the treble clef. This approach was fine for most of the 20th century and is still used by a small percentage of classical mandocello players. *The Mandocello*, however, will use the bass clef. This is the same clef used by the orchestral cello; it is both logical and convenient, as you will see.

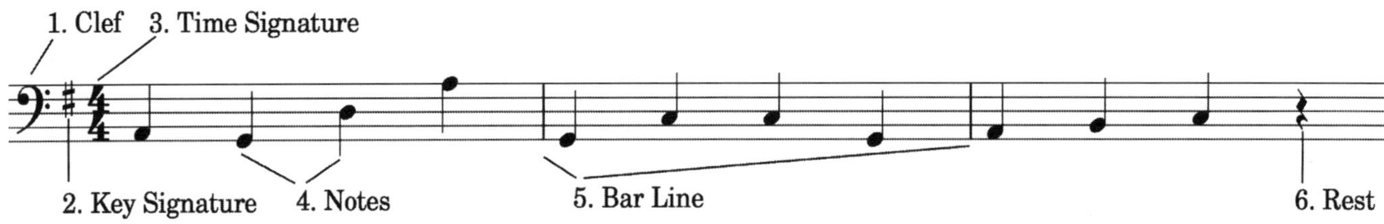

Figure 19: Essential Elements of the Bass Clef

1. Bass Clef – This clef is the normal clef assigned to the orchestral cello, and since we tune our mandocello the same, we will use this clef initially; we will discuss alternate clefs in later sections.
2. Key Signature – Identifies the major or relative minor key of the music.
3. Time Signature – Identifies both the number of beats in each measure (the top number), and the note value that receives one beat (the bottom number). In the above example, there are four beats per measure with a quarter note getting one beat.
4. Notes – The word "note," derived from the word *notation*, refers to how we notate the pitch and duration assigned to that sound on sheet music. Pitch refers to the perceived property of a sound and can be high or low, with respect to another note, or pitch. The words *pitch* and *note* are often used interchangeably.
5. Bar Line – The space between two bar lines constitutes a *measure*; in the example above, there are four notes per measure, so applying "musical math", each note or rest gets a quarter-note value.
6. Rests – A rest has the same duration of time as a note, but generates no sound. The example above is a quarter rest. The phrase "play the rest" is a euphemism; it actually means – stop the sounding of the preceding note.

Open Strings – The C string is the lowest sounding string on the mandocello; it is written below the bass clef. We call the two lines that appear below the clef **ledger lines**. So, unlike the guitar or mandolin, the lowest note or pitch of the mandocello is written just two ledger lines below the staff. Conveniently, the C note occurs on a line, which corresponds to our lowest string. The third string, the G note, occurs on the bottom line of the bass clef. The second string, D, lies on the 3rd line and the A string on the top line. Notice that no ledger lines occur unless needed. In between each note shown below, there is one more line and two spaces. They are assigned different note names, as you shall see.

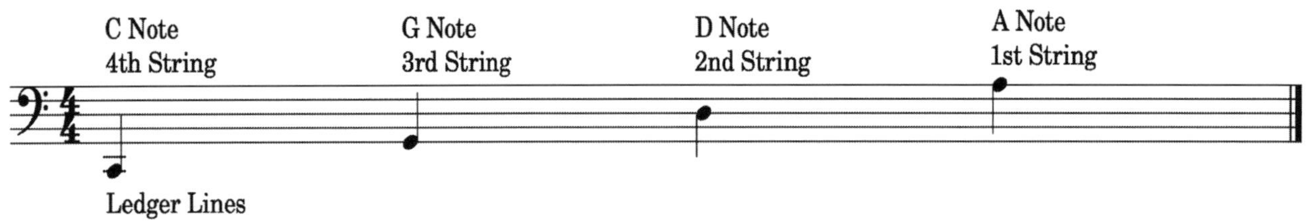

Figure 20: Open Strings – Note Names

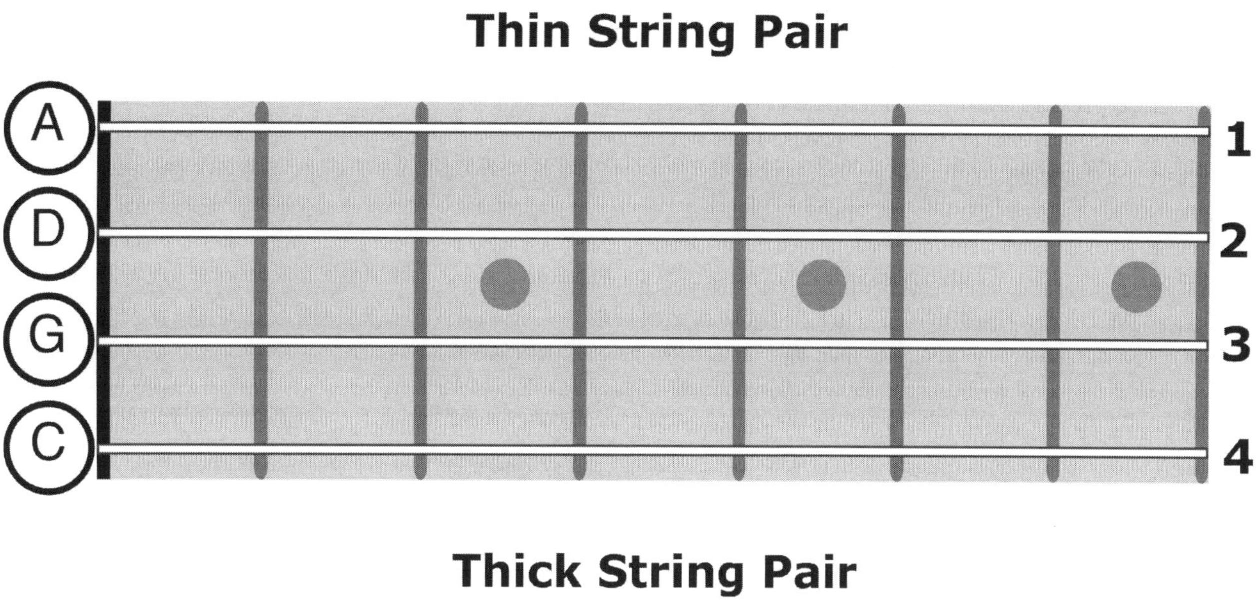

Figure 21: Open Strings – Fretboard view

Drop-and-Stop Exercise

Play the following open-string exercise. Apply the drop-and-stop method as introduced previously. Learn the names of the strings and notes, and play slowly. You will learn best by *saying-and-playing*:

"C, lift, Drop-and-Stop, return."

Be sure to rest the flat side of the pick on the upper string when returning. Rest long enough on the string to hear it stop vibrating. Each downstroke (drop) should sound like only one note even though you are playing the pair of strings. If each string sounds separately, that usually means you have not dropped the pick quickly enough but are trying to push the pick through the two strings. The new symbol (⊓) that appears in the first measure represents a *downstroke*.

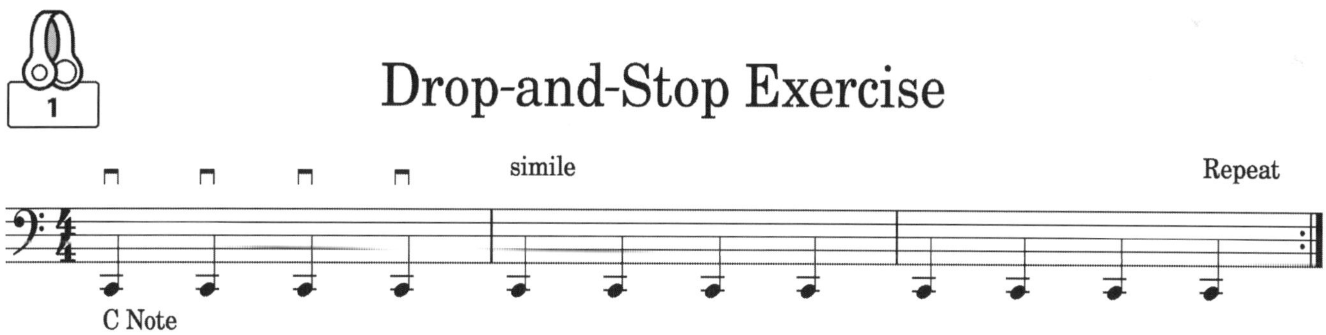

Figure 22: Drop-and-Stop Exercise

Play each note with a downstroke. Measure 2 has the word *simile* above it. It means to play "in a similar way." So the word "*simile*" indicates that you play all subsequent notes with a downstroke. Use the drop-and-stop method. (We will introduce an upstroke later.) A second new symbol appears at the end – a *repeat* symbol. Normally, this would mean to play this section of music (the 3 measures shown) one more time; for our purposes, repeat (return to the beginning) and repeat as many times as needed to get the feel of playing the C string.

If you are already familiar with the principles of reading music you might try to count the number of beats per measure. For this exercise and the ones immediately following, we want to emphasize the drop-and-stop approach and not the principle of counting; "Saying-and-playing" will slow down your playing, which facilitates learning the note names and proper pick technique. If counting is already a habit, change the phrase to:

"C, lift, Drop-and-Stop, 1, return; C, lift, Drop-and-Stop, 2, return; etc."

Continue with the next exercise and add the 3rd string, the G, and the 2nd string, the D. The drop-and-stop method always has the pick stopping on the string below the one you played. To play the first note on the G string, be sure to lift the pick and Drop-and-Stop, then Return. Do not play through the G string by merely pushing through the string; continue with the first step, the Lift. Likewise, the process is the same for the D string. Repeat this exercise on strings ④ ③ and ② until it feels natural and you are generating good tone. Do not forget to "*say-and-play*" to facilitate learning the note names on the bass clef.

You may have noticed that we have not yet played the A or the first string. We have deferred playing this string because we have no string below it to allow the full implementation of the drop-and-stop method. We have to stop the motion of the pick implicitly and return to the resting position. By learning the drop-and-stop method on the C, G, and D strings we facilitate the muscle memory needed to play the A string appropriately. Practice the following exercise on all four strings.

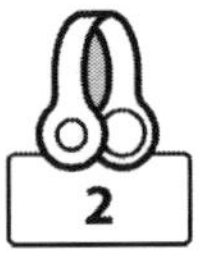

Open-String Exercise

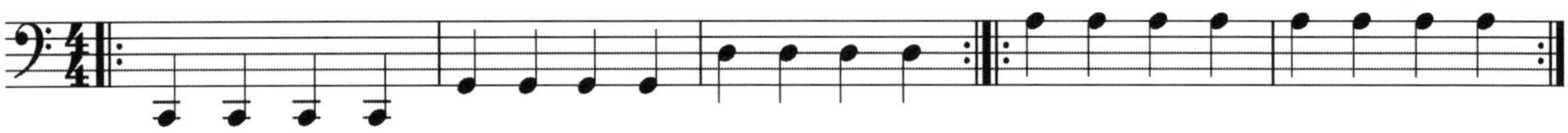

Figure 23: Open-String Exercise

In this exercise we have introduced an additional repeat symbol right after the time signature. This tells us to play the first 3 measures, repeat all 3, then go on to measure 4, play measures 4 & 5, then repeat measures 4 & 5. Be sure to repeat the whole exercise multiple times. Later we will introduce the symbol that defines how to repeat the entire section.

1.9 The Notes of the Bass Clef

We have shown that the open strings directly correlate to a line on the bass clef, or a ledger line in the case of the low C string. We memorize the remaining lines by a simple mnemonic – Good Boys Do Fine Always, as shown below.

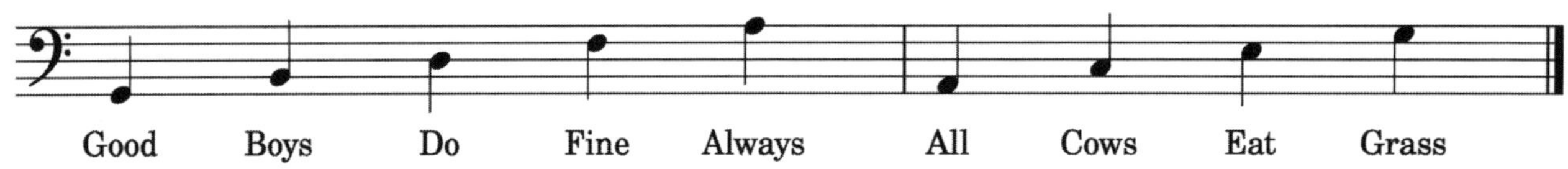

Figure 24: Bass Clef Notes Mnemonic

We learn the names of the spaces by the mnemonic – All Cows Eat Grass. The ledger lines that may appear above or below the bass clef simply continue the musical alphabet so are easy to learn. Use the illustration below to confirm you are playing the correct notes.

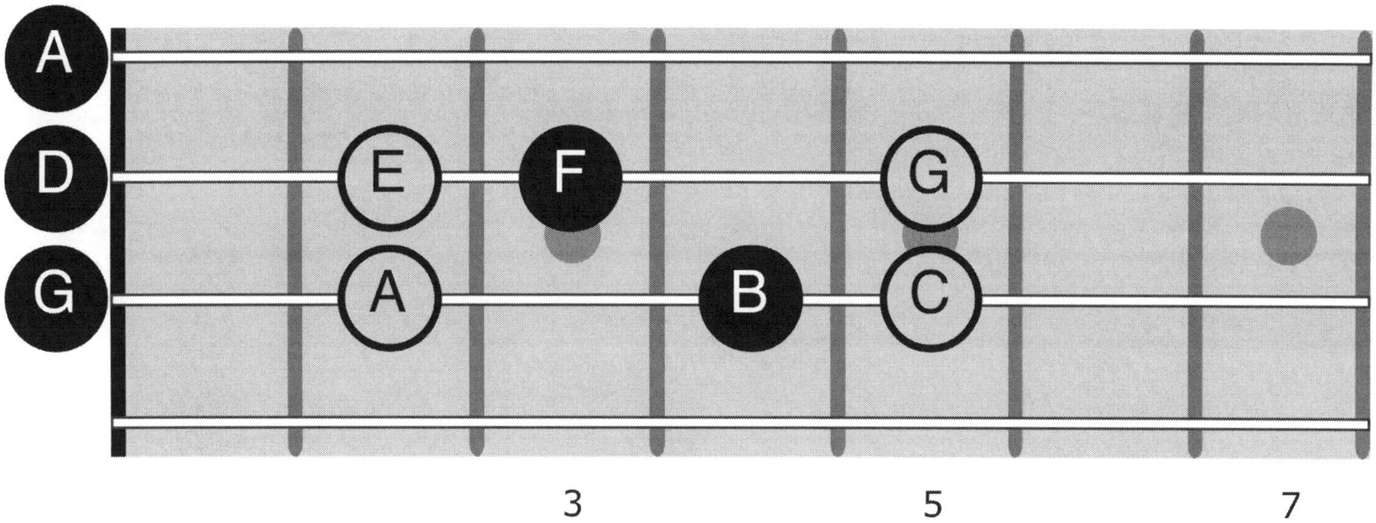

Figure 25: Bass Clef Notes Identified on the Fretboard

1.10 Proper Fingering of Notes

It is important that we learn to finger the notes by both fretting correctly and coordinating our fingers to play as a unit, rather than four isolated and separate fingers.

Preparing to Fret Correctly: to play any note other than the open strings requires that we finger the fretboard, or "fret the note". We do so by applying pressure just behind the fret. Review *Holding the Mandocello* diagram for the proper orientation of the left hand. Remember to place the thumb just past the number 2 fret; we consider this our **home position**. The mandocello is like the guitar in that we only play one note with one finger on one fret. It is important to coordinate the hand to play the next note with a different finger, as defined by the music. Before we even play one note, we need to orient the fingers so they are in proper alignment with each other.

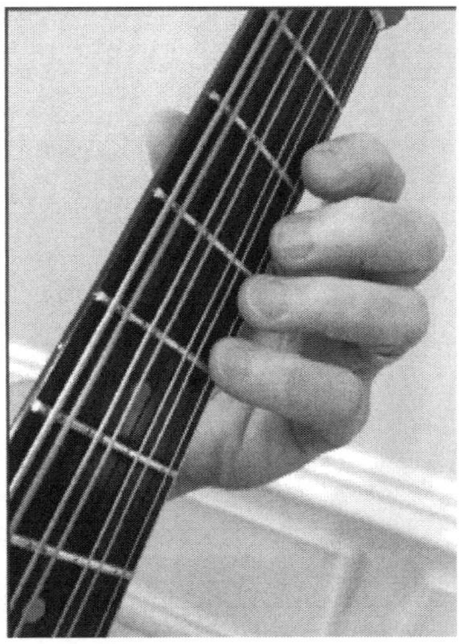

Figure 26: Finger preparation for fretting a note

In the illustration above you can see that the thumb is in the correct position and all four fingers are lightly touching the first string; no pressure is being applied yet. Place the index finger close enough to the 2nd fret to be ready to play. The middle finger is in between the two frets and may not be as close to the fret as finger one; this is OK for now. Fingers 3 and 4 are not in the position to play any note. This too is perfectly OK. We are preparing the entire hand to fret a single note with our first finger. Practice this hand-preparation motion by repeatedly lowering your left arm to your side and returning all four fingers to this fretting-preparation position.

Fretting the First Note: With the left hand in the preparation position, apply pressure with the first finger (behind the 2nd fret) and slightly raise fingers 2, 3 and 4, but keep them at-the-ready at all times. Do not lift the non-fretting fingers excessively.

To play the note at the third fret, keep finger 1 in the same position; apply finger 2, but move it closer to the 3rd fret than we had in the preparation position. Apply pressure with finger 2 and relax finger 1. Don't lift finger 1 off the string; just relax the pressure. Finger 2 is now applying pressure at the 3rd fret and fingers 1, 3, and 4 are relaxed, but at the ready for the next note.

Continue the process and play the next note on fret 4, using the third finger. We will wait until later to play any notes with the pinky.

We need to learn the music theory behind the notes we just fretted. I will introduce some fingering notation aids that will aid the process:

Bass Clef with Tablature

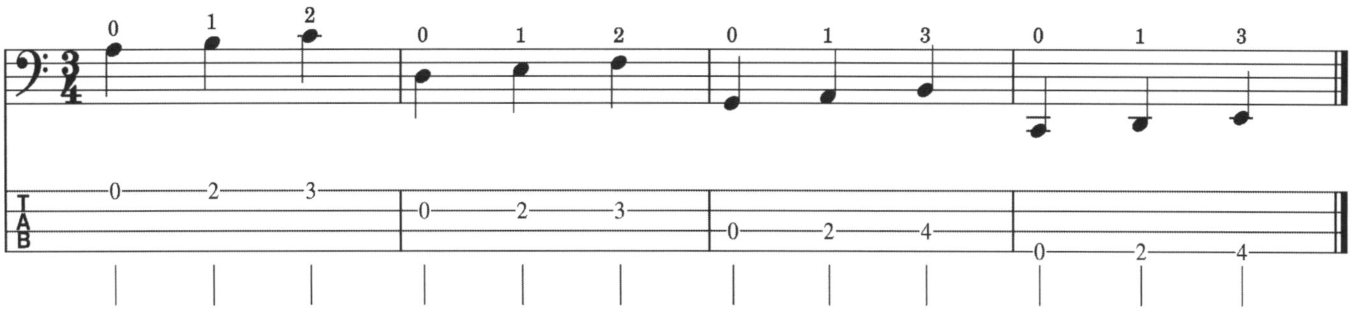

Figure 27: Bass Clef with Tablature

The illustration above illustrates bass clef notation and the equivalent fretboard tablature. The notation illustrates the time signature 3/4, so three beats per measure and a quarter note gets a beat. [More on that later.] The numbers 0, 1, and 2, in the first measure of the notation, above the three quarter notes, refer to the finger used to play that note. [Open string is 0, Index is 1, Middle is 2, Ring is 3, and Pinky is 4.] In the tablature, the numbers refer to the fret position for the associated string. [String one is on the top of the tablature.] So, in measure 1, play the open A string for one beat by using the downstroke. The next note in our musical alphabet, the B, is played with the first finger. The tablature illustrates that the B note occurs on the second fret. [We will discuss the note at fret one in a later section.] The third note on the first ledger line above the staff, is a C, played with the second finger on the third fret. Now play just the first three notes of measure 1 – A, B, C; be sure to apply the drop-and-stop method even though there is no actual string to stop the pick. How long did it take to play just the one measure of 3 notes? That depends on how quickly you plucked each note. Tempo is the rate of speed of the musical performance. Play slowly, so as to achieve accuracy.

The second measure moves to the second string, the D string. Here we see the notes D, E, and F. Notice that we also arrange the notes on the staff as – line, space, line, just as we did on the A string. We also play these three notes with the same fingers we used on the A string. Understanding this symmetry will facilitate learning how to read and play notes on the mandocello. Play this measure alone, then start at the beginning and play measures 1 and 2 sequentially.

We already discussed the concept of symmetry; notice how it changes on strings 3 and 4. Our fingering changes from fingers 1 and 2, to fingers 1 and 3. The three notes on the G string are G, A, B; the three notes on the C string are C, D, E. Did you notice that the note names ended at G and started again at A? As we use only seven letters from the musical alphabet, they must repeat. This simplifies both reading and writing musical notation. The A note on the second fret of the G string is exactly one octave (8 notes) lower in pitch than the open A string.

Practice the above four-measure exercise, remembering that the repeat symbol means to go back to the beginning (measure 1). Play along with a metronome and return to measure 1 while keeping the same tempo. Remember, the metronome does not understand measures, it only plays beats-per-minute. Set the metronome so it does NOT emphasize the first beat. Start by counting 1, 2, 3, 4 – then play. When you make a mistake, just restart when you are ready; you control the starting time if the metronome does not emphasize beat one. This is the best approach for beginning players and will also be the same method used for learning a challenging tune or passage. Later we will set the metronome to emphasize the first beat.

1.11 The Bass Clef – Combining Notes

Continue practicing the previous exercises until you are comfortable playing three notes on each string and have learned the principles of the musical alphabet – seven letters, from A to G. Remember, each open string coincides with a line in the bass clef staff.

Let's combine all the notes we've learned and play a random sequence of notes. The first three measures include the fingering, along with some nonsense lyrics where the first letter of the word matches the note name. Saying or singing the lyrics will accelerate the learning process. The second line uses *solfège*, for those familiar with that method.

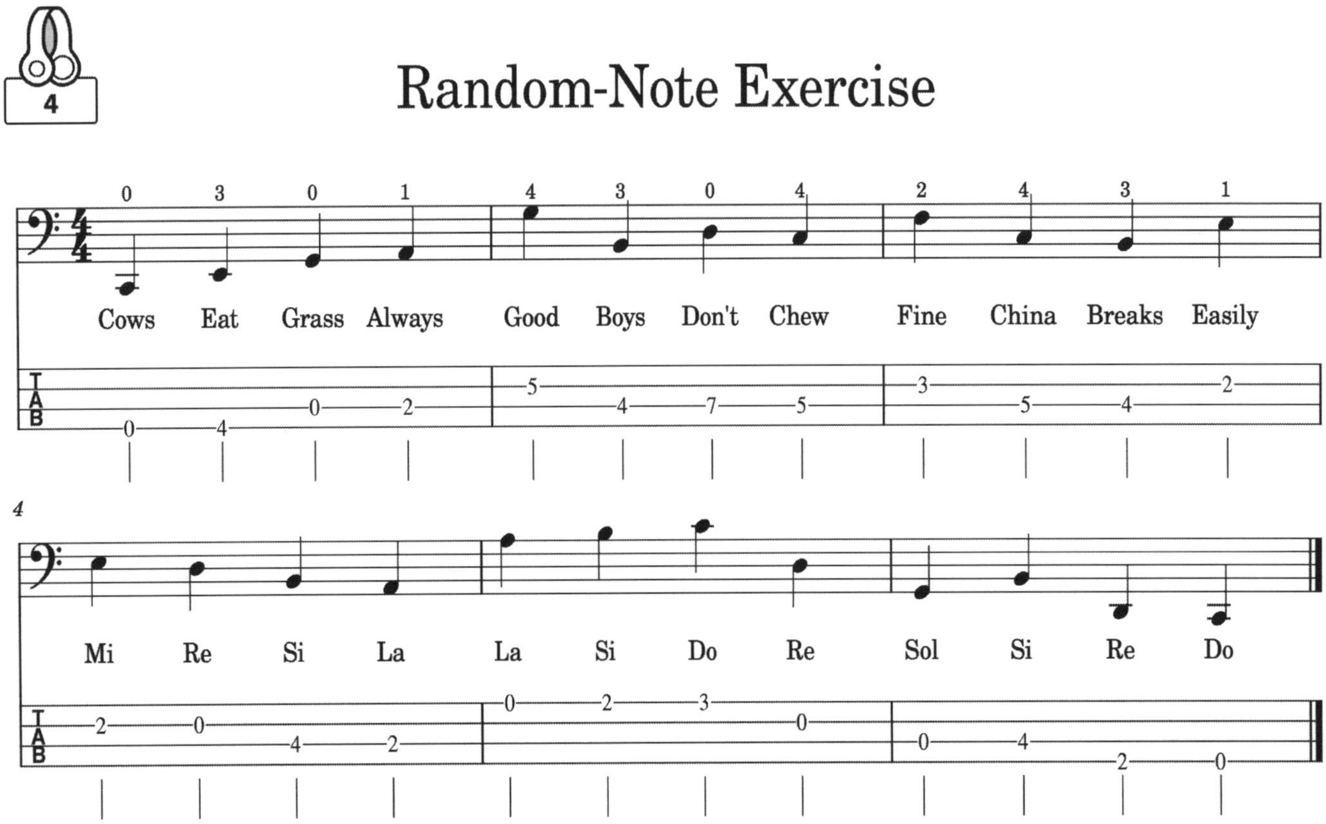

Figure 28: Random-Note Exercise

For those who "play by ear": If reading bass clef notation is new to you, this exercise will be a challenge because the melody is so random it will be difficult to memorize and play by ear. Play it slowly, using the drop-and-stop method, and say the note names out loud. This will facilitate learning both the fretboard and the bass clef. Practice keeping your eyes on the music and not on your hands.

Try to play the exercise above without looking at your left hand. Your fingers are not yet instinctively playing the notes as you read the bass clef; you need to "talk your fingers into place."

Twinkle, Twinkle, Little Star

The following exercise is an adaptation of the common tune "Twinkle, Twinkle Little Star." Again, "say and play" the note names.

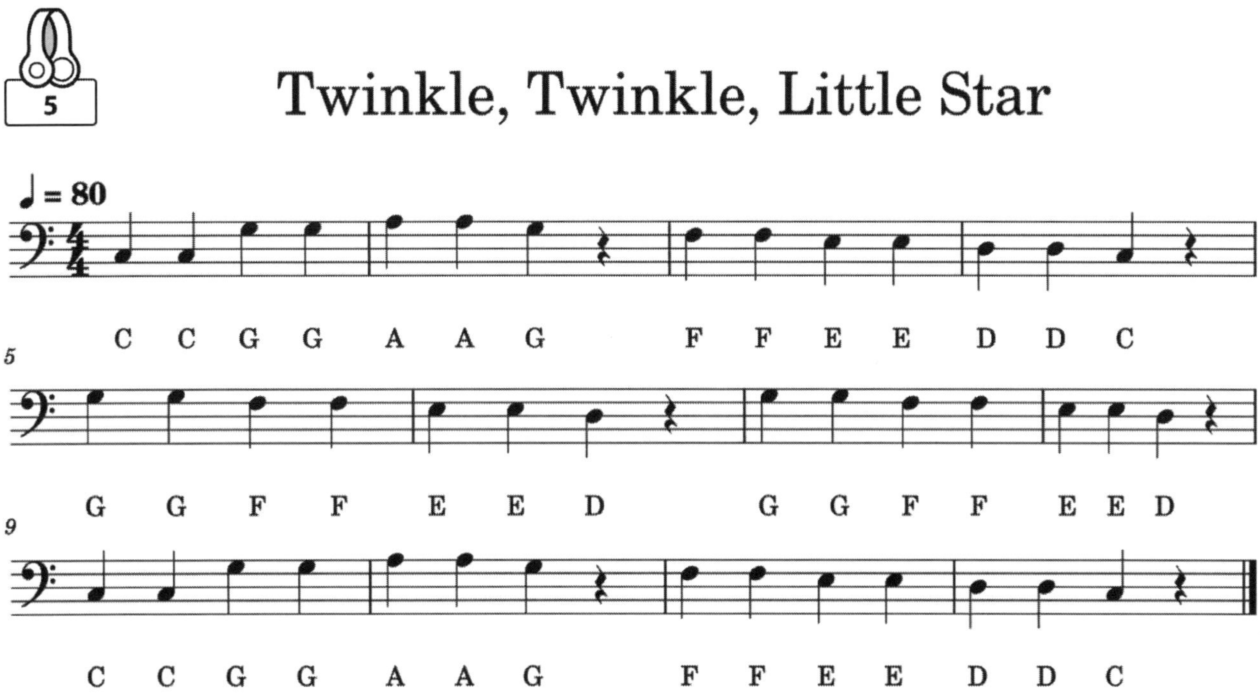

Figure 29: Twinkle, Twinkle, Little Star (Simplified)

London Bridge

The next exercise is also a well-known tune. Notice the repeat symbol that appears at measure 1 and measure 8. Measure 8 also includes a half note rest, which receives two counts. Use a metronome set to 120 beats per minute to ensure that you do not rush the last measure when returning to measure 1 to play the tune again.

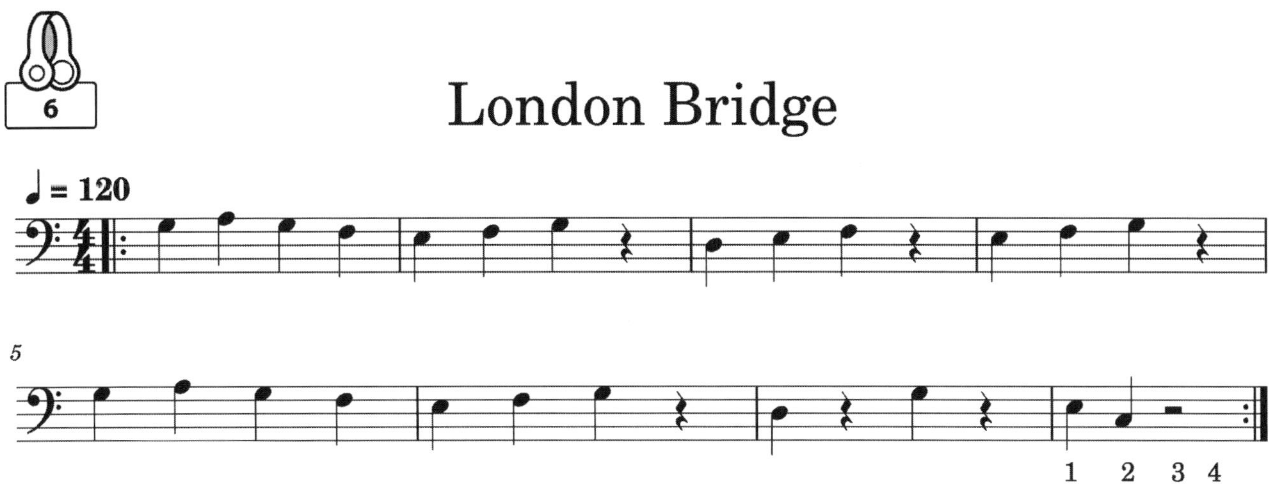

Figure 30: London Bridge

Hava Nagila

The next exercise is a traditional Jewish folk song, "Hava Nagila." It is included to demonstrate the critical role any bass clef instrument may play within an ensemble setting. The bass instrument, in our case a mandocello, plays a quarter note on every beat. Play with a metronome to maintain proper tempo. This tune normally increases in tempo as it is performed. Start with a slow, comfortable tempo and slowly increase the tempo as you repeat the exercise. For those already familiar with the tune, the melody (not shown) starts at measure 3.

There is a dot symbol immediately below or above each quarter note. This is a *staccato* mark and indicates the note should be played short and distinct. This is accomplished by releasing the pressure of the left-hand finger after picking the note. Do not remove the finger completely off the string; just release the pressure. If you are familiar with the principle of string muting, you can apply it to the notes played with the open D string.

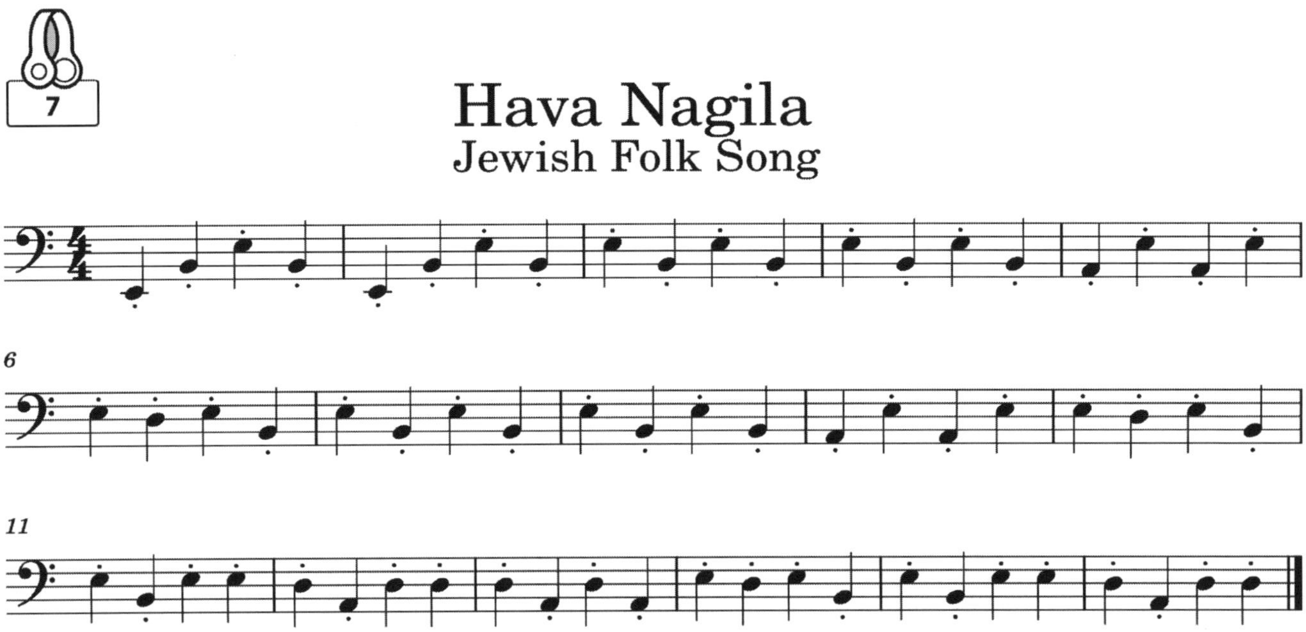

Figure 31: Jewish Folk Song – Hava Nagila

1.12 Relationship of the Fretboard to the Bass Clef

So far we have only learned to play the "alphabet notes". We know our 20+ frets on the mandocello allow us to play a lot more notes, so let's investigate both the details of the bass clef and the fretboard.

The note C is the lowest note on the mandocello, located two ledger lines below the staff. If we play a note at the first fret of string ④, we are playing a C-sharp, notated as C♯. (Pronounced "C-sharp"; this is not a hash or pound symbol in musical notation.) A C♯ is a half tone or one fret higher in pitch than a C. Play each note on the C string, starting with the open string, then fretting the first position, moving to the second fret, etc. Play up to the twelfth fret. The twelfth fret marker is normally shown on fretted instruments with two dots on the face of the fretboard, and sometimes on the edge of the fretboard as well. Play with only the first finger, for now, and shift fret-by-fret. Make sure the thumb remains in the same orientation to the first finger. Listen to the changes in pitch. Be sure to apply the drop-and-stop method.

An *interval* is the relationship or space between two notes or tones. The relationship of one fretted note to the next fretted note, up or down the fretboard, is an interval of a half-step. In modern Western music the half-step is the smallest interval we play. We mentioned before that our musical alphabet uses the letters from A to G, or only seven letters but you just played twelve notes from the open C string to another C, one octave higher on the twelfth fret. That means there are twelve half-steps in each octave.

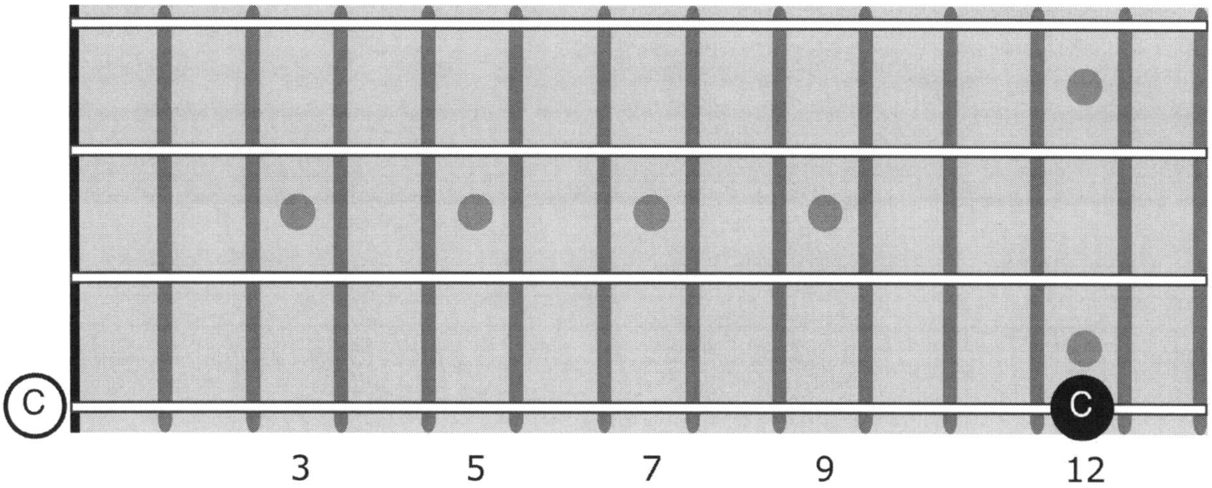

Figure 32: One Octave Range on Fretboard

One Chromatic Octave on the C String

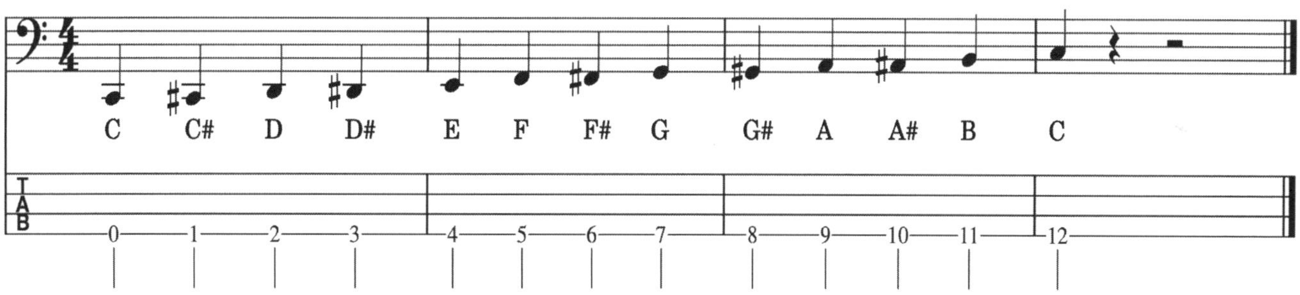

Figure 33: One Chromatic Octave on the C String

Open: C
Fret 1: C♯ (pronounced "C-sharp")
Fret 2: D
Fret 3: D♯
Fret 4: E
etc.

In measure 2, notice that between the E and the F note we do not see a sharp symbol. This is because the interval between E and F, is a half-step. You see this again between the B at fret 11 and the C at fret 12; so from B to C is only a half-step. So the complete musical scale is:

C, C♯, D, D♯, E, F, F♯, G, G♯, A, A♯, B, C

We will examine the relationship of half and whole-steps later. For now, remember that E – F and B – C are the **natural half tones**, respectively located one fret away from one another.

The notation below illustrates all the notes on the bass clef staff starting on the open C string and going up to the E two ledger lines above the staff.

Location of C on the Bass Clef Staff

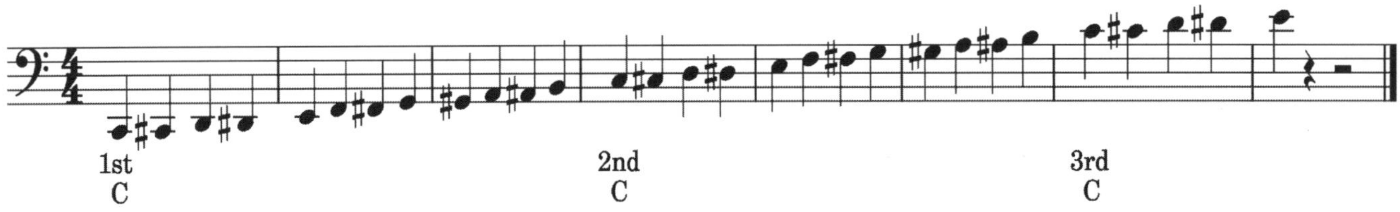

Figure 34: Location of C on the Bass Clef Staff

The three C notes in the example above are identified by the reference below the staff. Previously we introduced the first three notes on the G string: G, A, B. To play the C on the G string we play the note at the 5th fret. As we learned, the interval from B to C is a half-step, so the note C is just one fret higher up the fretboard. One principle of all fretted instruments is that the same note, or pitch, can occur at more than one fret and string position. What is critical to understand, and see on the fretboard, is that the C on the G string at the 5th fret is the same pitch C as the one played on the C string at the twelfth fret. In the fretboard diagram below, the twelfth fret illustrates the note name, a C, which corresponds to the first note of measure 4 in the above notation.

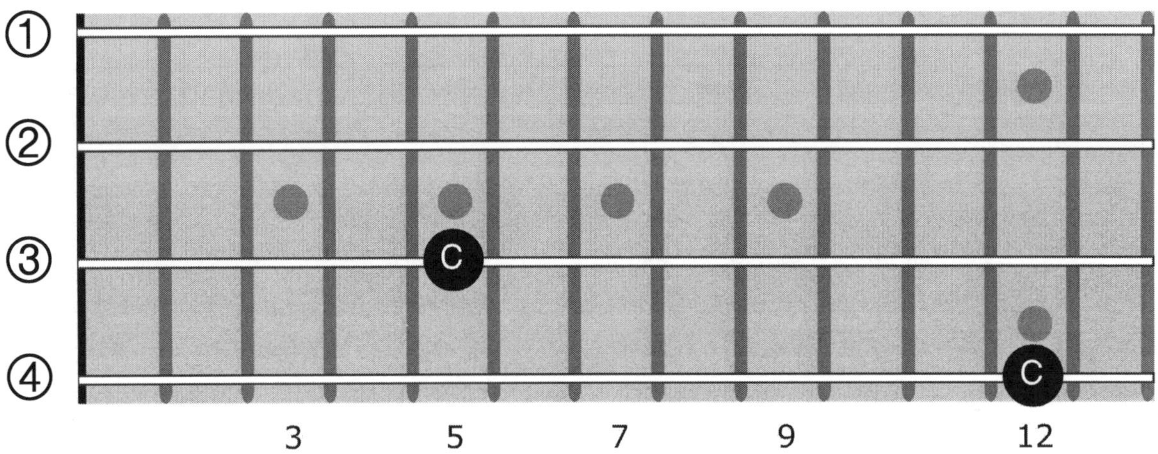

Figure 35: Location of Identically-Pitched C's

The point of all this discussion is this: When you read measure 4 above, you know to play a C. But where do you play it? – on the 5th fret of the G string, or the 12 fret of the C string? The answer is – it depends! There may be alternative locations to play a note, but there is often a logical location that dictates which position to use. The logical concepts include:

1. What notes come next? You want to play the next note as close as possible to the note you just played. (There are exceptions to this rule, which we will address later.)
2. What note sounds best? If you stay on the same string for adjacent notes, each will generate a similar timbre [the tonal quality or color of the sound, based on multiple factors; pronounced – tăm′bər.]
3. Which finger will you use? You may play an open string for convenience, rather than playing the same note at the 7th fret of the adjacent string.
4. Where is the music going? For example: If the music is moving up the bass clef staff by one octave or more, we will want to move our fingers higher up the fretboard.

For a good example of the difference in timber, play the D note on the 14th fret of the low C string and compare the tone to that of the open D string. Same pitch, different timbre.

1.13 Identifying the Notes of the C Major Scale on the Fretboard

The previous section identified the notes at every fret on each string. We detailed the C string and identified the twelve notes from the open string to the twelfth fret. In the C major scale, the notes identified on the staff are only the natural notes of our musical alphabet: C, D, E, F, G, A, B. The major scale is a series of seven distinct pitch classes plus the octave. Unlike the piano, we don't have any black and white keys as a visual aid, so we need to both memorize the note location (by fret) and the relationship between notes.

On string ①, the open A and B are two frets apart, which is a whole-step. B to C is only one fret apart, so it is a half-step. C to D is two frets, so a whole-step, and D to E is likewise a whole-step. If you examine string ②, you will see that E to F is a half-step. The two pairs of notes that are a half-step apart in the key of C are the E – F, and B – C, the **natural half tones**.

It is important to remember that the relationship between notes is defined by the key in which they appear. We will consider how they change when we examine different keys.

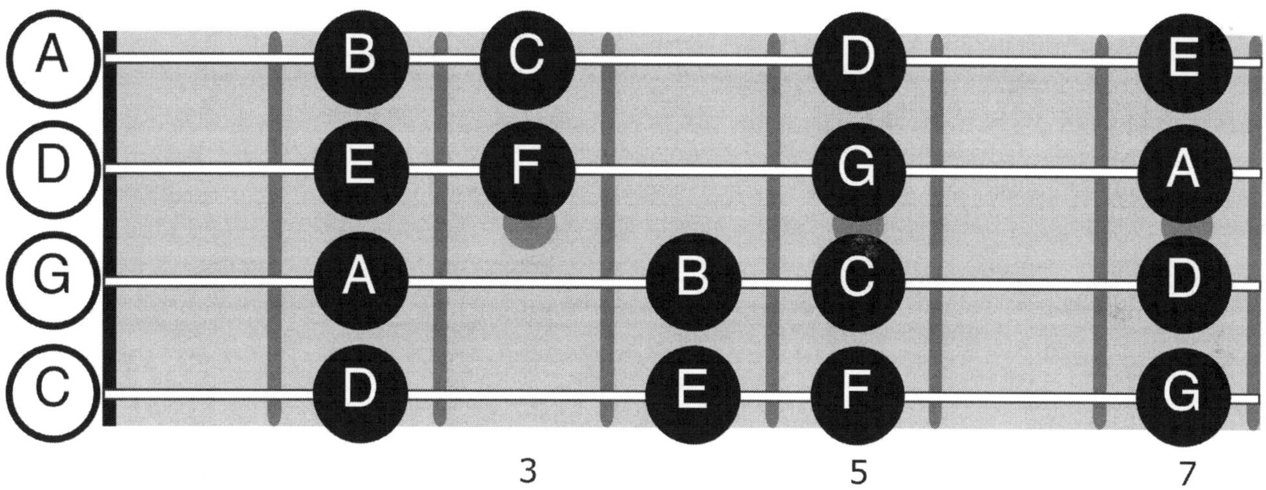

Figure 36: Notes of the C Major Scale on the Fretboard

1.14 C Scale Study and Pinky Exercise

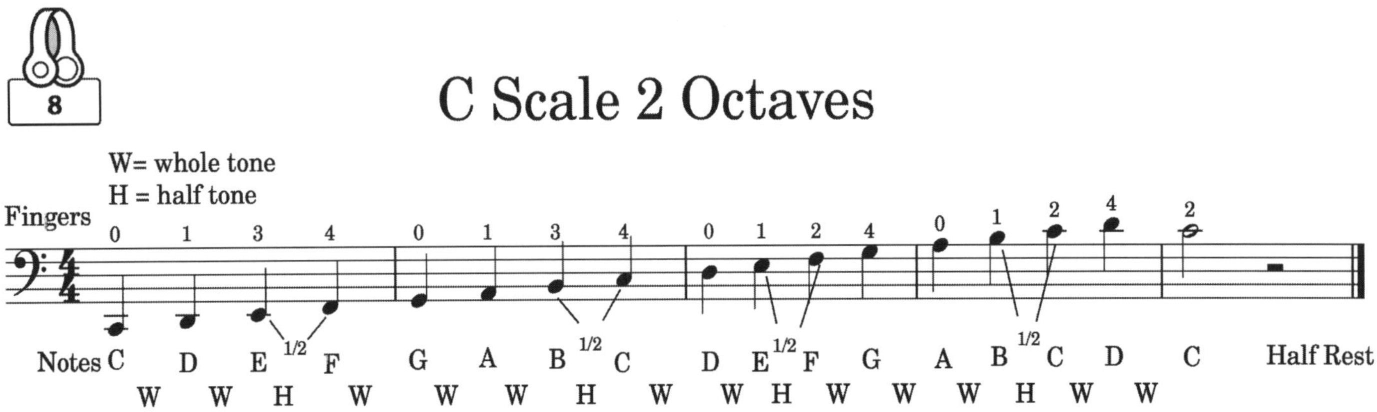

Figure 37: C Scale 2 Octaves

One of the basic principles of learning how to play any musical instrument is to learn how to play scales. A scale is a set of musical tones, or pitches, used to create melody and harmony. The first scale everyone learns is the C major scale with no sharps or flats. Here we have a significant advantage with the mandocello: Our lowest string is a C, so learning the C scale is easy. When we play the low C string and advance up the musical alphabet, the relationship between notes remains the same. When we get to a G, because our alphabet must start over, the next note in the sequence is an A. The distance between notes remains the same too. From the open C string to the D is two frets, or a whole-step. D to E, 2 frets, or one whole-step. E to F is only one fret, or a half-step. The exercise above illustrates which fingers to use above the staff with the note names below for the notes of the C scale.

In order to play the F in the first measure it is necessary to use the pinky, or finger 4. This will probably feel like a big stretch at first. Remember to keep all 4 fingers “at-the-ready”. Play the E with finger 3 and simply add the pinky to play the F. Do not push too hard with the third finger, but provide enough pressure to make the effort required by the pinky seem minimal. The pattern is the same for the next measure with B to C being a difference of one fret, using fingers 3 and 4. On the D and A strings the fingering changes. Fingers 1 and 2 are required to play E to F on the D string and B to C on the A string. The new stretch challenges are from F to G and C to D. It is more difficult to go from finger 2 to finger 4 than from finger 3 to finger 4. If you find playing the note with the fourth finger too much of a stretch, check the position of the thumb. When finger one is close to fret number 2, the thumb should extend just past fret number 2. This provides greater leverage and eases the effort needed by the pinky to fret the note. Additionally applying pressure with the second or third finger (simultaneously with the pinky), is a good practice; this technique is also beneficial when playing a long performance or concert.

The following exercise will assist in strengthening the pinky. Consider warming up with this exercise both before and after playing the C scale shown above.

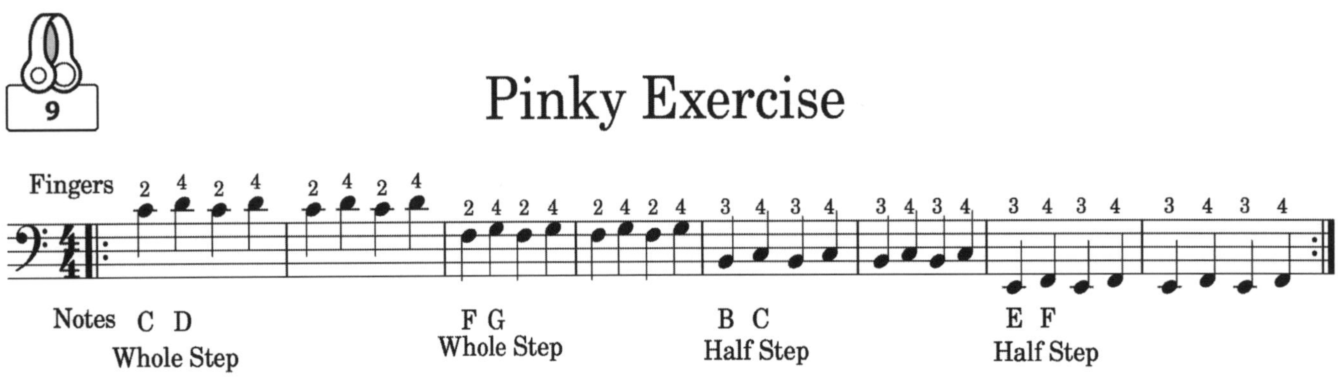

Figure 38: Pinky Exercise

1.15 Learning Proper Fingerings, with Scale Exercises

Proper fingering technique is important in playing the mandocello, just as it is with the guitar or mandolin. The mandocello is more like the guitar in that, because of the scale length of the neck, it is typical to assign one finger per fret, unlike the mandolin, in which each finger addresses two frets. The best approach to learning both note location and which fingers to use is to play all scale exercises in a descending manner. Learning the notes and which finger to use takes almost no time to "learn", but "teaching" your left-hand fingers to do the job correctly will take sufficient repetition to develop muscle memory. Why would we practice scales in a descending manner rather than ascending? Two reasons – we all have the alphabet memorized in ascending order, but try to say the alphabet from G to A. We rarely think this way, so we have to re-train our brain to recognize that the musical alphabet needs to work both ways. The second advantage is – by starting with the higher notes on the staff, we can start playing on the slimmer A string, then progressively move to the thicker strings. The thicker the string, the harder it is to play with the correct picking technique.

Practice each scale below slowly. Place all 4 fingers "in position" before fretting the first note with your fourth finger. We don't use the second finger in the keys of C, G, and D, but the fingers should remain in proximity to the fretboard.

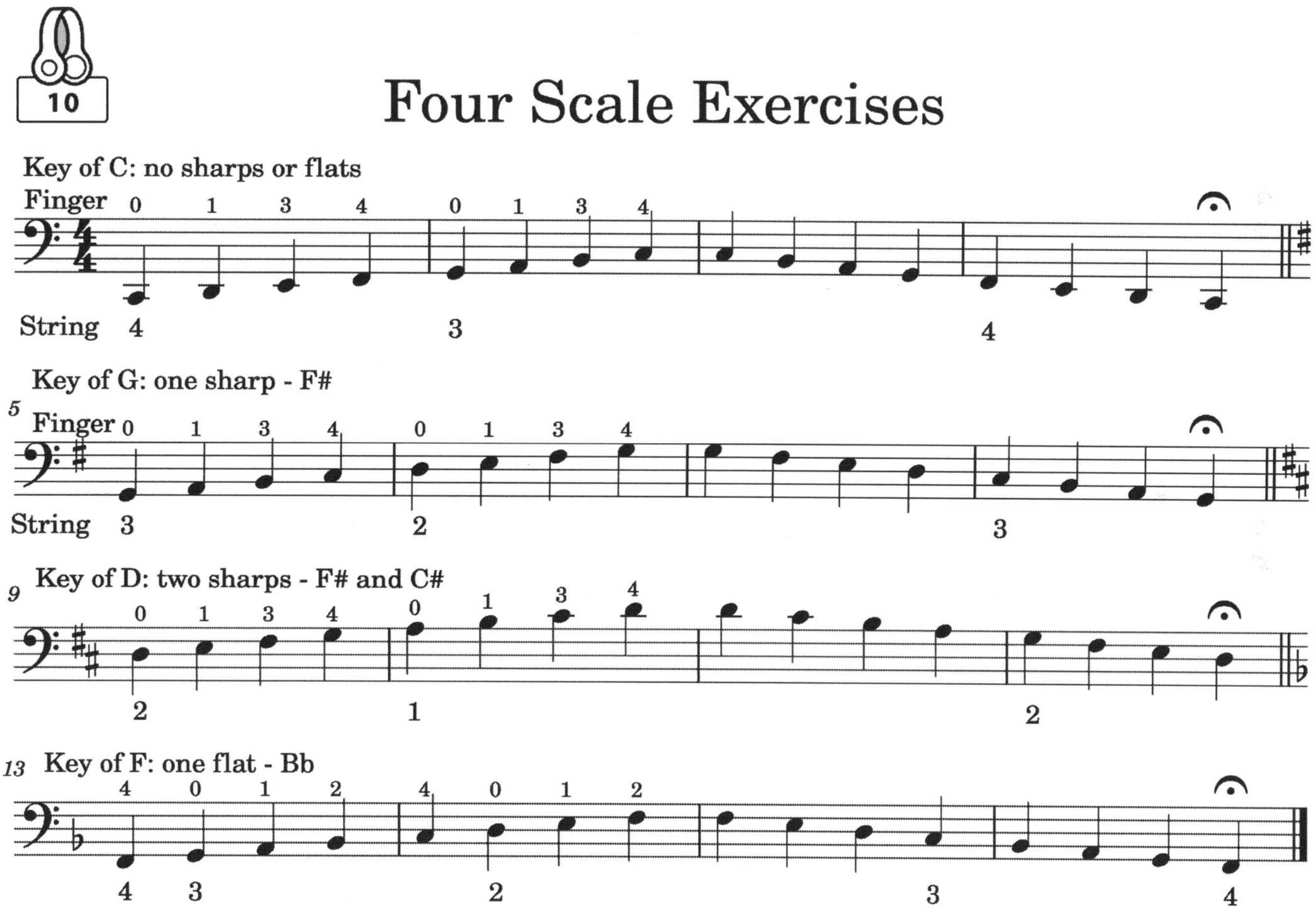

Figure 39: Four Scale Exercises

Did you notice how the fingering was the same for the keys of C, G, and D major, then changed for the key of F major? Let's examine the fretboard to better understand the underlying music theory.

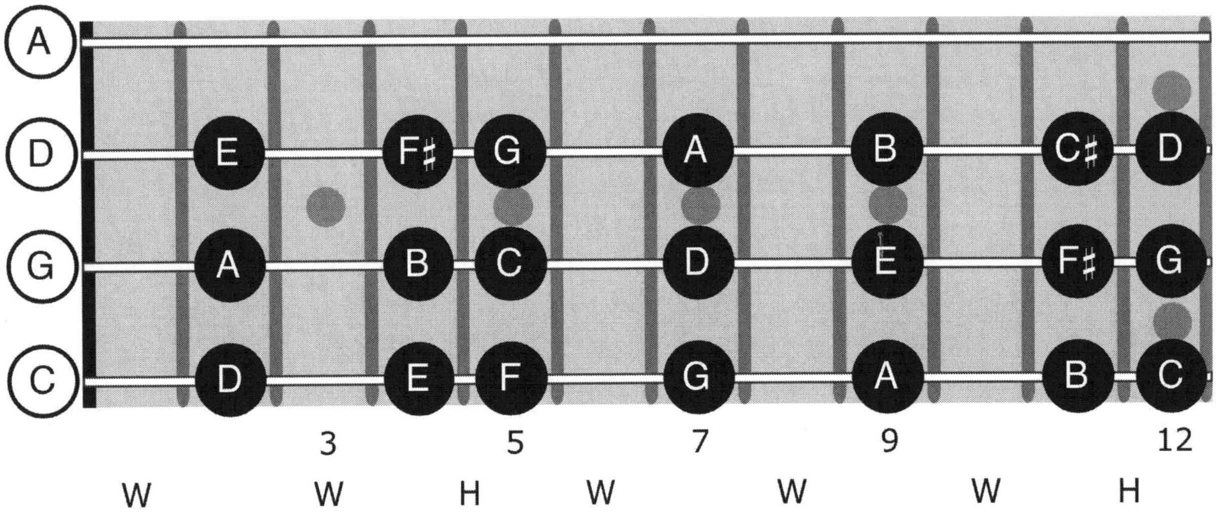

Figure 40: Three Major Scales on the Fretboard

In the diagram above we have shown all the notes of the C scale on the fourth string. Likewise for the key of G major on the third string and the key of D major on the second string. In the previous "C Scale Study," we mentioned that the interval between E – F and B – C is a half-step, or one fret. The relationship of all the notes in the C major scale is as follows:

C – D: a whole-step

D – E: a whole-step

E – F: a half-step

F – G: a whole-step

G – A: a whole-step

A – B: a whole-step, and

B – C: a half-step

So the pattern is WWHWWWH. On the mandocello, mandolin and guitar, this is equivalent to:

2 frets, 2 frets, 1 fret, 2 frets, 2 frets, 2 frets, 1 fret.

Apply this knowledge of the major scale's relationship to the fretboard by playing the A scale on the first string from the open string to the twelfth fret. Repeat the same pattern shown above. Now, identify which notes you played. The third note of the A scale is a C, but notice in the pattern it is a whole-step away from the B. So it must be a C♯. Likewise, there is an F♯, and G♯. The pattern remains the same – WWHWWWH.

The fourth scale exercise in the example on the previous page (Figure 39) is in the key of F major. The notation identifies the key of F as having one flat, a B♭. The F scale is analyzed as follows:

Note:	F		G		A		B♭		C		D		E		F
Interval:		W		W		H		W		W		W		H	

The B must be a B♭ because it is only a half-step from the third to the fourth note of the major scale. The Whole – Half pattern for any **major scale** is consistent, but it is not as easy to see when we are crossing multiple strings, as in the F scale exercise above. The interval from F to G is a whole-step, so it can be played on the open G string or on the seventh fret of the C string. As a separate exercise play the F scale on the D string, starting on the third fret. The upper F in the scale occurs on the 15th fret.

The key signature can be identified by the number of sharps and flats by using the following two mnemonics:

Sharps: Go Down And Eat Breakfast Fast
1 2 3 4 5 6

Flats: Fat Boys Eat Apple Dumplings Greedily
1 2 3 4 5 6

The order of the sharps and flats always remains the same. This facilitates reading the key signature in the music notation.

This has been a very brief introduction to the major scale. For a more detailed study of music theory, independent of the mandocello, consult the Mel Bay book, *Theory and Harmony for Everyone* [93790].

1.16 Introducing the Half Note

The half note 𝅗𝅥 receives two beats, so one half note is equal to two quarter notes. In the example below notice how measure 2 applies beats 3 and 4 to the last note, a half note, completing the 4 beats in the measure.

Half Note – Example Tune

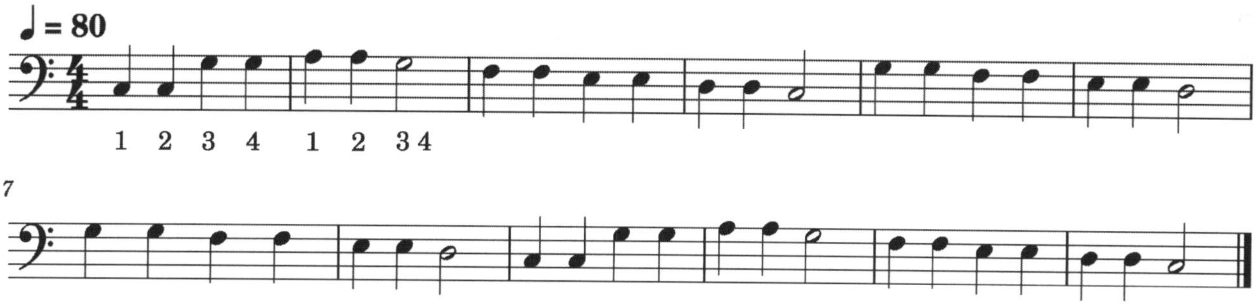

Figure 41: Half Note – Example Tune

Ode to Joy (Simplified)

The next exercise is a simplified version of "Ode to Joy." The use of only quarter and half notes provides the opportunity to practice with a metronome.

11

Ode to Joy
(Simplified)

Ludwig van Beethoven

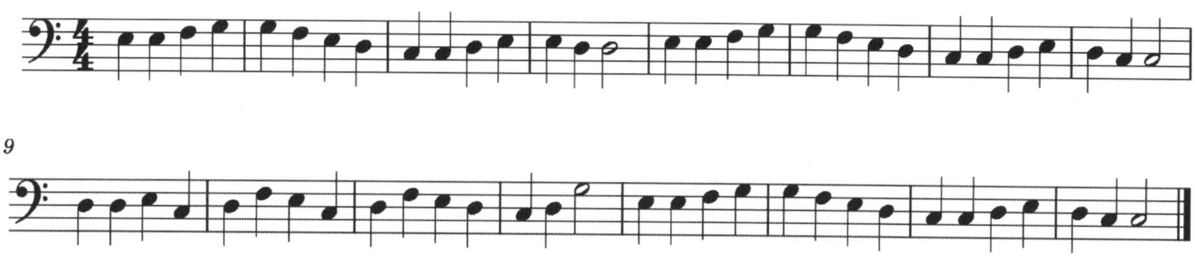

Figure 42: Ode to Joy (Simplified)

1.17 The Eighth Note

Two eighth notes are equal to one quarter note. Say the count out loud as demonstrated in the first line of the etude below. Use a metronome set to beat only on the quarter note. The symbol in measure 3 (⊓) illustrates that the pick direction should remain as all downstrokes. Do not try to apply alternate picking for this exercise; the intention is to internalize the count.

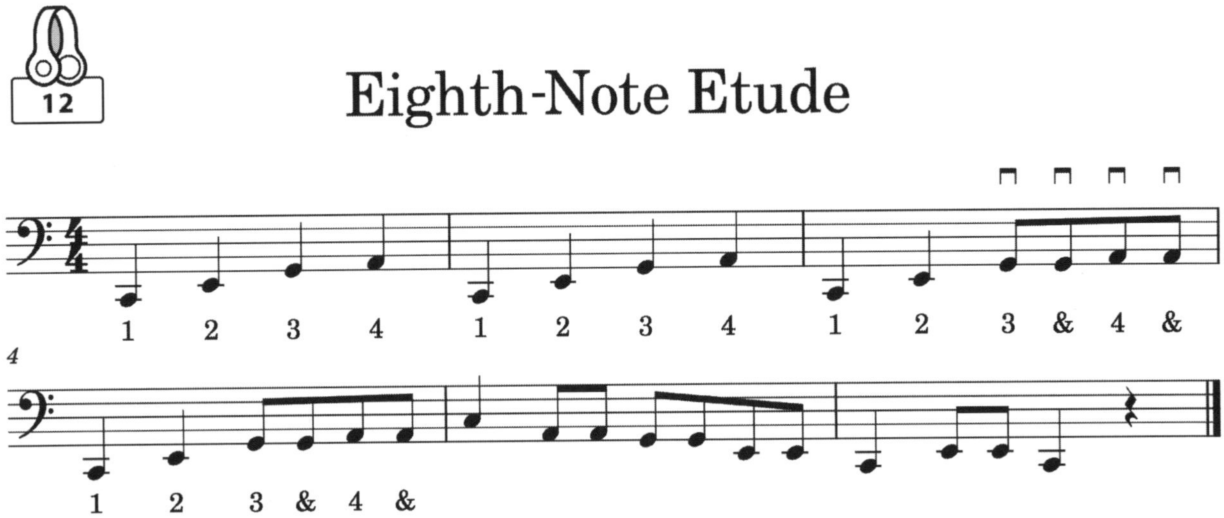

Figure 43: Eighth-Note Etude

The next tune is not identified; it is a common nursery rhyme. You might have to play the tune a few times before the words come to mind. If they do, notice how the lyrics assist you in keeping proper time.

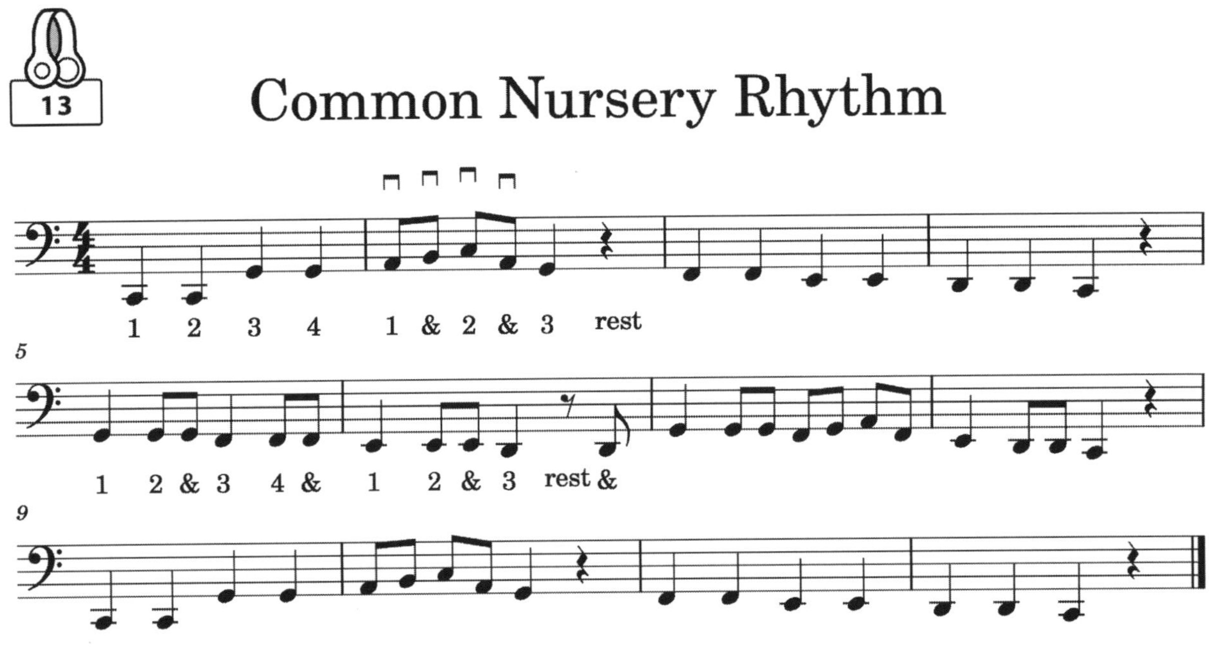

Figure 44: Common Nursery Rhyme

The next tune includes all the rhythmic values introduced so far.

14

Cripple Creek

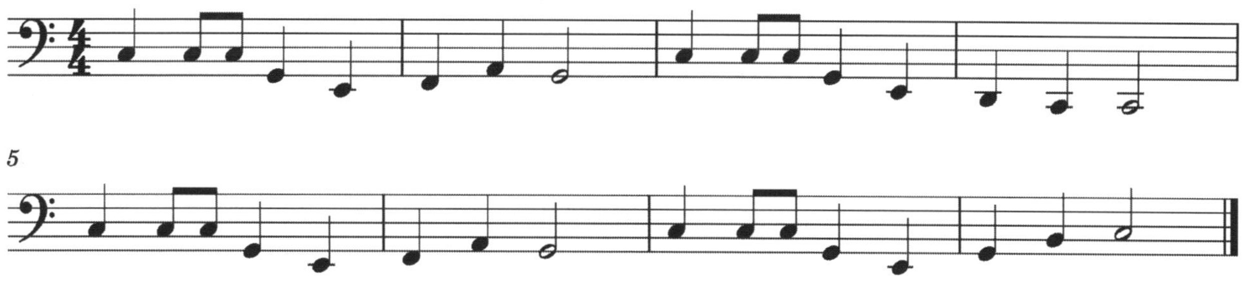

Figure 45: Cripple Creek

1.18 The Dotted Quarter Note

A dot on a quarter (or eighth note) increases its duration (length) by half of its original value. So, a dotted quarter is equal to 1½ beats.

Previously, you played a modified version of "Ode to Joy." The next tune is the original version which has dotted quarter notes in measures 4, 8 and 16. Notice: All three measures have the same rhythm even though the notes may change. Count this measure "1 and 2, and, 3 4."

15

Ode to Joy

Ludwig van Beethoven

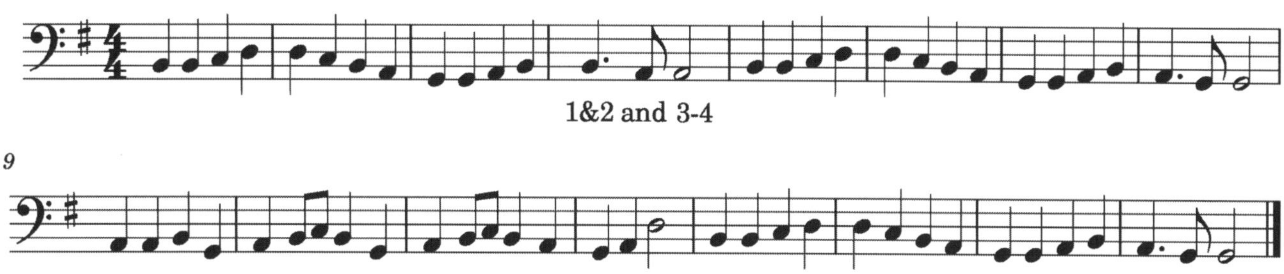

Figure 46: Ode to Joy

1.19 The Upstroke and Alternate Picking

You may be surprised that we have covered so much material with no mention of the upstroke. We have been concentrating on playing the downstroke with the drop-and-stop method because it is so critical to establish this habit for proper technique and tonality. If you have been using the upstroke out of habit, then please review the section "Picking the Open Strings" before continuing. So, why the emphasis on downstrokes using the drop-and-stop method? Because the principle of playing a smooth upstroke is just a minor variation of the downstroke. You cannot play a second downstroke without lifting the pick to get ready for that downstroke, or any downstrokes to follow. All we need to do is to play the same string again during the lift phase. Ideally, your right hand will be at an angle to the strings, as shown below:

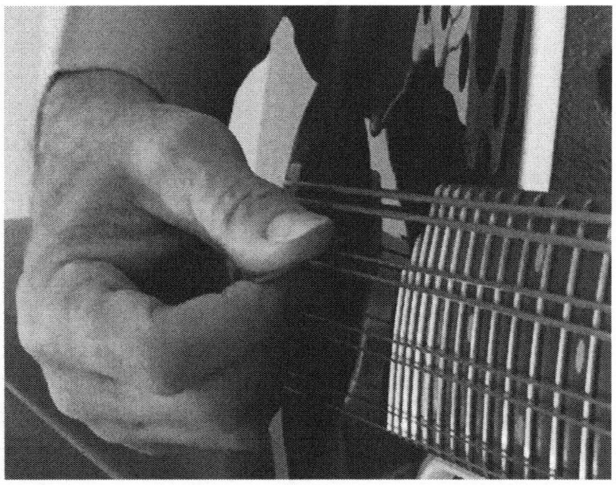

Figure 47: Correct pick angle for starting the upstroke

From the player's perspective, you should be able to see the bottom of the palm of the right hand. This is the correct angle for starting the upstroke.

Alternate Picking Etude

The following example, "Alternate Picking Etude," explains the principles of alternate picking [down and up strokes with the pick] and movement between strings. We want a "sweet" tone, not a harsh tone.

Play slowly; alternate picking is not a speed drill. Every change in pick direction is also a change of notes, so this is also a coordination exercise.

Start on the A string, and go "up the alphabet" – A, B, C, D. Play the open A string with a downstroke; be sure to lift and drop through both strings. The upstroke, for the B, is just as precise: with the pick at the defined proper angle, **it should only strike the lower A string, not both, during the upstroke**. The etude continues with this alternating pattern. It should become second nature so that you don't even need to think about the pick movement.

What happens after the first four notes? Having played the fourth note (D) with an upstroke, you can immediately play the next downstroke on the second string, a D one octave lower. The symbol in measure 7 that looks like a half circle with a dot in the middle is called a ***fermata***; it means to hold the note, or let it continue to sound. It is there to give you the time to mentally prepare for the next note on the next lower string. The up-down pattern continues, as before. A *fermata* stops the normal rhythmic counting, so, as written, you cannot play this exercise with a metronome. The tempo of the tune does not change, it merely has a pause at the *fermata*.

At measure 8 the scale descends from the upper C and starts with an upstroke. It may not be immediatley apparent why you should start with an upstroke, until you get to the first note on the next string. The G is played with a downstroke. Starting measure 8 with an upstroke enables the alternating pattern to continue when changing strings.

Play through this exercise initially without the metronome. Pause only as long as necessary to prepare mentally and physically for the shift to the next string. Eventually, you should use a metronome and ignore the *fermatas*. The following exercise should be played daily. This pattern requires a change of finger to play a different note for each movement of the pick.

16

Alternate Picking Etude

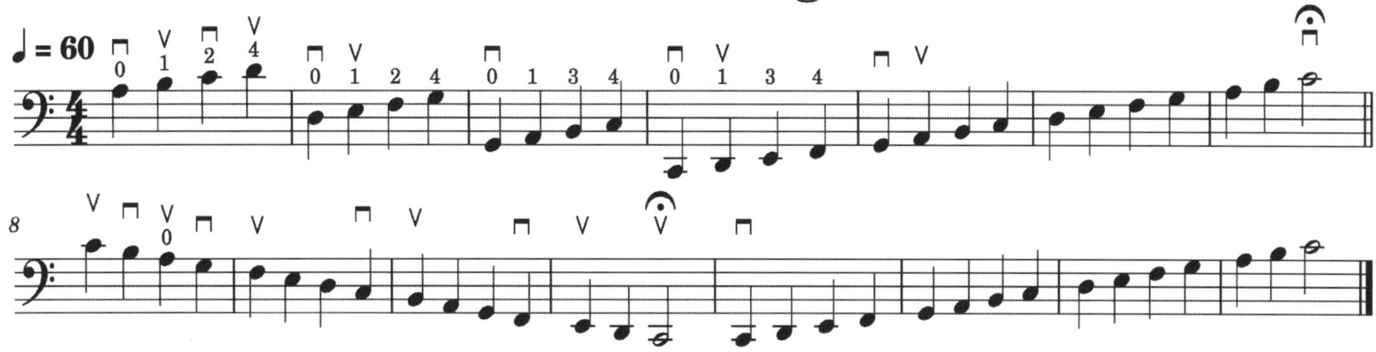

Figure 48: Alternate Picking Etude

The next example requires eighth notes to be played with down/up strokes on the same note. In measure 1 you see the implied upstroke, which is there to remind you to lift the pick to prepare for the next downstroke. So, how do you "play" an eighth-note rest? Simply stop all the strings from vibrating. In this example, it's the one string you have just played. To "play" the rest, lift the appropriate left-hand finger slightly, relieving the pressure holding the string to the fretboard without completely lifting the finger off the string. The *fermata* symbol for each quarter note is there to allow "mental preparation" for the upcoming alternate picking pattern. At the end of measure 4 there is both a *fermata* and a quarter rest. The A needs to stop sounding, but since it is an open string, you will need to mute it with the heel of the right-hand palm. Do not slap the string; gently place the heel on the vibrating string, and adjacent strings, to stop the sound. The last measure applies the same principle "in time" as there is no *fermata* pausing the song.

17

Alternate Picking Eighth Notes

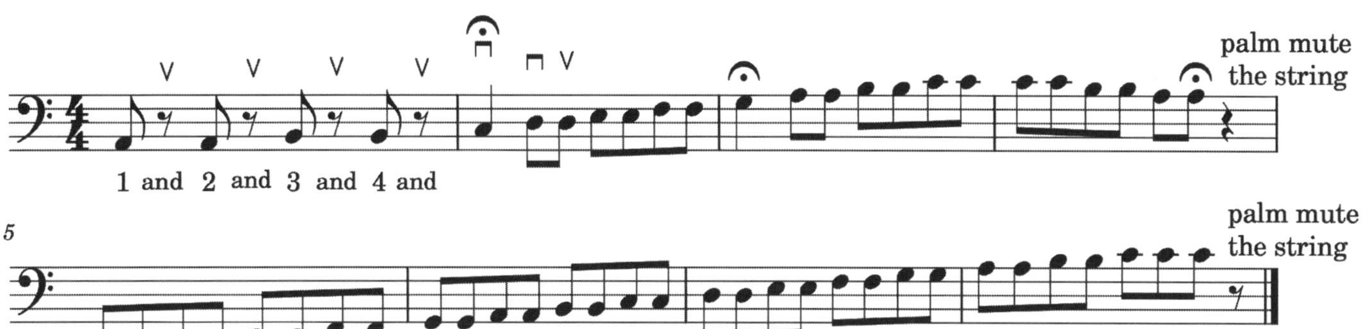

Figure 49: Alternate Picking Eighth Notes

Now, let's apply the principles of alternate picking to a common French tune.

18

Alternate Picking Applied to a Common French Tune

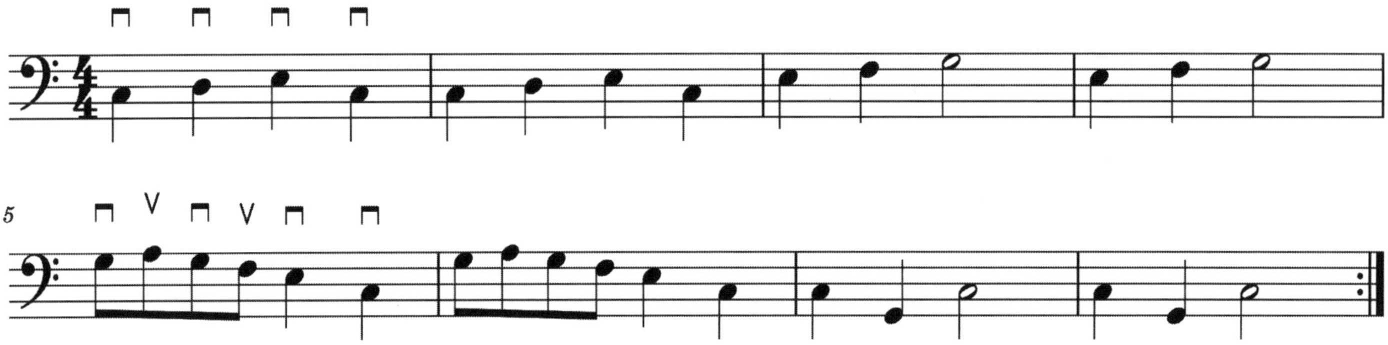

Figure 50: Alternate Picking Applied to a Common French Tune

The following well-known tune includes quarter notes, eighth notes and half notes. While tempting, try not to play too fast. Use alternate picking on only the eighth notes.

19

Old MacDonald

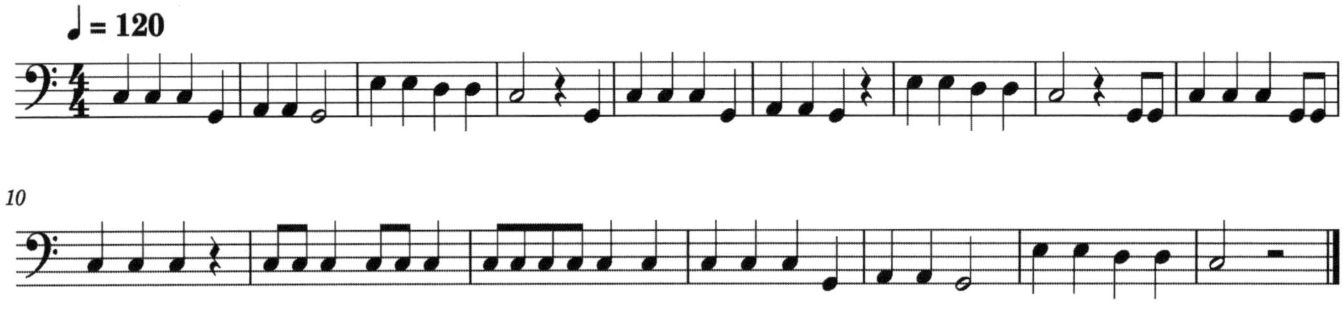

Figure 51: Old MacDonald

Below is another alternate picking exercise based on a J. S. Bach Musette. The time signature is in 2/4, so the beats are included to facilitate proper counting.

20 Alternate Picking – Musette

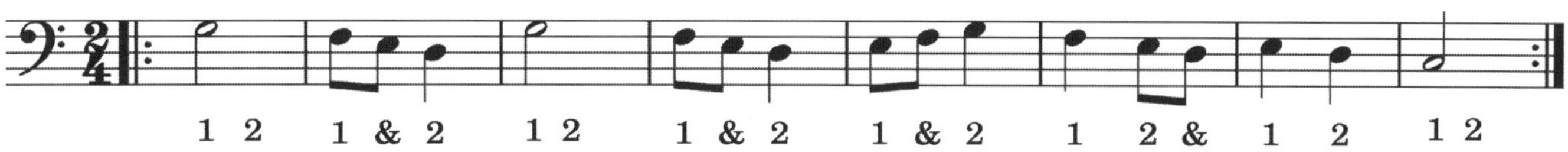

Figure 52: Alternate Picking – Musette

For the following exercise, play all the half, quarter, and eighth notes with downstrokes and use an alternating pattern only for the 16th notes. Like eighth notes, sixteenth notes are beamed together if part of the same beat. Sixteenth notes are typically counted – 1, e, &, a. The ampersand (&) is pronounced "and." The "a" is normally pronounced as "uh."

21 Alternate Picking Etude – 16th Notes

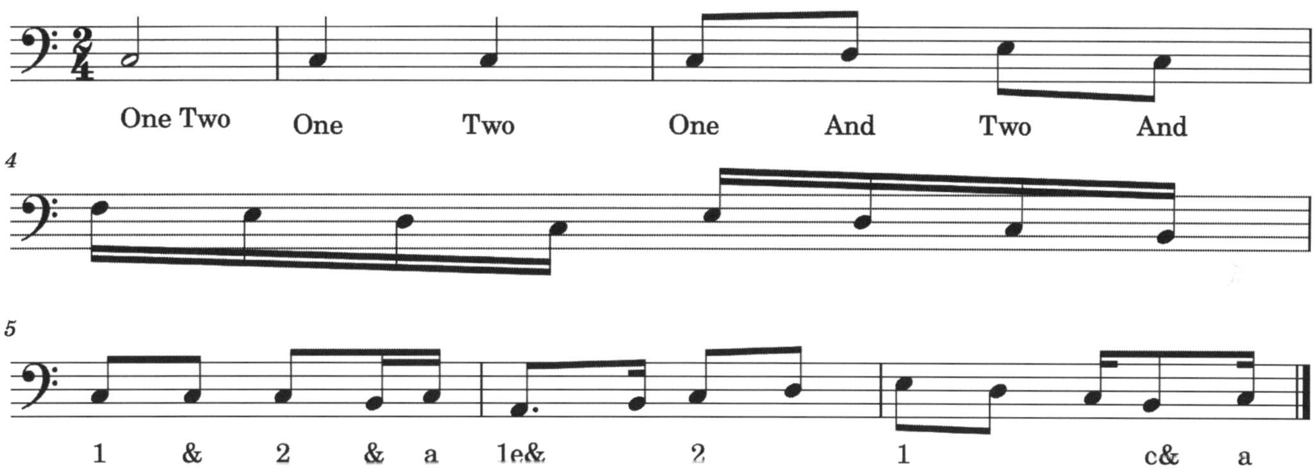

Figure 53: Alternate Picking Etude – 16th Notes

Bickford's Left-Hand Technique

The following exercise, from Bickford's section on "Studies in Left-Hand Technic," includes a helpful introduction to the challenge of coordinating the left and right hands.

> *"To insure a clean and reliable technic, it is absolutely essential that the fingers of the left hand work exactly in conjunction with the pick. This is to be taken literally and means that when the pick moves for a down or an up stroke, the required finger must start at the same instant, either to drop against the string or to leave it, as the case may be. It is essential that the fingers remain in their places as long as possible, so long as the playing is confined to any one string. (In) the following study...the right hand plays an important part and the strokes must be very quick and decisive, the pick remaining exactly where it lands in either direction until it starts in the opposite direction."*
> (*The Bickford Method for Mando-cello* by Myron A. Bickford, page 16.)

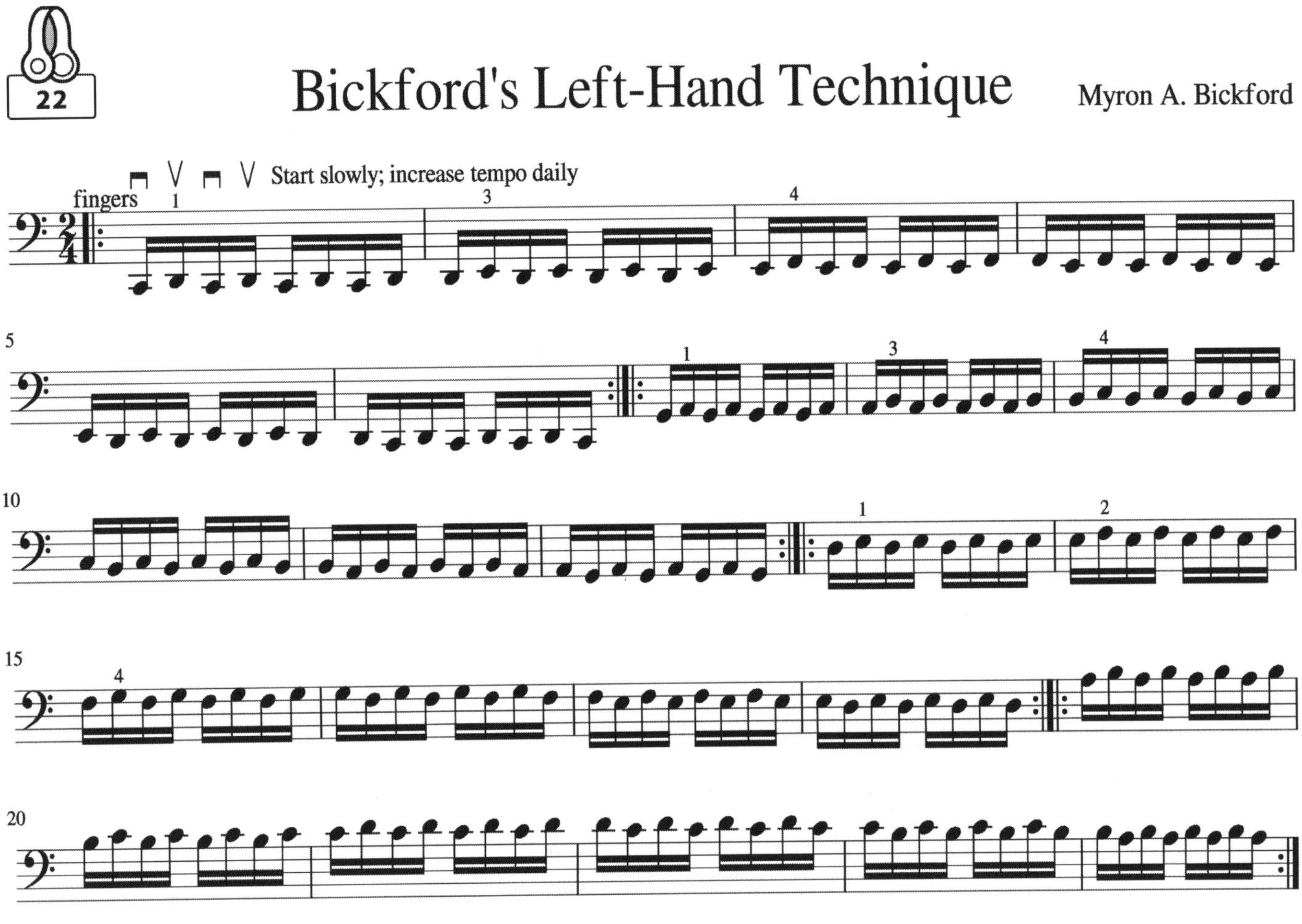

Figure 54: Bickford's Left-Hand Technique

1.20 Preparation for Playing a New Tune

Our next example "Studies in Waltz Time," by Myron A. Bickford, will serve as the template for the preparatory steps to take before you play any new tune, consider:

(1) In what key signature is the tune written?

With no sharps or flats, it's likely the key of C, but check the last note of the tune; it might be in the key of Am, the relative minor to the key of C.

(2) What is the time signature?

It's in 3/4, or waltz time.

(3) Is there a tempo marking?

Here, yes, but not all waltz tunes specify the tempo.

(4) What is the shortest note value played?

An eighth-note. What does that tell us? To subdivide with "1 and, 2 and, 3 and."

Be sure to play all quarter notes with a downstroke and all eighth notes with an alternating down and up stroke. Don't forget to mute the strings during rests. This tune provides two methods of muting the strings: in measure 12, mute the D by resting the palm of the right hand on the strings; in measure 4, mute the A with the palm, or by lifting the first finger slightly off the fretboard. Do not remove the finger from the string entirely as the open string may resonate slightly; just reduce the pressure applied by the first finger.

23

Studies in Waltz Time

Myron A. Bickford

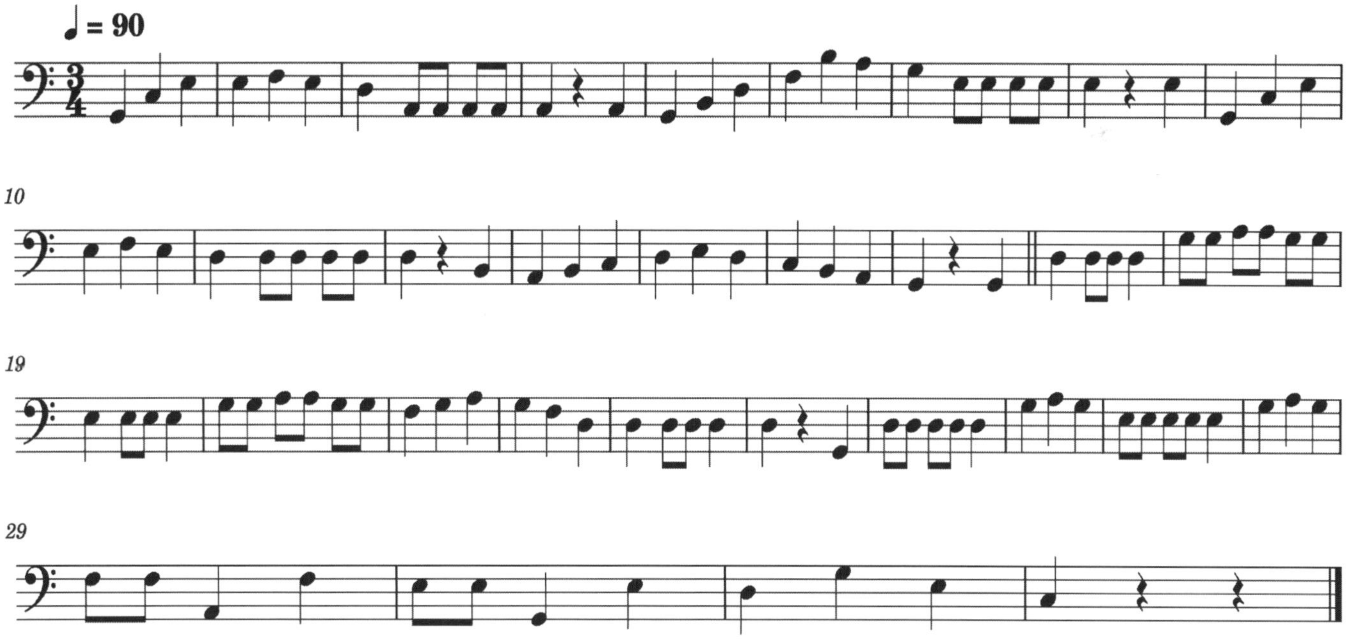

Figure 55: Studies in Waltz Time

1.21 Etudes and Waltzes in 3/4 Time Signature

Here is a simple arrangement of a popular waltz. Apply the principles from the previous section: There are no sharps or flats in the key signature, but the piece ends on the note A. Even before playing it, we can be confident that this waltz is in the key of A minor.

24

Chopin Waltz

Arr. Mark E. Freemantle

F. Chopin

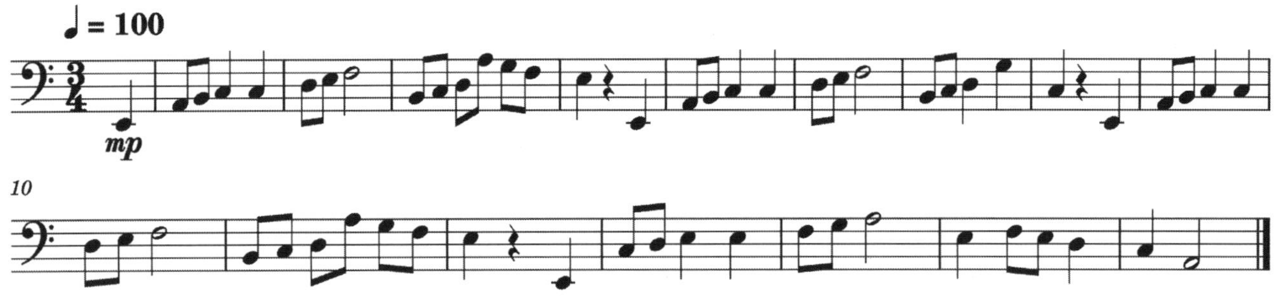

Figure 56: Chopin Waltz

The following tune, another waltz, introduces more musical terms and principles of reading sheet music. Notice that the first measure contains only one quarter note, called a **pickup note**, or technically, an *anacrusis*. Because it is not a full measure, we do not consider it measure 1. Count off the 3 /4 time, and start playing on beat 3. The repeat symbol at measure 8 takes us back to the beginning of the tune, but notice that measure 8 only has 2 quarter beats; the third beat is provided by the pickup measure. The second time playing this section the third beat is provided by another anacrusis after the repeat symbol. There are two musical terms to learn: *Fine* and *D.C. al Fine*. The Italian musical term fine (pronounced fee'-nay) marks the end of the tune, or movement. *D.C. al Fine*, or *Da Capo al Fine*, means "Play from the beginning to the end." So, play section 1, repeat section 1, play section 2, go back to the top of the tune and end at the *Fine*.

25

German Dance Waltz

Arr. Mark E. Freemantle

Ludwig van Beethoven

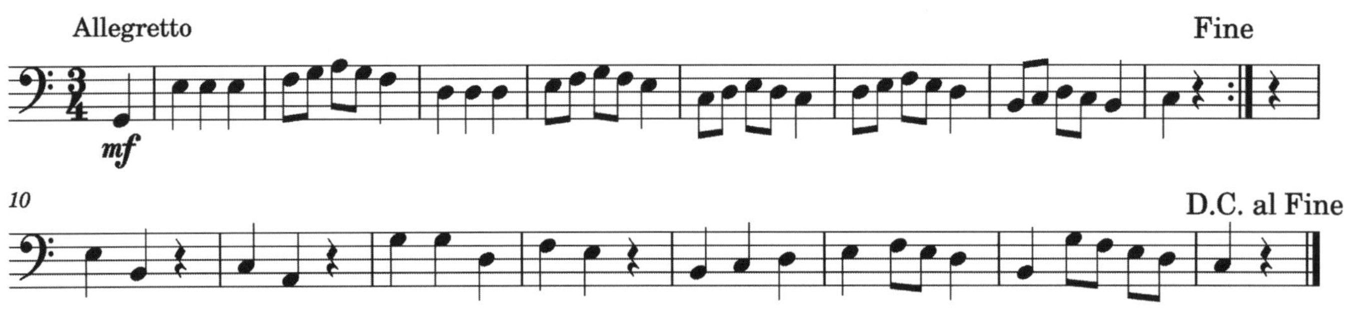

Figure 57: German Dance Waltz

1.22 Introducing the Key of G Major with One Sharp

Most of the exercises up to this point have been in the key of C major, which has no sharps or flats. The next key and scale we need to master is the key of G major, which has one note in the scale raised one fret, the F to F♯. The G scale still uses the same musical notes of our alphabet, and the scale is still comprised of eight notes, so, starting at G, the scale is:

G, A, B, C, D, E, F♯, G

Let's examine a single-octave G scale. First, notice that the G scale only requires strings two and three, and that the pattern of notes on the fretboard is symmetrical, yielding the Whole-Whole-Half-Whole-Whole-Whole-Half-tone diatonic major scale formula, as discussed previously. In the key of G major the two pairs of notes that are a half-step apart are the B – C and F♯ – G.

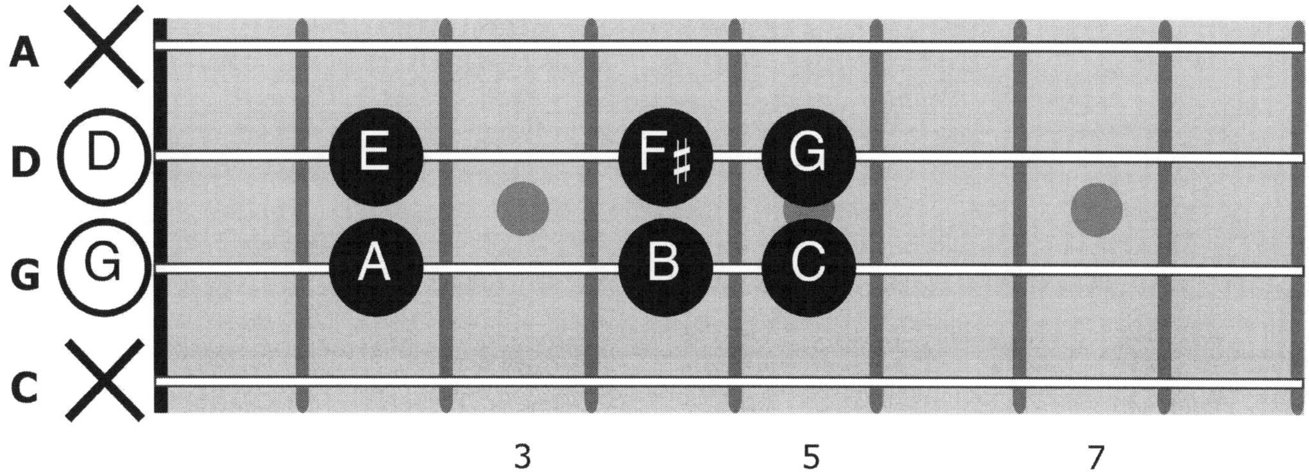

Figure 58: G Major Scale – on Strings 2 and 3

We play the A and E with the first finger, the B and F♯ with the third, and the C and G with the pinky. Notice too that the relationship for B – C remains the same: a half-step. The relationship between E – F♯ has changed to a whole-step, while the F♯ – G is now the second half-step in the scale. All Major scales have two pairs of notes that are a half-step apart. The scale is notated below:

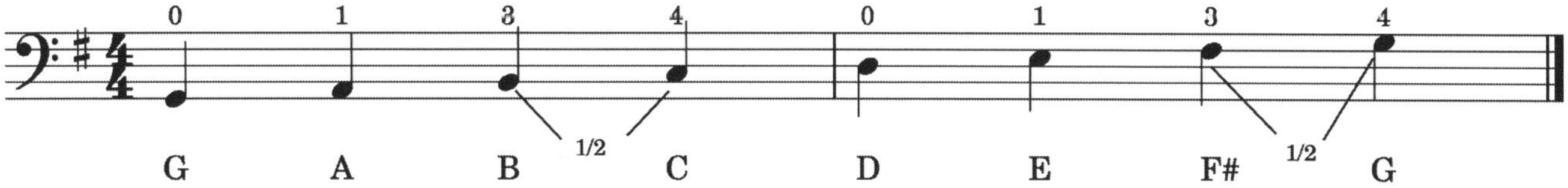

Figure 59: G Scale – One Octave

Notice the sharp symbol ♯ is located just to the right of the bass clef symbol. Its location on the fourth line identifies its name. The fourth line is the note F, so in the key of G, the F becomes an F-sharp [F♯]. Remember that ALL F notes played in the key of G are F♯, not just the F♯ identified on line 4. So, in the two-octave scale on the next page, the second F♯ in measure 4 is played with the 3rd finger (as noted) on the 9th fret. As you know, the space between the E and F natural is only one fret, but in the key of G major, the F becomes an F♯, so it is two frets away from E.

Play the two-octave G scale, below, and be sure to notice the fingerings. Measure 4 includes the Roman numeral VII, which identifies the 7th fret and indicates that a shift is necessary to play the remaining portion of the scale. It is always a good habit to examine a new piece of music, identify the key signature, and play the related major scale. This facilitates proper fingering as well as getting the key signature "into your ear."

26

G Scale - Two Octaves

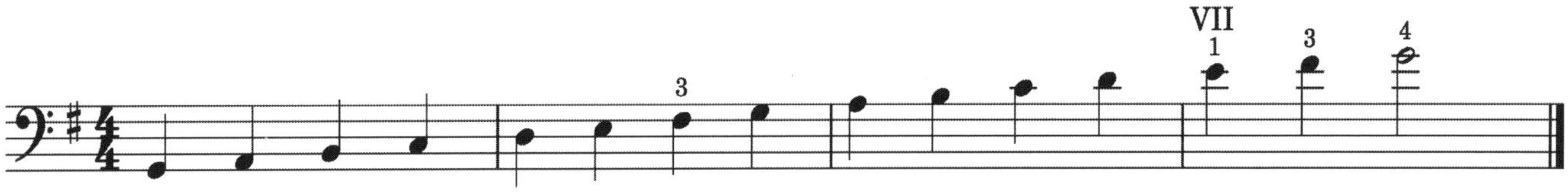

Figure 60: The G Scale – Two Octaves

Play the scale again, but this time play an F natural in measures 2 and 4, not the F♯ notes required for the key of G. Notice how it sounds completely wrong? Playing the scale correctly helps to "tune the ear" too.

When we first introduced the bass clef, we pointed out that the mandocello's strings correlate with the lines in the bass clef staff:

> The low C string is sitting on the second ledger line below the staff.
>
> The G string is represented by the bottom line of the bass clef staff.
>
> The D string lies on the middle line.
>
> The A string corresponds to the top line.

As mentioned previously, memorize the five lines of the bass clef by using the mnemonic: Good Boys Do Fine Always. For the four spaces in between use – All Cows Eat Grass. [Since we cannot go lower than the C string, we just memorize the notes below the staff: C, D, E, and F. See the fretboard diagram in Section 1.13 for reference.] The good news is – we can repeat the All Cows Eat Grass mnemonic starting on the top line and continuing up to three ledger lines.

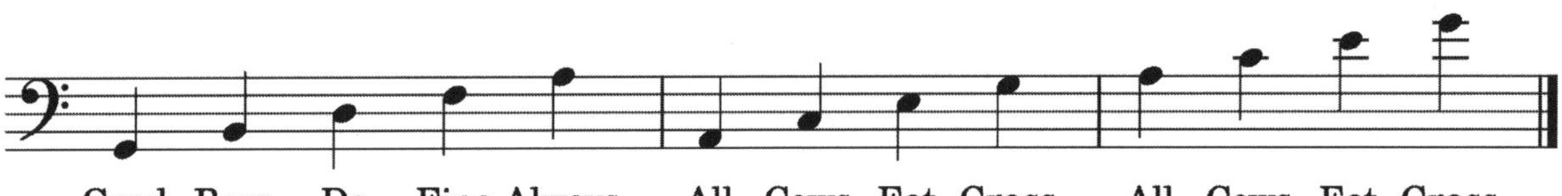

Figure 61: Extended Bass Clef Mnemonic for Lines and Spaces

1.23 Tunes in the Key of G

The following tune, "Aura Lee", written in 1861, is a highly recognizable tune. You may know it as "Love Me Tender," from the movie of the same title, set in the time of the U.S. Civil War.

27

Aura Lee

George B. Poulton

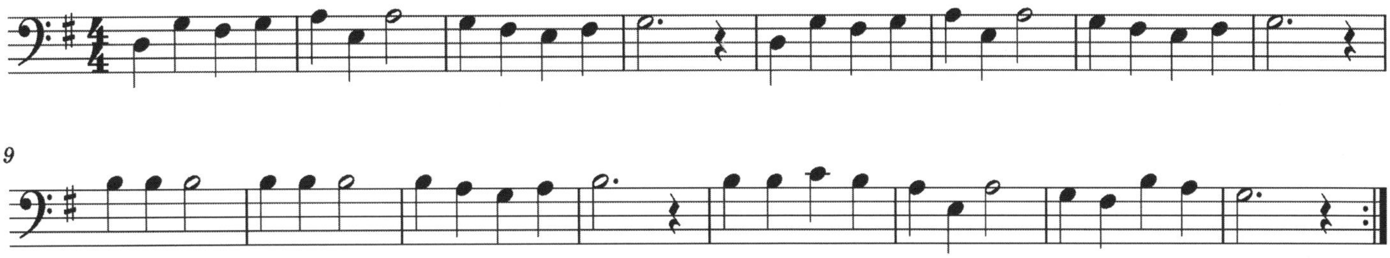

Figure 62: Aura Lee

"Go Tell Aunt Rhody" is an American folk song from the 18th century, derived from various European sources.

28

Go Tell Aunt Rhody

Folk Tune

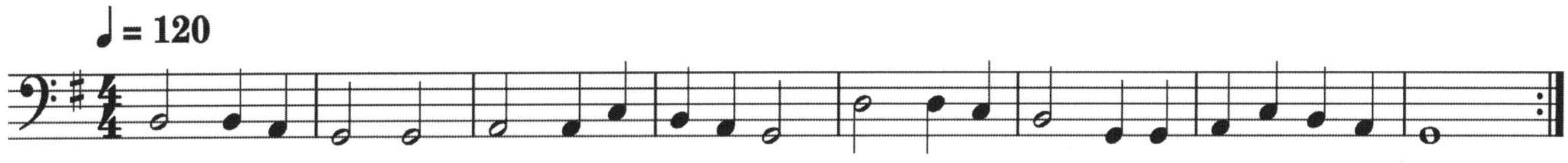

Figure 63: Go Tell Aunt Rhody

We associate the following melody with the national anthems of multiple countries. Pay special attention to measures 12 and 13, which include suggested pick directions.

29

Nation's Anthems

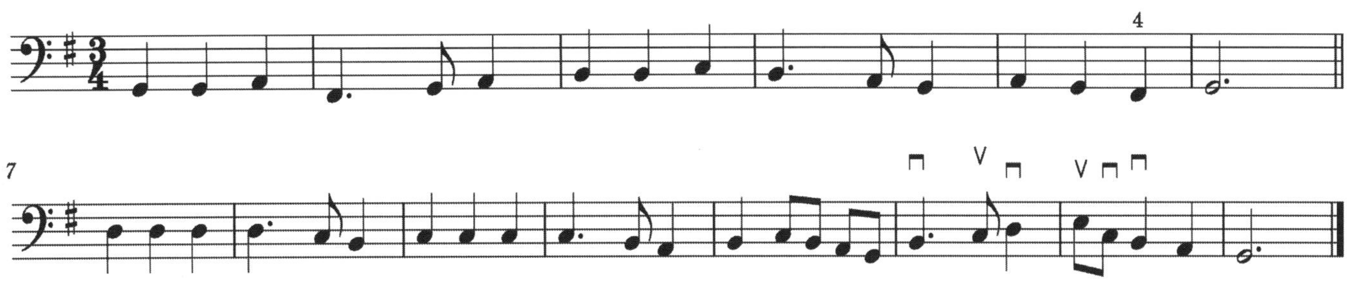

Figure 64: Nation's Anthems

1.24 Tremolo

Music notation often requires that a note be sustained for a long time; this presents a challenge for the mandocellist as compared to the cellist. The cellist can sustain a note as long as desired by playing "long bows" or *tenuto*. The mandocello, like all plectrum instruments, requires a different technique to sustain the note. That technique is the **tremolo**.

The tremolo technique is the application of the down and upstroke at a much faster rate. It sounds simple enough, but often challenges players. Most guitarists and mandolinist find that "*...since the mandocello, owing to the size of the strings and the consequent larger sphere of the vibrations, will not permit as rapid a tremolo as the mandolin...*" [Bickford, page 20.] Changes in right-hand technique may be required to achieve the best tremolo possible. The first critical question to answer is – "How many alternating strokes are required for it to be considered tremolo?" Again, Bickford provides the answer – "*The impression that any certain number of strokes is necessary for each beat or for notes of the same denomination, in all cases is erroneous.*" [*ibid.*] **The general principle for playing an effective tremolo is to play more alternating strokes than the shortest note in that tune.** For example: If the music's shortest duration note is an eighth note, then it may be appropriate to play sixteenth-note strokes when applying the tremolo technique to a whole note in one measure. It may not be possible to play twice as many notes as the shortest duration note, but it is a worthy target and, on slower-tempo pieces, it may sound better with **more** alternating strokes.

The ideal approach to the tremolo is to continue the drop-and-stop method for alternate picking, applying the Down on Two strings, Up on One String approach. If this method does not provide an effective tremolo, it will be necessary to change the right-hand approach. Consider the following two aspects of right-hand technique:
1) How to hold the pick, and 2) The movement of the right arm.

How to Hold the Pick:

If the pick is held in flexion, as described in Section 1.4, it minimizes the amount of surface tension between the pick and the strings. The result is a sensation of the pick "gliding" over the string more consistently. We can achieve similar results with a very rounded point on the pick. It may be necessary to compromise tone for speed. Experiment with different picks in both thumb positions [extension versus flexion.] Using a thinner pick may also facilitate the playing of the tremolo, but sacrifices tone quality for speed.

The Movement of the Right Arm:

In playing tremolo, the movement of the right arm may also require a unique approach. In step two of the drop-and-stop method, the right forearm is rotated to raise and lower the pick. Try this same approach for the tremolo but minimize the rotation in such a manner as to **not** be able to see the heel of the hand on the upstroke. In this approach, the lower string does not impede the motion of the hand and pick. Think of the hand as "vibrating" across the strings. If this still does not produce the desired tremolo effect, there is one more approach to try.

Because of the diameter of the mandocello strings and the challenge of getting them to vibrate sufficiently, it is possible to increase the force upon the strings by using the weight of the forearm. In this approach, hold the pick at an angle to the strings [flexion] and raise and lower the entire arm in one motion, moving only from the elbow. The wrist does not rotate but remains in a relaxed state.

No matter which method you use, hold the pick as loosely as possible to minimize tension in the hand, wrist, arm, and even the shoulder.

The exercise below illustrates tremolo starting on the D string. The D string facilitates the drop and stop method by having the A string below it to stop the pick. Repeat each picking pattern as often as necessary. The last measure illustrates two new symbols: 1.) The two slash marks [//] below a whole note signify "play with tremolo," which is precisely what you were doing in the previous two measures. This is the normal way to mark tremolo. 2.) The initials *D.C.* signify *Da Capo*, Italian for "return to the top", or start over from measure 1. Each time you repeat, increase the tempo. Play with a metronome and if your electronic app includes a practice mode, set it to increase the tempo during each cycle. Be sure to continue counting the four beats, preferably out loud. Do not count the strokes. For this exercise only count "1,2,3,4". Do not count "1, e, &, a, 2, e, & a" etc. as you will want to play faster than you can say the sub-divisions. Start at the defined 60 bpm and practice daily, gradually increasing the tempo. Repeat the process on the G string next, then the C string, which will be harder to implement due to the increased thickness of the strings. Finally, move to the A string, whereby muscle memory will aid in implementing the implied stop motion.

30

Tremolo Preparatory Exercise

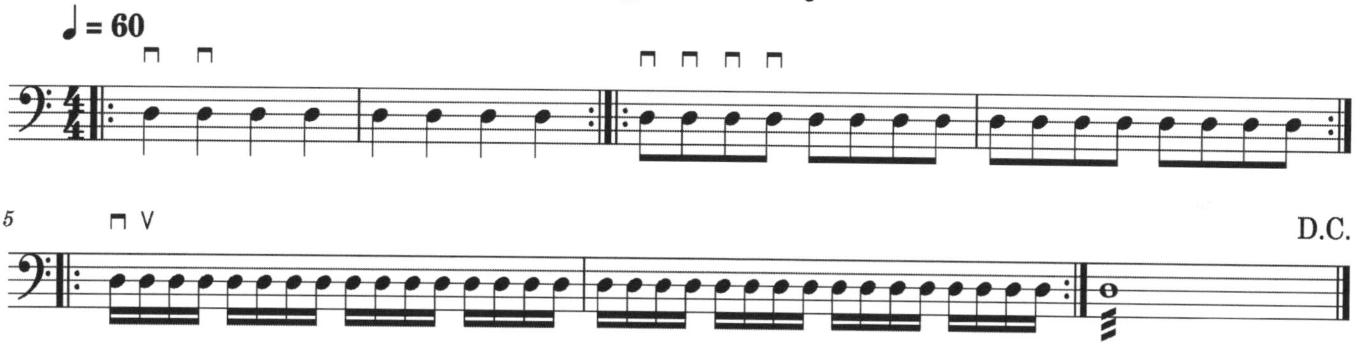

Figure 65: Tremolo Preparatory Exercise

The following tremolo etude was designed to provide a logical transition from fast alternate picking to the sustained tremolo. While 220 bpm is the target goal, start at a slower tempo if necessary.

31

Tremolo Etude 1

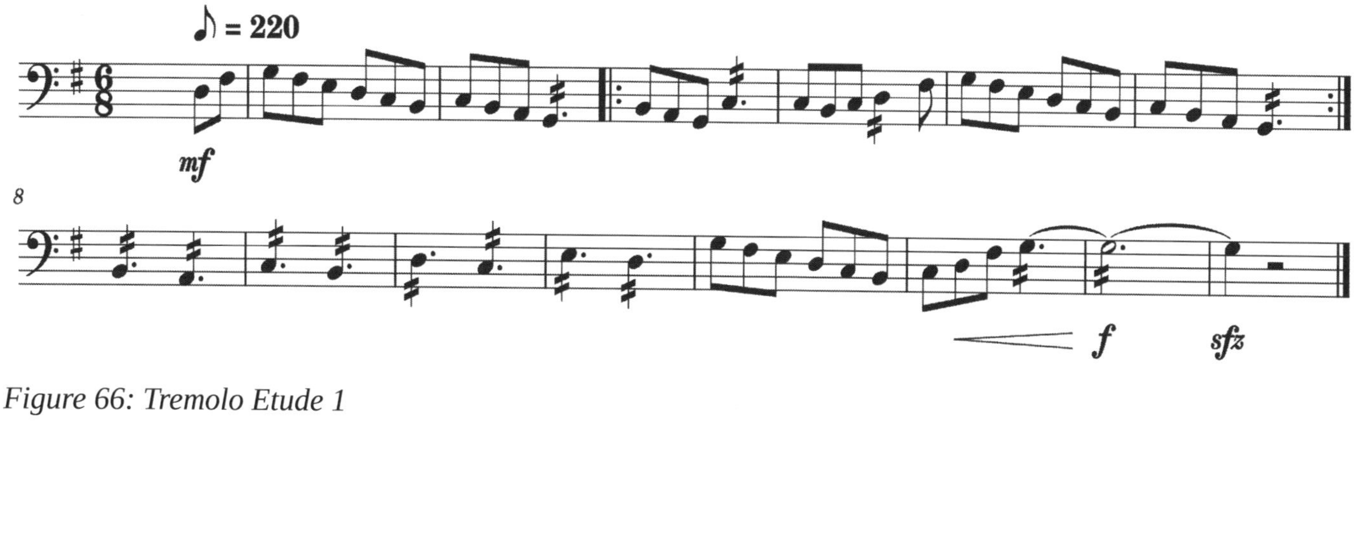

Figure 66: Tremolo Etude 1

1.25 Tremolo and Musical Phrasing

In the previous etude, we transitioned from fast alternate picking to the tremolo, applied to only the quarter and dotted quarter notes. The following tune, "How Can I Leave Thee," applies the tremolo to a complete musical phrase. The curved line that appears over the notes of every two measures is a phrase marking; in this example it is a melodic phrase, as identified by the original lyrics. A singer would normally take a breath at the end of each two-measure phrase. Practice this etude one phrase at a time. This will facilitate the desired aim of making an obvious transition from one melodic phrase to the next. Actually taking a breath at the end of the phrase can also facilitate proper technique.

32

How Can I Leave Thee?

Thuringian Folk Song

Apply tremolo technique to each 2-measure phrase.

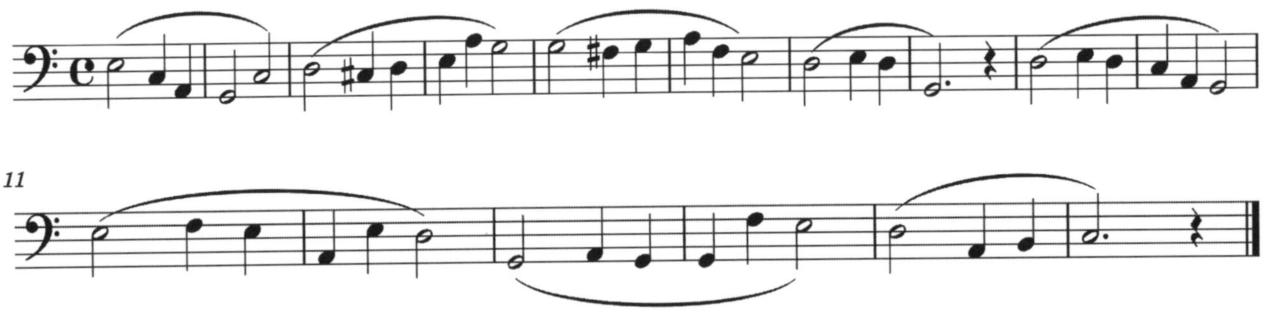

Figure 67: How Can I Leave Thee?

Bickford's Andante, in C

Andante is an Italian word that means "walking," so perform this piece at a slow, moderate pace, typically between 76 and 108 beats per minute. Bickford's version (transposed from the original key of F) has been modified to introduce some new musical elements. The first 8 notes are written with two small slashes through the stem of the notes, which indicates – "play with tremolo." A composer may identify how many strokes they expect you to play. Since this tune is in 3/4 time, you would play a minimum of 6 alternating pick-strokes. Two dash lines would then double that amount, etc. The tremolo indication is not shown past measure 8 because it is implied by another musical element – the slur. The arcing line above the note is a slur and indicates a smooth, connected manner of playing. You can achieve this effect by playing with tremolo. Additionally, measure 9 indicates "sim"; this is an abbreviation for "simile" and indicates to play the following passage in a manner similar to the previous passage. Notice the quarter rest at measure 8; stop the tremolo and mute the sound of the open string at beat 3.

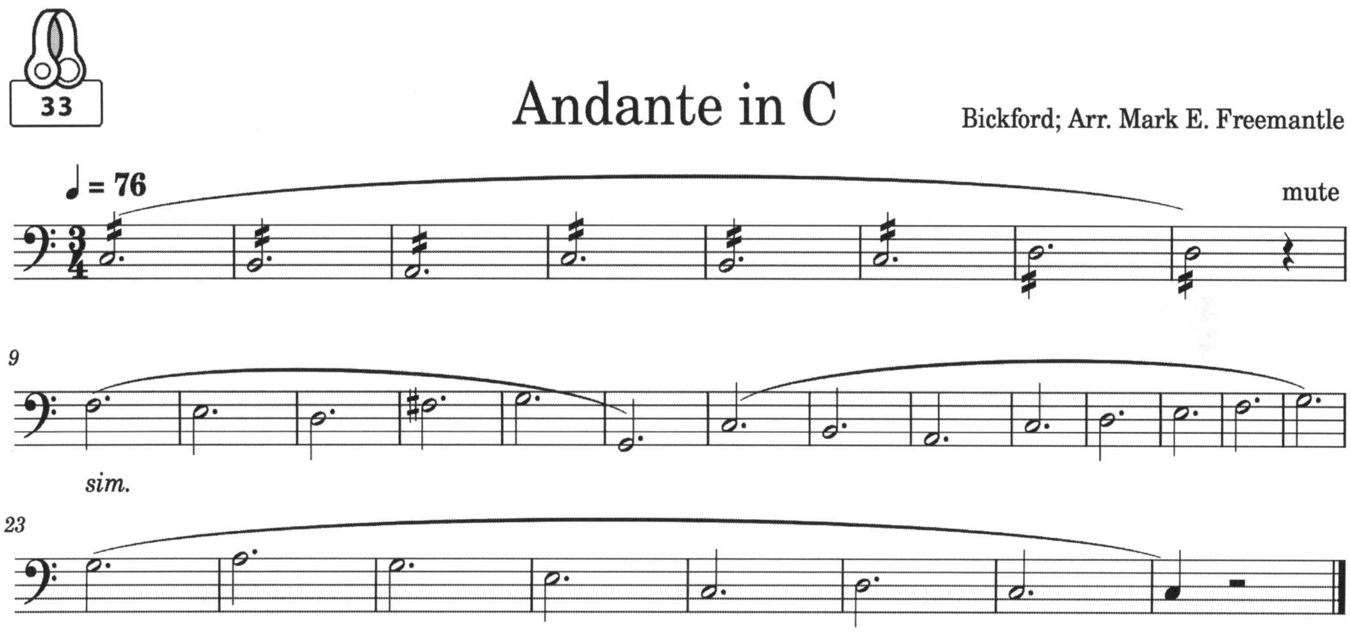

Figure 68: Andante in C

Slurs and Phrases

As already mentioned, the long arching line that appears over measure 1 to 8 of "*Andante in C*" is a slur marking. However, it may also be interpreted as a phrase marking. A phrase may cover a longer passage, as in this example, but it still implies a sense of connection. A bowed instrument might interpret the phrase markings by moving the bow in one direction only throughout the phrase. Since we play with a pick, we cannot connect the notes that precisely. Measure 8 includes a rest, so we must stop the tremolo at the rest by muting the open D string with the heel of the right hand then start the tremolo again at measure 9. Notice that the slur or phrase continues to measure 14 so the tremolo is continually applied throughout the phrase. At measure 14 the G is played on an open string. Again, the tremolo must stop and the open string is muted. Notice that we play the same note at measures 22 and 23. The two phrases are separated by slightly lifting the finger at the end of the phrase in measure 22.

Wondrous Love

This selection has no tremolo marking indicated, but there are several reasons why we might want to apply tremolo. To begin, the tempo is defined as 76 beats-per-minute, which is relatively slow. It is also marked as "*Andante Cantabile.*" "*Andante*" is a tempo reference and signifies "play at moderate tempo," or "walking pace." [Check your metronome for the range covered by "*andante.*"] The second term "C*antabile*" means to play in a lyrical manner. Combining the two terms means to play at a moderate tempo with a singing effect, or flowing and songlike. Many of the quarter notes are connected by a slur marking, which advises the performer to connect the two notes; this is best done with the tremolo technique.Use tremolo technique on all half notes.

34

Wondrous Love

Folk Hynm, 1811

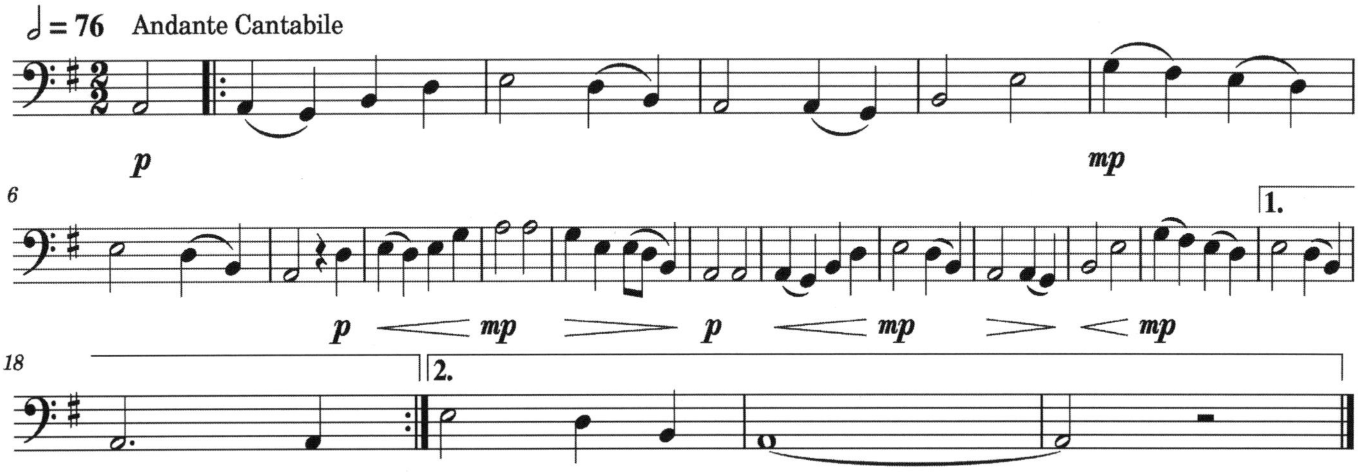

Figure 69: Wondrous Love

Beautiful Dreamer

"Beautiful Dreamer" is written in 9/8 time signature, i.e., nine beats per measure and the eighth notes get one beat. We count the first dotted quarter note in measure 1 – 4, 5, 6; and 7, 8, 9 for the second dotted quarter note. The dotted half note in measure 2 is six beats long. The tune is marked as *Dolce* which is the Italian musical term for "sweetly". The best way to accomplish this is to apply tremolo to all the dotted notes.

35

Beautiful Dreamer

Stephen Foster

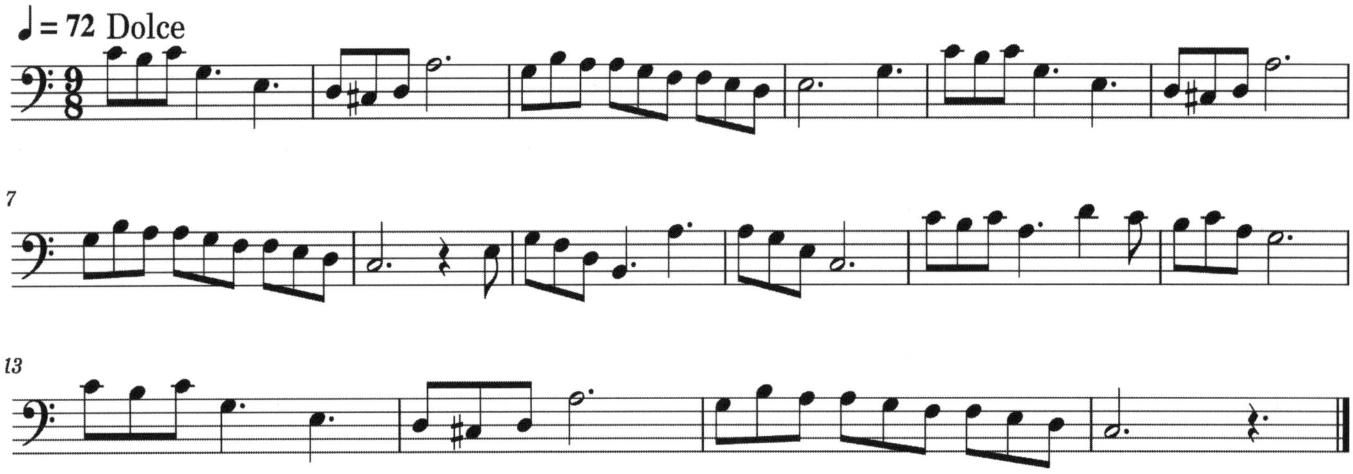

Figure 70: Beautiful Dreamer

1.26 Introducing the Key of F with One Flat

The key signature of F major contains one flat, B-flat. The F Scale provides us with a challenge: We must shift our left-hand position to be able to play a two-octave scale. The fretboard diagram below illustrates the note locations. Both the open strings and equivalent fretted notes (on fret 7) are shown.

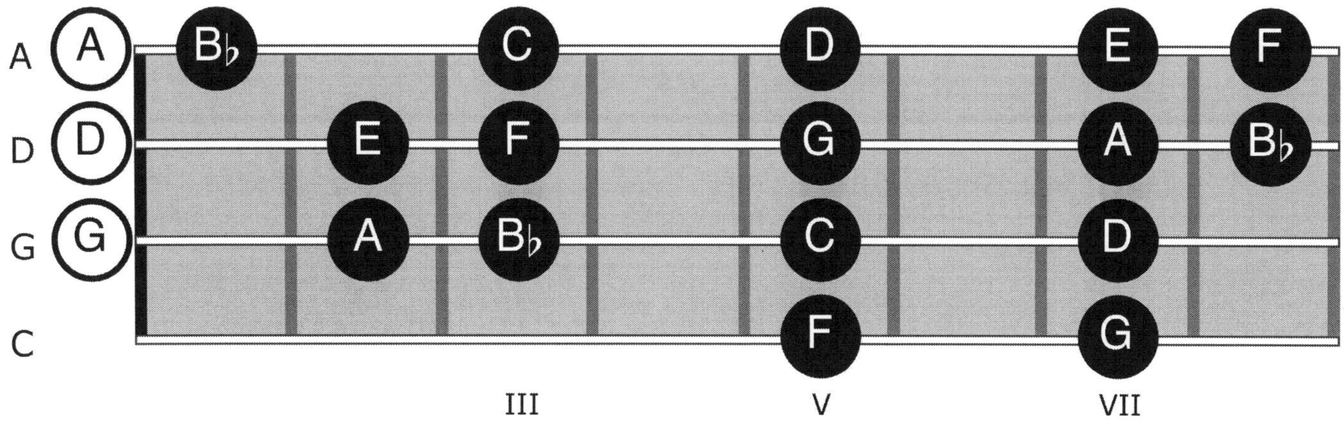

Figure 71: Two-Octave F Scale Fretboard Diagram

Most guitarists are comfortable playing scales in one position covering four frets. Stretching for an additional fifth fret is often necessary and not too challenging on guitar. On the mandocello it is not possible to play a two-octave F scale without shifting the left hand since we need to cover more than 5 frets. Looking at the diagram above, you can see the B♭ on string ①, fret 1 will require a stretch to reach while remaining in home position. This assumes playing the G, D, and A open strings, but you cannot reach the F on the seventh fret without shifting. Here is one approach to playing the two-octave F scale:

Start with the pinky on string ④, 5th fret. Play F, open-string G, A (finger 1), B♭ (finger 2), C (pinky), open-string D, E (finger 1), F (finger 2), G (pinky) open-string A, then shift (or reach back) to play the B♭ with finger 1. Now it gets challenging: you can shift to position III and play the C and D with fingers 1 and 4, then shift to position VII and play the E and F with fingers 1 and 2. An alternative is to play "stretch position"; play the B♭ with finger 1, the C with finger 2, and the D with finger 4. Then shift the left-hand, first finger to fifth fret. Finger 1 is now on the D note, but is only placed there for orientation. Play the E with finger 3 and the F with finger 4.

F Scale Exercise 1

The following exercise illustrates a simple two-octave F scale, ascending and descending with suggested fingering. The “stretch and shift” is required to play measures 4 and 5. Measure 1 includes a “courtesy” flat symbol. Measure 3 ends at the start of the second octave. Measure 4 starts with the F note repeated and played with the same fingering.

36

F Scale Exercise 1
Stretch and Shift

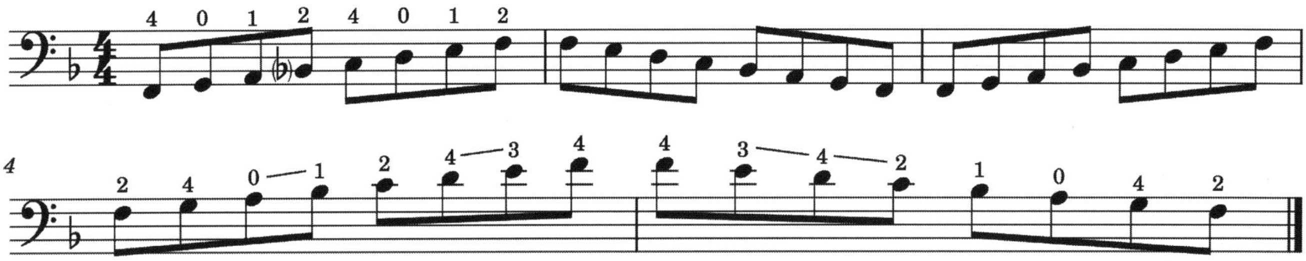

Figure 72: F Scale Exercise 1

Stretching and shifting can be challenging, especially if you need to keep your eyes on the music and not the fretboard. An alternative approach is to continue to play with “one finger, one fret” and shift to a new position as needed.

F Scale Exercise 2

The following example presents the same two-octave scale but with the recommended position shift and fingering. This example includes a *fermata* symbol at the end of each octave. The *fermata* ensures slower playing and allows preparation time to determine the fingering and shifting needed to complete the playing of the next octave. Measures 4 through 6 include Roman numerals above the fingerings to illustrate the fret location or position. The numerals follow the guitar tradition rather than the cello tradition since the mandocello is a fretted instrument. At measure 4, shift the first finger to the third fret and play the F. Shift again to the fifth fret to play the G. Play the A with the third finger on the seventh fret rather than with the open A string. Play the B♭ (with no courtesy accidental) with the pinky on the eighth fret. Shift back to the third fret for the C on the A string, then shift again up to the fifth fret for the D. The E and F fall right into place with fingers 3 and 4. The descending scale follows the same fingering and shifting patterns.

37

F Scale Exercise 2
Position Shifting

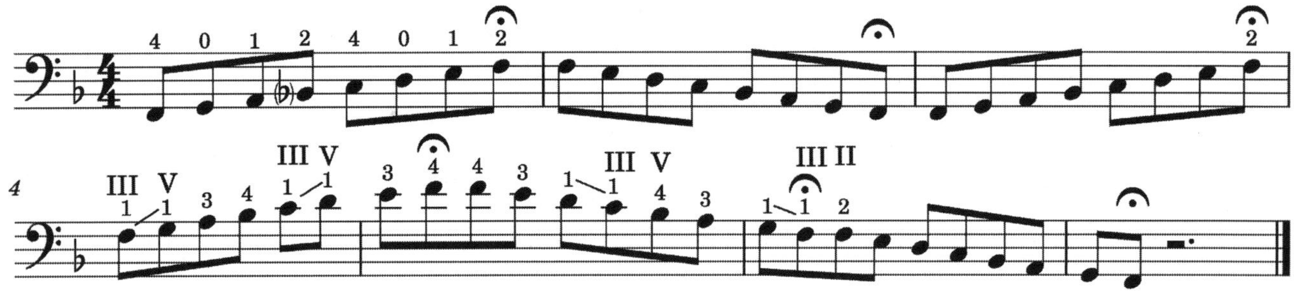

Figure 73: F Scale Exercise 2

There is one more alternative to consider when playing scales or tunes in the key of F major: Play in positions V and VII only and use no open strings. I find it possible to play this scale without looking at my hands since the shift, up or down, is only two frets. See the fretboard diagram below for reference.

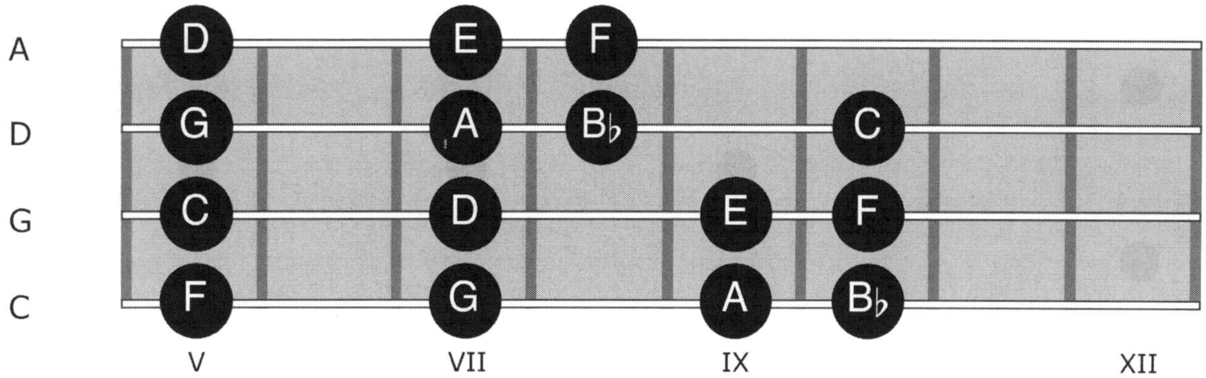

Figure 74: Fretboard Diagram - F Scale in Positions V and VII

Play all position V notes with finger 1 then shift to position VII. Notice the symmetry of the fretboard is such that fingers 3 and 4 are placed on strings ④ and ③, and fingers 2 and 4 are placed on strings ① and ②. This approach can be implemented easily with practice and negates the need to watch the fretboard. Try this approach with a 2-octave F scale.

1.27 Tunes in the Key of F or D Minor

Barbara Allen

The next tune, "Barbara Allen," in the key of F, includes the lyrics, which aid in understanding the flow of the melody. Notice that the first measure contains only one eighth note, called a **pickup note**, or technically, an *anacrusis*. Because it is not a full measure, we do not consider it measure 1. Count off the 3/4 time with the eighth note subdivision (1 & 2 & 3 &), and come in on the "and" of beat three. Don't rush playing the last eighth-note of measures 1, 2, 4, 5, 6, or 7. Imagine the singer taking a breath (') just before playing the eighth note and it will aid you in playing the tune in proper time.

38

Barbara Allen

Trad. English Folk Song

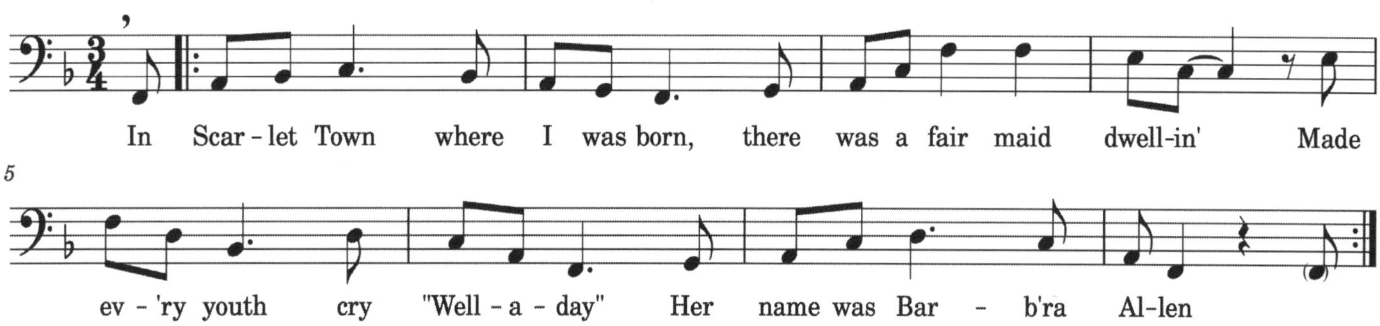

Figure 75: Barbara Allen

Interpretation: Even a simple folk melody should be played with an awareness of **interpretation**. The most direct approach is to vary the dynamic level by playing as if you are singing the tune – softer on low notes and louder to support the high notes, with *crescendos* and *decrescendos* between extremes. On the repeat, you might change the *tonal* color by playing closer or further from the bridge and applying a *ritardando*, gradually slowing towards the end. Attention to such details will greatly enhance your overall musicianship.

Gavotte in D Minor

A *gavotte* is a lively dance originating in France in the 17th century. Notice that it starts on beat 3, which is typical for a Gavotte. This tune is in the key of D minor, which is the relative minor of F. [If this concept is confusing, consult Mel Bay's *Theory and Harmony for Everyone*.] The following excerpt was chosen to introduce another important concept to consider when reading sheet music. The opening measures 1 to 4 have the same rhythmic pattern as measures 15 to 18, but the notes are not identical. Those individuals who find it easy to memorize a melody will need to pay particular attention while playing the last four measures.

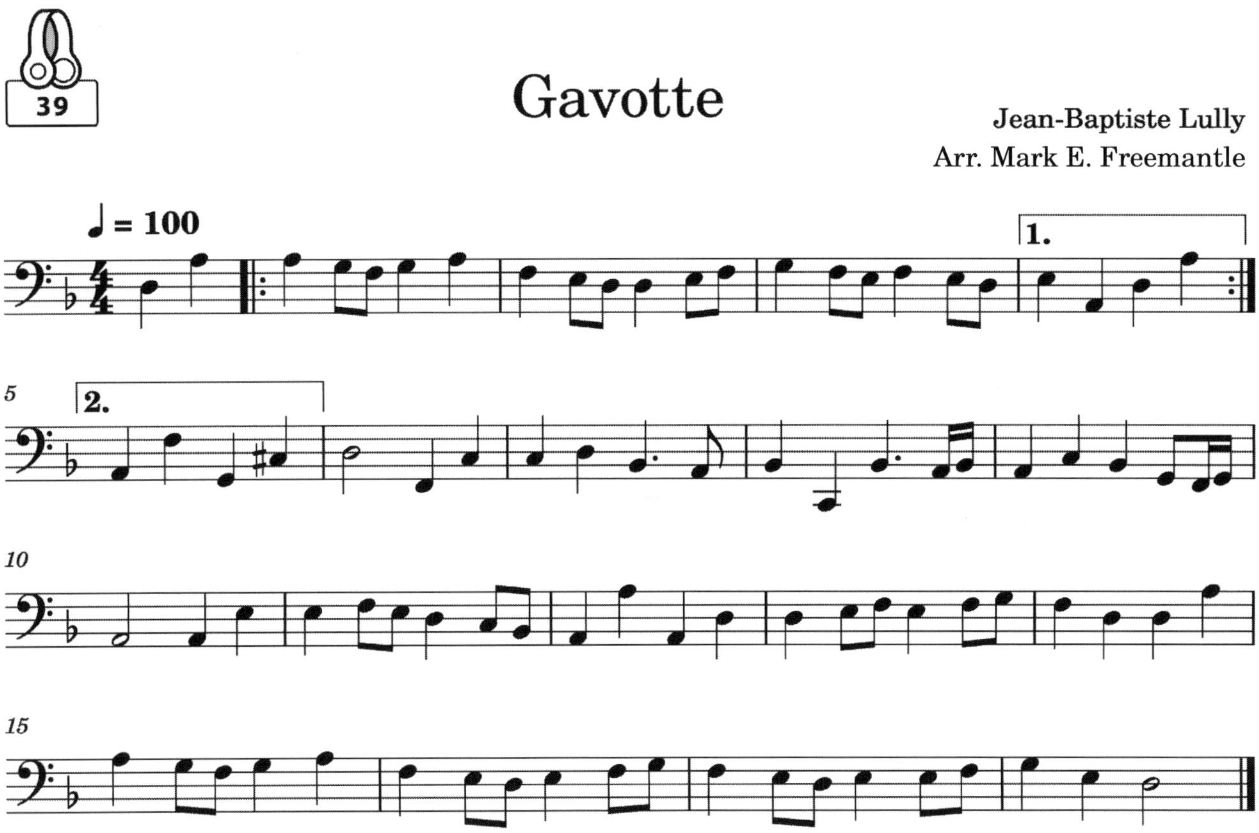

Figure 76: Gavotte

Come, Thou Long-Expected Jesus

The next tune, “Come, Thou Long Expected Jesus,” is a popular hymn; it is arranged to be played “sweetly” [*dolcemente*] by the use of tremolo, phrasing, rests, and tempo. Tremolo is applied to all slurs and half notes. In measure 3 the tremolo ends and the eighth note is played with the upstroke. Be sure to stop the tremolo at the end of each phrase, even if the next measure starts with a phrase; for example, in measures 4 and 5. Measures 9, 11, and 13 start with a tremolo on the half note, then are followed by an eighth note and an eighth-note rest. Suggested positions are indicated in measures 17-21. Remaining on the same string facilitates proper tremolo technique and maintains the same tone color.

40

Come, Thou Long-Expected Jesus

R. H. Prichard, 1831
Arr. Mark E. Freemantle

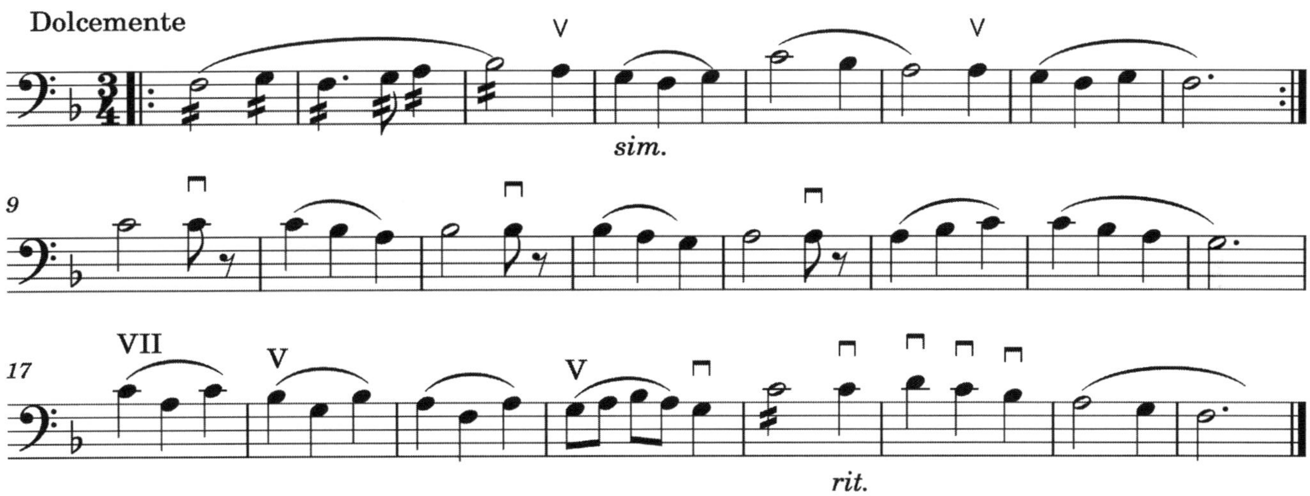

Figure 77: Come, Thou Long-Expected Jesus

Section 2 Tunes, Techniques and Theory

In *Section* 2 we expand our musical horizons by learning more technical aspects of playing the mandocello. The tunes included in this section use the basic playing principles you have already learned and add more complex techniques and music theory as we introduce new tunes and etudes.

2.1 Accidentals and Enharmonic Notes

When a composer includes a note that does not naturally occur in the established key, it needs to be identified in a manner that illustrates their intention. This is done by using *accidentals*. We place accidentals to the left of the note heads to illustrate that the note is raised (♯) or lowered (♭) one half-step. The example below is written in the key of G, so the expectation is that we will play all F notes as F♯. In measure 1 there is one F note, at beat four. No unique designation is needed because in the key of G, all F notes are normally played as F-sharps. The first note of measure 3 includes a new symbol called a **natural** (♮). It tells the musician to disregard the F♯ in the key signature and play a natural F note. The second note of measure 3 adds the sharp symbol ♯, which tells us to play the F♯, as normally expected in the key of G. The most important fact about all accidentals is that they only apply to the measure in which they occur. The bar line cancels the accidental unless that note continues into the next measure. (Tie lines will be introduced later.) The fourth note of measure 3 is an F♯ and is written with a courtesy accidental (♯). A courtesy accidental is not required, but serves as a helpful reminder to play the F♯ as expected in the key of G. A courtesy accidental is normally written within parenthesis.

Courtesy Accidental – Example 1

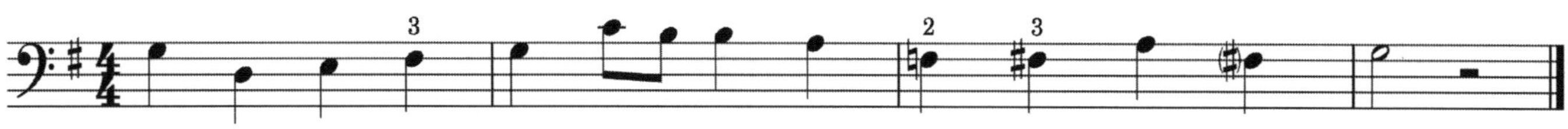

Figure 78: Courtesy Accidental – Example 1

The next example is in the key of F with one flat, a B♭. The accidental symbol in measure 2 tells us to play a B-natural, not a B-flat. Remember, the B♭ in the key signature tells us that ALL B's are B♭'s, not just the one on line two from the bottom of the stave. Notice the B♭ in measure 3 does not include a courtesy accidental as it occurs within a new measure and consequently defaults to the key signature.

Courtesy Accidental – Example 2

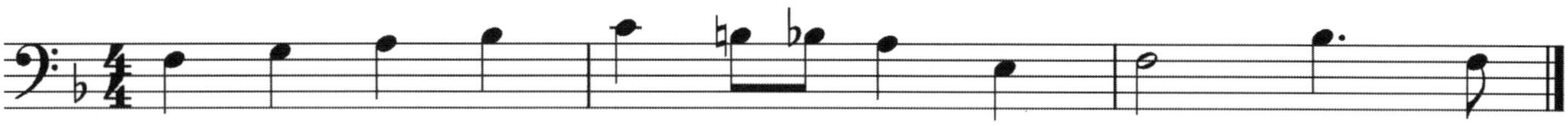

Figure 79: Courtesy Accidental – Example 2

Finally, the last theory-related aspect of note-naming conventions is the enharmonic note. Enharmonic notes represent the same pitch but have two different names. For example, a D♯ has the same pitch as an E♭. Enharmonics may occur within a chromatic progression. In the example below, the key signature is G, so all F notes are F♯s. The third note is an E and the fourth note is an E-sharp, or E♯. Remembering that E – F and B – C are the "natural half-tones," E-sharp is the same as F-natural. The three measures below represent the same pitches; they are merely notated differently. In measure 3, the F♭ is the same as the E that follows. Sharp symbols are used to indicate accidentals in rising passages and flat symbols are used to illustrate accidentals in descending passages. For more related theory, consult the aforementioned theory book.

Enharmonic Notes

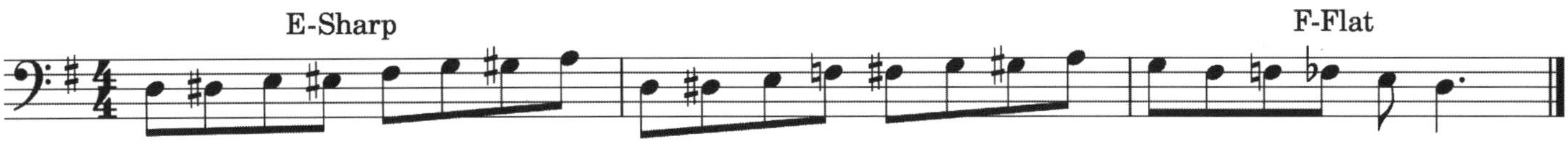

Figure 80: Enharmonic Notes

Bickford's Recreation in F – Including Accidentals

The following tune "Recreation in F", by Myron A. Bickford, includes our first use of accidentals. The exercise is identified as a "lively" tune, which means that eventually it should be played rather fast. The pick directions and fingerings were marked to facilitate learning the tune. Measure 5 presents the first challenge: We should play the open A note with an upstroke, which requires crossing over the A string, then plucking upwards. Practice this motion several times until it becomes second nature to alternate pick directions not only on the same string but while crossing strings. Measure 7 includes a B♭, played on the first fret of the A string and written with a courtesy accidental. You should be able to play this note by shifting the left hand backwards without moving the thumb out of position. The first accidental is in measure 9, where the F becomes an F♯. In measure 10, the second D has a flat accidental, so we lower the pitch a half-step and it becomes a D♭. The fingering for the D natural in the next measure reminds us that the flat accidental only applies to the measure in which it occurs. Measure 13 also includes one sharp accidental, which again, applies for the whole measure.

Recreation in F

Myron A. Bickford

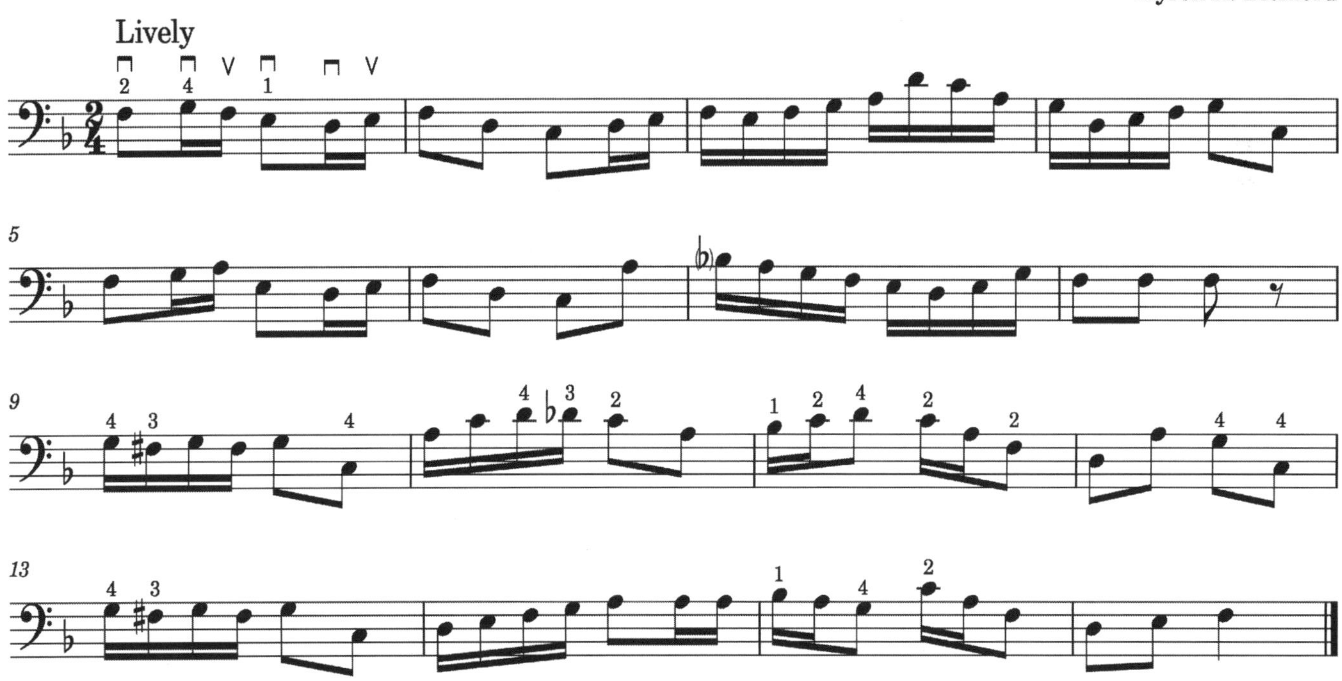

Figure 81: Recreation in F

Greensleeves

This arrangement of the classic tune "Greensleeves" has several accidentals and includes a specific anomaly to illustrate the principle of enharmonic notes. Measure 6 introduces the first accidental, a D♯, which is not in the key of E pure minor. "Greensleeves" is in the key of E melodic minor. E minor is said to be the relative minor of G major as it has the same key signature. It is common to write the raised 6th and 7th degrees of the harmonic minor scale using accidentals. Measure 8 also has one accidental, an E♭. D♯ and E♭ are the enharmonic equivalents! It would not be typical for a musical score to include both of the enharmonic notes, but you may come across it, especially with older music created without music notation software. Also, remember that the accidental applies only to the measure in which it appears. We identify no dynamics or references with tremolo; vary the dynamics and additionally add the tremolo for effect. There is no repeat symbol, but we can play the tune again with varying dynamics.

"Tagging" Music for Convenience

Measure 28 has a reference applied to the last note, identified as a "tag". Instead of writing a longer score that repeats the last four full measures (and one pickup note), the composer specifies that we play the tune to the end and then return to beat three of the previous measure to the note identified as a "tag," then play to the end. The rough classical music equivalent to a tag would be a Coda.

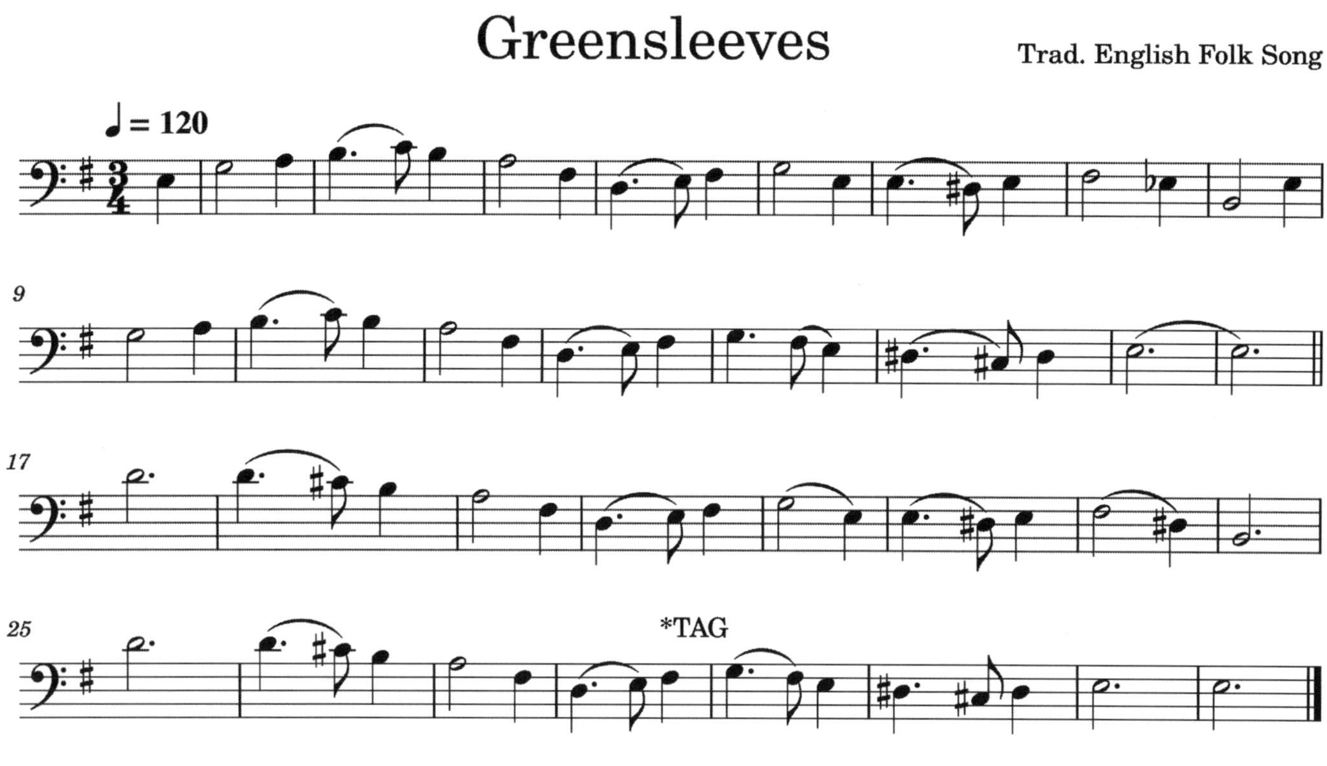

Figure 82: Greensleeves

2.2 Alternate Picking – Crossing Strings

Alternate picking of notes on the same string is simple; the challenge comes when we need to alternate the pick direction while changing between strings. We first saw this technique in Bickford's "Recreation in F." In the exercise below, the first three notes are on the second string. The fourth note, a B, is on the third string. As the pick-direction symbol illustrates, we need to play the B with an upstroke. The right hand wrist needs to relax, with the pick held in the same manner but not at the same angle as used in the introductory drop-and-stop method. We cannot stop on the first string because the pick needs to "jump over" the second string to play the B on the third string. This exercise requires alternating between the second and third strings.

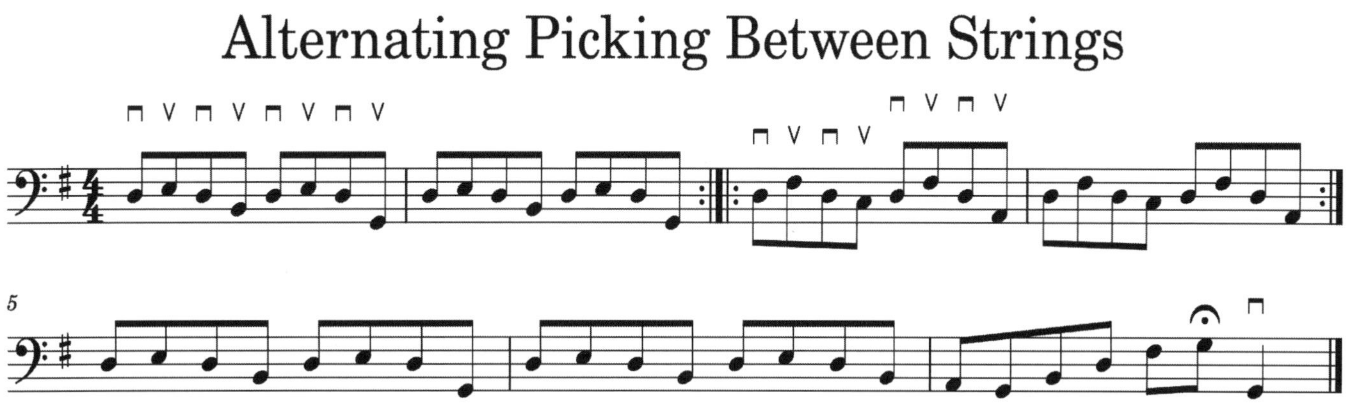

Figure 83: Alternating Picking Between Strings

Frère Jacques – Redux

We played this tune earlier, but in the key of C. Here in G, measures 5 to 8 require alternate picking while crossing strings. Be sure to use alternate picking only on the eighth notes and not on the quarter or half notes.

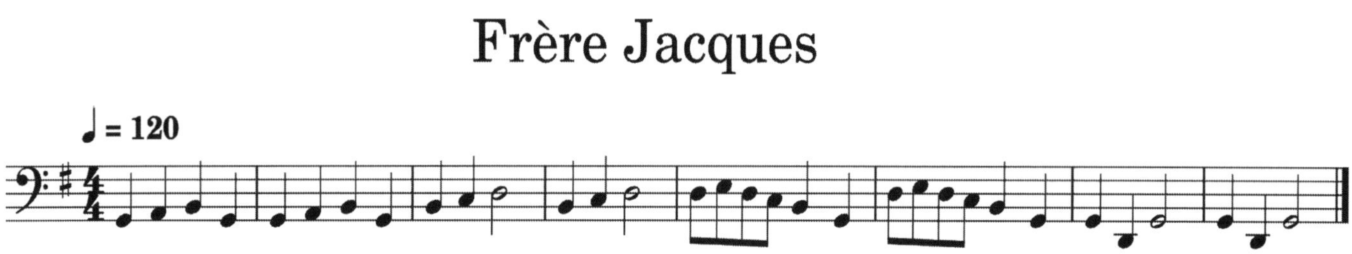

Figure 84: Frère Jacques – in G

Recreation in G

"Recreation in G" is written in the key of G in 2/4 time, at 60 beats per minute. Notice that measure 8 ends with a double barline. This illustrates the end of a phrase that your ear will recognize as you play this tune. Play slowly at first, with all downstrokes for the eighth notes and alternate picking for the sixteenth notes.

Look at the second G in measure 3: We should play it as a 16th note with a downstroke. It may seem natural to play this note with an upstroke because the note just before it, the open A string, was played with a downstroke. While it is not technically wrong to play this note with an upstroke, it is not ideal for learning proper technique, and critically important – for keeping proper timing. The target tempo is 60 bpm; set the metronome lower than that to begin studying this exercise. Measures 19 and 20 include notes on the C string and a "courtesy fingering" is included to serve two purposes:

1) To remind you that the F is played as an F♯ (on the 6th fret) and,

2) To prompt you to play it with your pinky.

You will need to shift your left hand, including the thumb, to play the F♯ and E notes. Place the thumb two frets higher up the neck to play with the pinky. The third finger can be lightly pressed on the 5th fret to support the pinky. A double bass player never plays the pinky by itself. Always support it with the third finger pressing down as well. Start the shift just after playing the open G.

Recreation in G

Myron A. Bickford

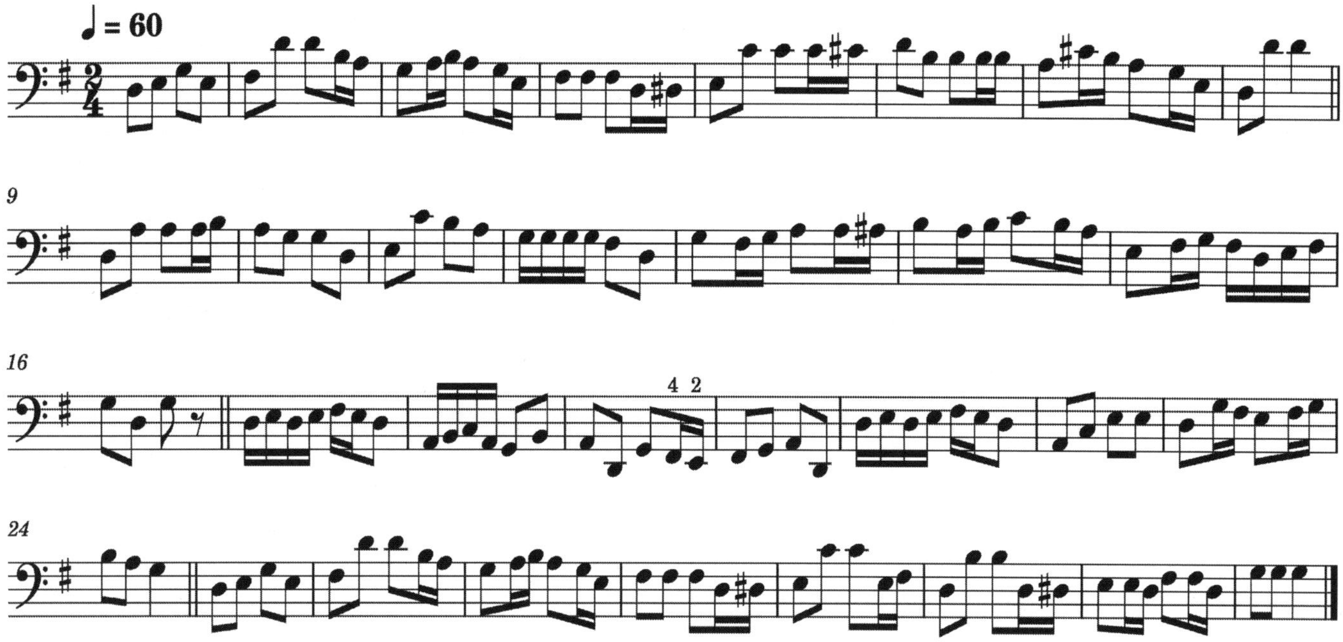

Figure 85: Recreation in G

Simple Gifts

This popular Shaker tune includes alternate picking that requires crossing strings. Measure 1 shows the challenge: We play two C notes with downstrokes followed by a cross-string upstroke to play the open string D. Then a downstroke E note followed by a cross-string upstroke for a C note. Practice this tune using two techniques:

1) All quarter notes start on a downstroke; all eighth notes (on the beat) start with a downstroke and the next beamed eighth note gets an upstroke. Measures 9 and 10 end with a single eighth note, played with an upstroke.

2) Begin each measure with a downstroke, then use alternate picking, crossing strings as needed.

Many players prefer the second approach since it seems to flow naturally. One caution: Those using the second approach have a tendency to rush the tempo. Practice with a metronome to guarantee accuracy, no matter which method you choose.

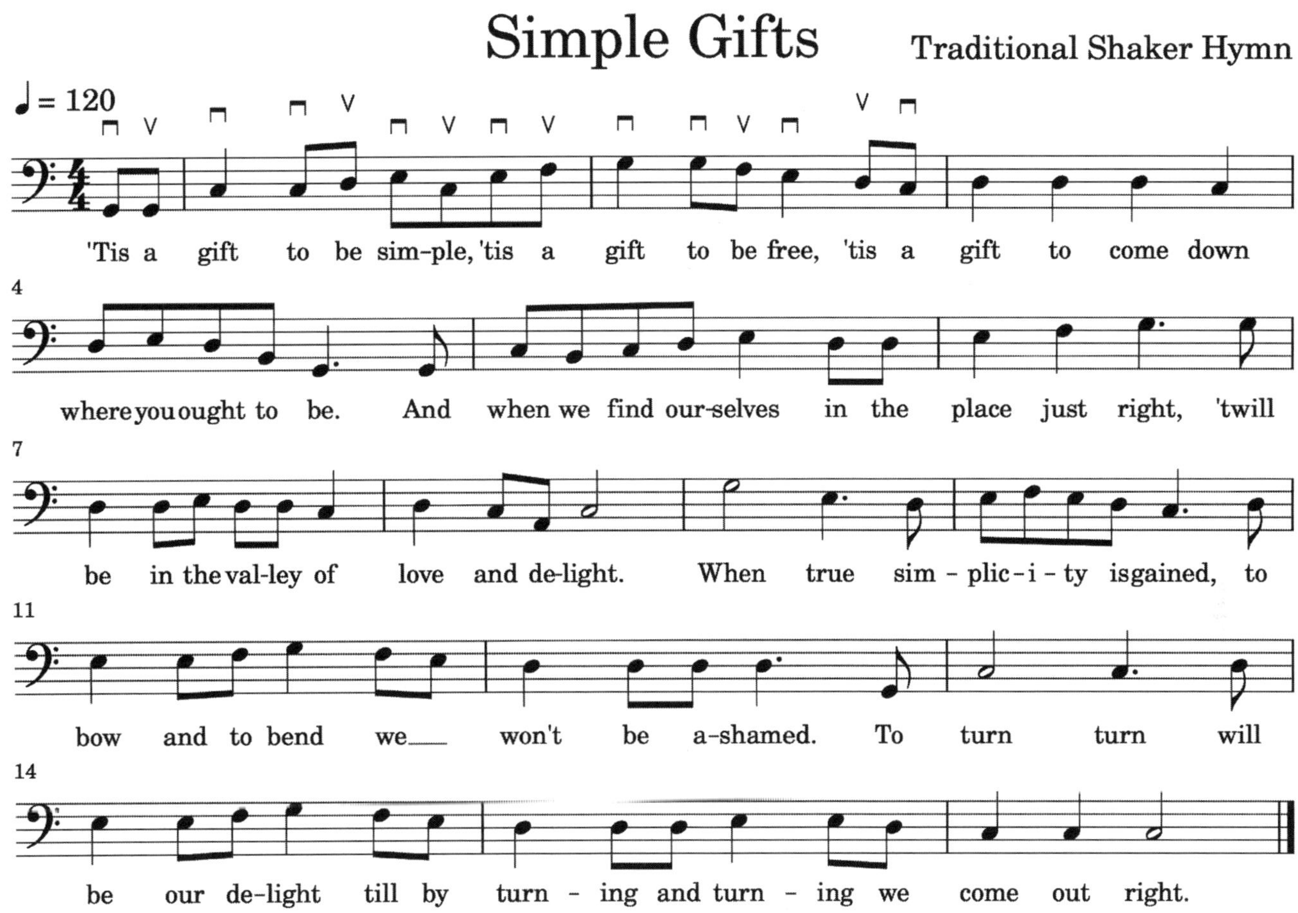

Figure 86: Simple Gifts

Bach's First Cello Suite No. 1 in G Major

The following Bach selection was chosen because of the opportunity it presents to develop the crosspicking string technique. This selection is approximately one-half of the whole tune. Advanced players will surely want to learn the whole tune. In addition to the crosspicking technique, we have other techniques to consider, not only for playing this selection but, in general, for any cello piece of music. Consider the first measure:

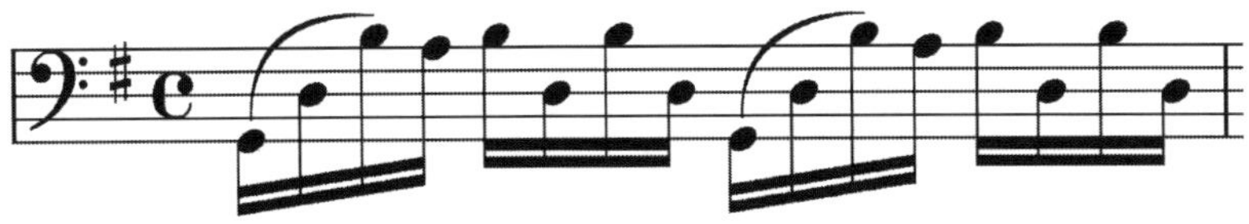

Figure 87: Prelude from Bach Cello Suite in G Major – Measure 1

The first three notes have a slur connecting them. Consider how a cellist would play this: The bow would start on the G string and in one continuous motion, connecting the D and A with a single down-bow motion. Rather than alternating the pick direction for every sixteenth note, it might be advantageous to **sweep** the pick downward across the first three strings, then alternate the next five notes. The second half of measure 1 repeats the same phrase. Consider applying the same technique to the first four measures. Study each measure separately to see what similar patterns might emerge. Not all slurs cross three strings, so the same approach is not always available. Experiment, but try to be consistent in your technique.

Cello Suite № 1 in G Major

1. Prélude (excerpt)

J. S. Bach

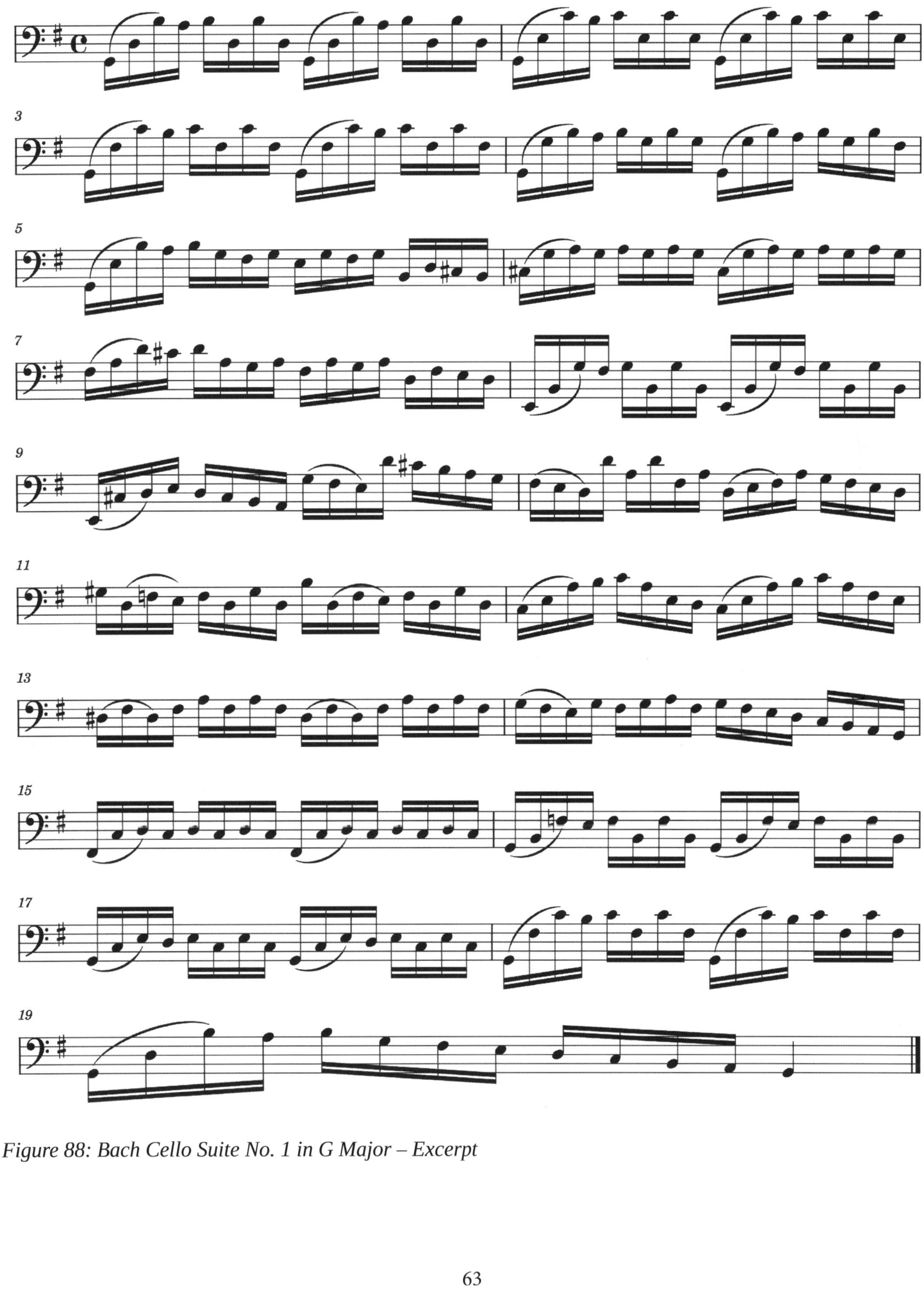

Figure 88: Bach Cello Suite No. 1 in G Major – Excerpt

2.3 Introducing the Key of B♭ Major

The key of B♭ major has two flats, B♭ and E♭. Think about the organization of the fretboard. Where do you find those two notes? The answer is at fret one (strings one and two) and fret three (strings three and four.) To play the notes on fret one, we need to either change our hand and thumb location to position I or "pivot" the hand between the range of notes from fret one to fret five. Try playing the B♭ scale below, measures 1 to 4, while remaining in the default, or home, position II. Do not move your thumb; but rather, "reach back" to fret 1 to play the B♭ and E♭.

B♭ Scale

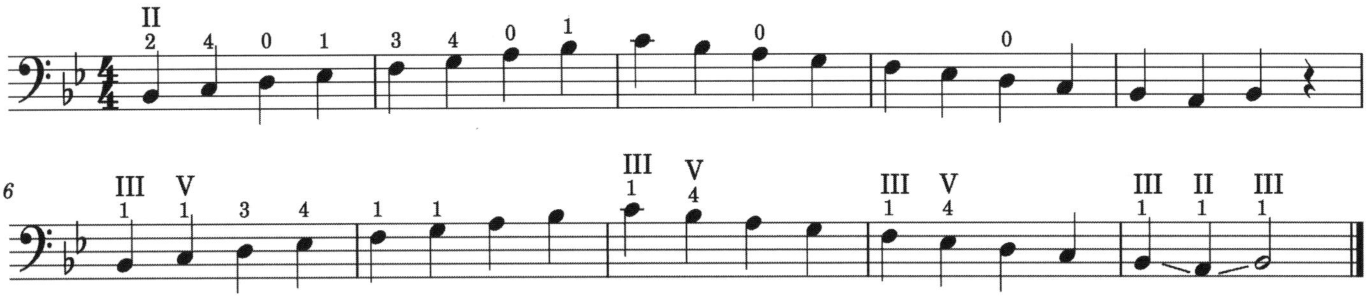

Figure 89: B♭ Scale

The proposed fingering positions, as marked at measures 6 to 10, may be necessary if the "reach back" to fret one is a challenge. Remember, it is not just a question of "*Can you reach the notes*?" but "*Can you reach them while still reading the sheet music*?"

The following etude will assist in determining which method will work for you. (No fingerings or positions are provided.) The *fermata* is provided to facilitate the transition to playing the descending scale.

B♭ Scale – Moving Thirds

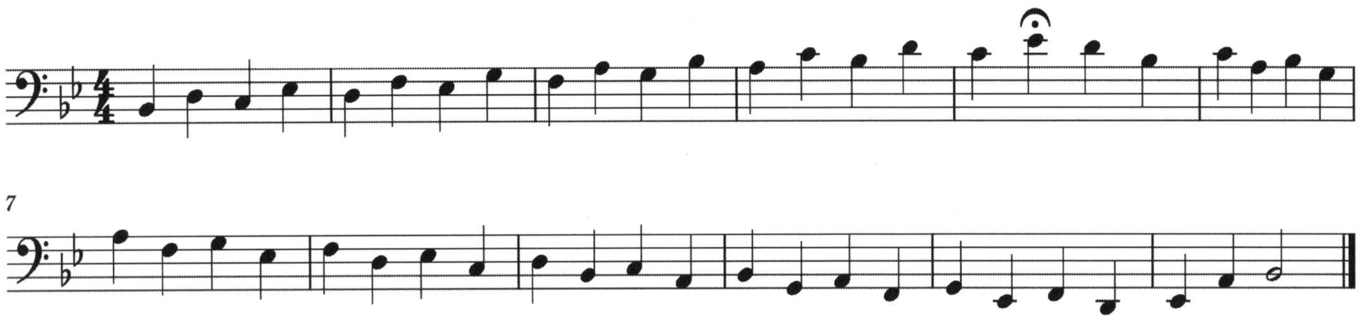

Figure 90: B♭ Scale – Moving Thirds

2.4 Tunes in the Key of B♭ Major

Greenville

This tune was originally written as a gavotte or dance tune; it was composed by Jean-Jacques Rousseau for an opera in 1752, but included no lyrics. By the 1820s, the tune was identified as "Greenville" and was utilized in many church hymns. You will no doubt recognize that it was later adapted to become the well-known tune "Go Tell Aunt Rhody."

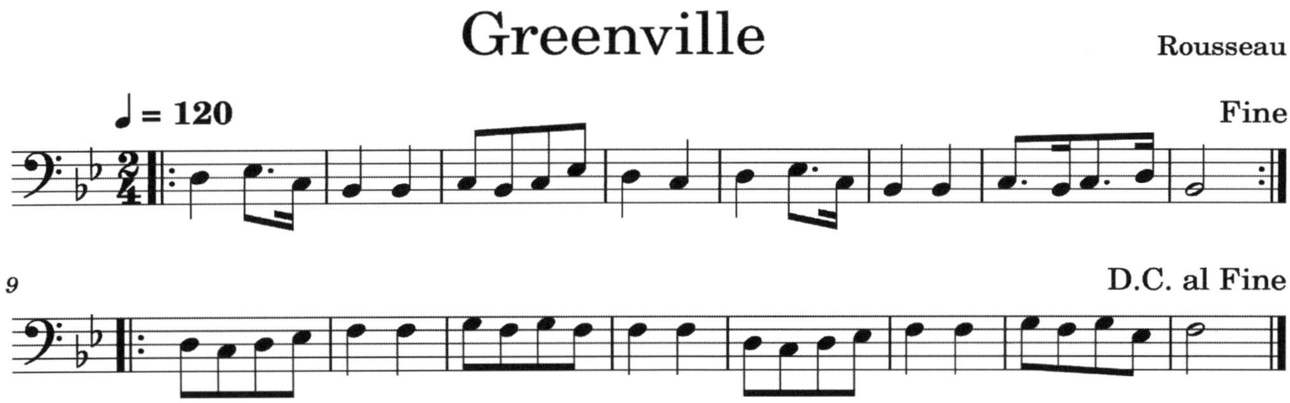

Figure 91: Greenville

Au Claire de la Lune

This ever-popular French tune is a good starting point for learning to play B-flats. [Notice that, although there are 2 flats in the key signature, there are no E♭'s in the melody.] Play all G and D notes with open strings; the pinky will get a workout with the C notes on string ③ and the one F note on string ④. Practice slowly until you can play at the suggested 160 bpm. No phrasing is provided. Play the tune and identify where the phrases occur. Consider using tremolo for half notes or for selected phrases.

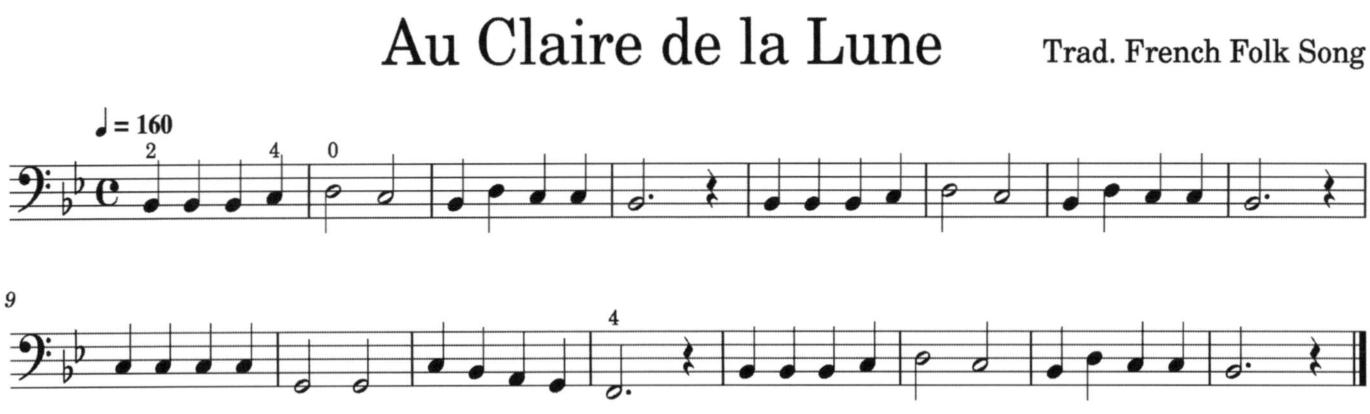

Figure 92: Au Claire de la Lune

Annie Lisle

"Annie Lisle" is a tune commonly associated with colleges or high schools as their respective alma maters. The E♭ on string ①, fret 6 will most likely require a shift; the stretch approach can also work with only that one note requiring a quick shift, possibly without moving the thumb. Consider using the two-position shift approach, in this case, from positions III – V.

This arrangement introduces the use of double-stops in the last three measures. The tune consists of four four-bar phrases, as indicated. Phrases one and two are identical rhythmically and might be played with the same application of tremolo. Consider changing phrase three by stopping the tremolo for the sixteenth notes only. Measure 14 introduces the term "*rubato*," which means you are free to vary the rhythm (to the end of the tune). The double-stops provide a greater harmonic impact when the tempo is slowed down considerably. A double-stop is simply the playing of two notes (on different strings) at the same time. A classical guitarist would do so with separate fingers. On the mandocello, it is implemented by applying a downstroke to both strings in a quick, fluid motion. For those familiar with this technique, commonly used in jazz guitar, it is also possible to apply hybrid picking, combining the pick with middle and ring finger strokes. [Double-stops are also addressed in *Section 2.16.*]

Annie Lisle
(Alma Mater)

H. S. Thompson
Arr. Mark E. Freemantle

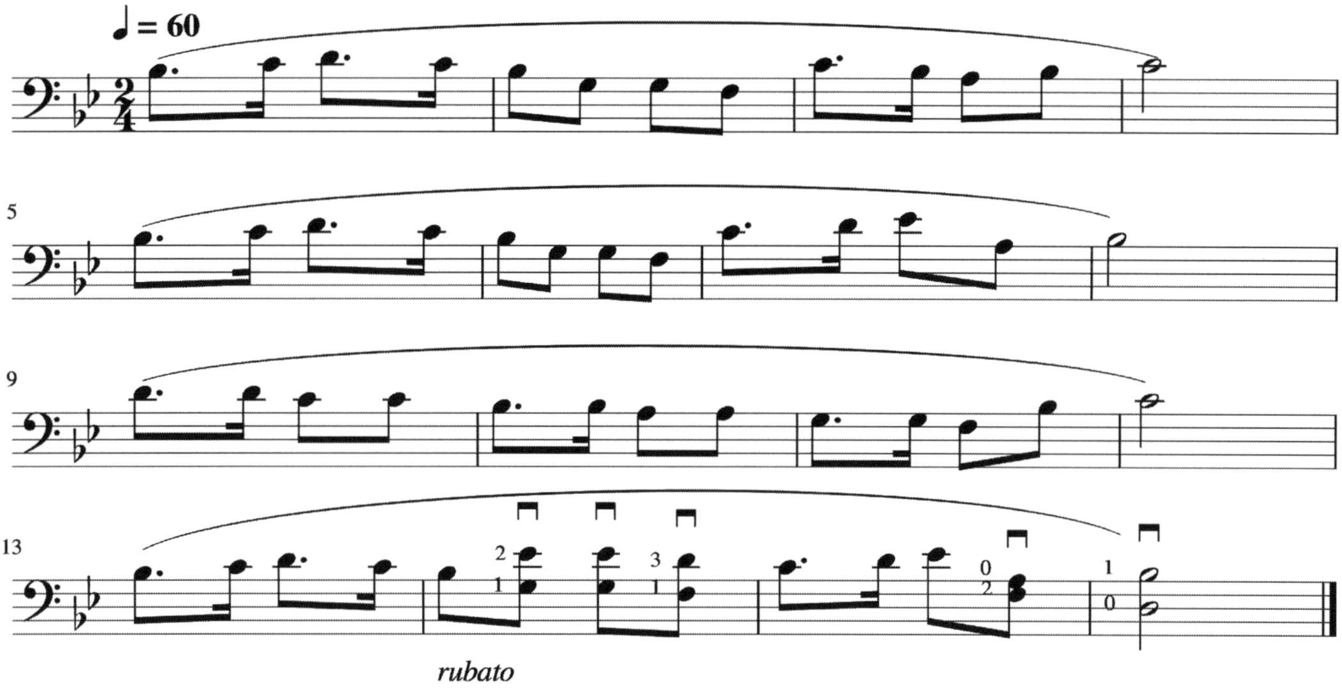

Figure 93: Annie Lisle

Hope Waltz

Pay particular attention to the fact that an accidental on a note applies only to the one measure where it occurs. Suggested positions and fingerings are included. The application of tremolo may not be necessary as this arrangement is set at a faster tempo.

Hope Waltz

Johann Strauss I

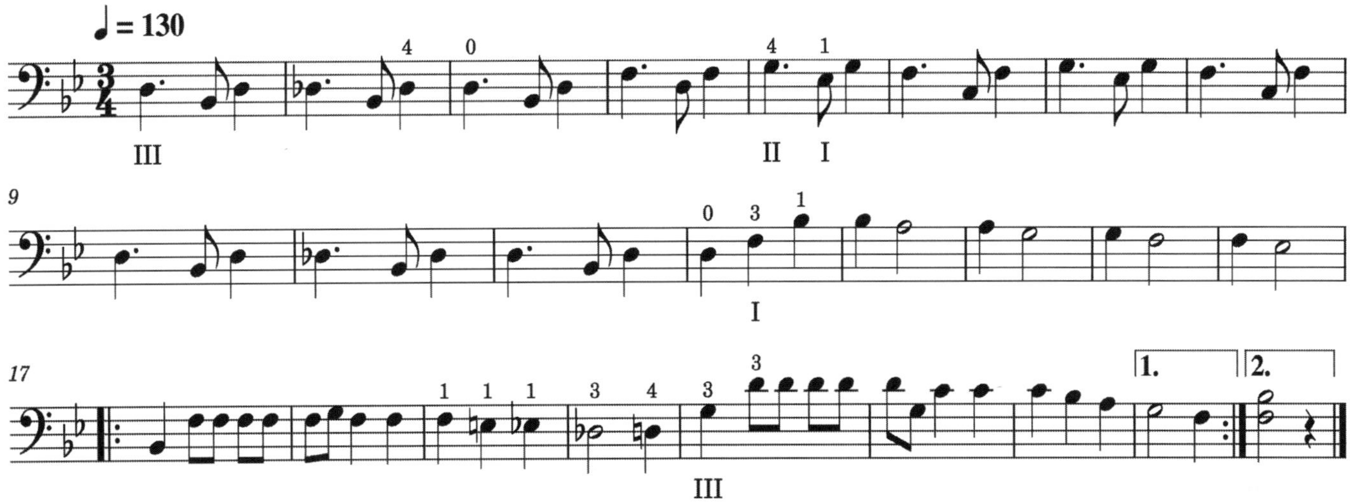

Figure 94: Hope Waltz

Hornpipe in B♭ Major

Purcell's "Hornpipe in B♭ Major" is a popular Baroque piece, written in 1695. Dynamics are included to provide variety during the repeated sections. Notice the dynamics at measure 1: the first time, play *mf*, the second time, play *p*. The new symbol < starting at measure 9 is a *crescendo*; it means to gradually increase the volume. In this case, from *piano* to *mezzo-forte*; *piano* (*p*) means "quiet" and *mezzo-forte* (*mf*) means moderately loud.

Hornpipe

From Abdelazer Suite

Henry Purcell (1659-1695)

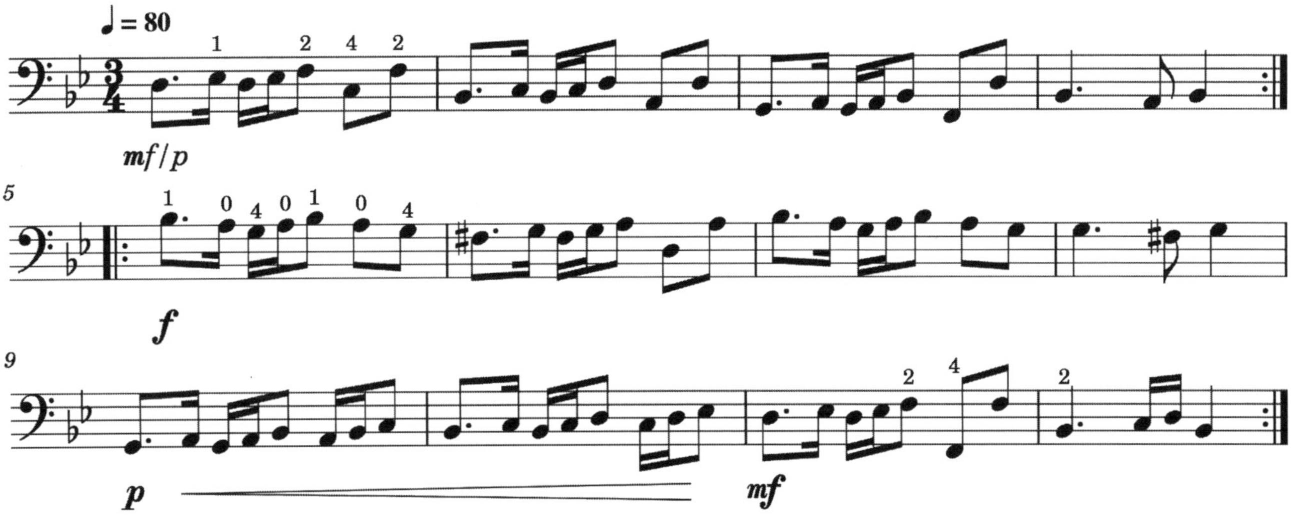

Figure 95: Hornpipe in B♭ Major

2.5 Introducing the Key of D Major with Two Sharps

The key of D includes two sharps – F♯ and C♯. This presents a challenge for the mandocellist with an average-sized hand. Try playing the D, E, and F♯ notes on the fourth string, starting with the index finger on the D. It requires either a big hand, a big stretch, or a hand shift. We will consider two methods of playing the notes in the D scale.

When playing a D major scale, it is normal to play only three fretted notes on one string before changing to another string. Speaking from the perspective of the scale or tune progressing upward in pitch, there are two methods to play three fretted notes on one string: The first method is to shift between two different positions; the second method is to stretch the fingers while maintaining the thumb in position. We present the two options in the following one-octave D-Scale exercise. Notice the fingering references and the position locations in Roman numerals. As a reminder, we are using the guitar method of defining positions; we base the position number on what fret the first finger would naturally lie on, depending on where you are on the fretboard.

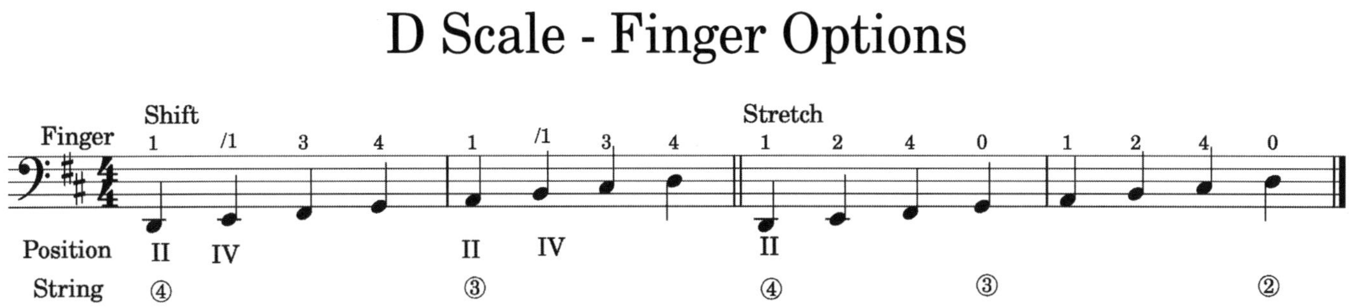

Figure 96: D Scale – Finger Options

The first two measures illustrate the *shift* method. The first finger plays the D on string ④, second fret position II, then shifts immediately to position IV. The pinky plays the G on the seventh fret rather than the open G on the string ③. When all notes are fretted or "stopped," we call this <u>closed position</u>. The other option, the *stretch* method, requires the hand to stay in place [in position II] while stretching the second and fourth fingers to reach the required notes. In the stretch position for the key of D, it is normal to play the open strings for the G and second octave D notes. If you have very large hands or long fingers, either option may work. The following exercise will assist in determining which approach may most likely "fit" your hand-size. No fingerings or positions are provided, so you may determine what best works for you.

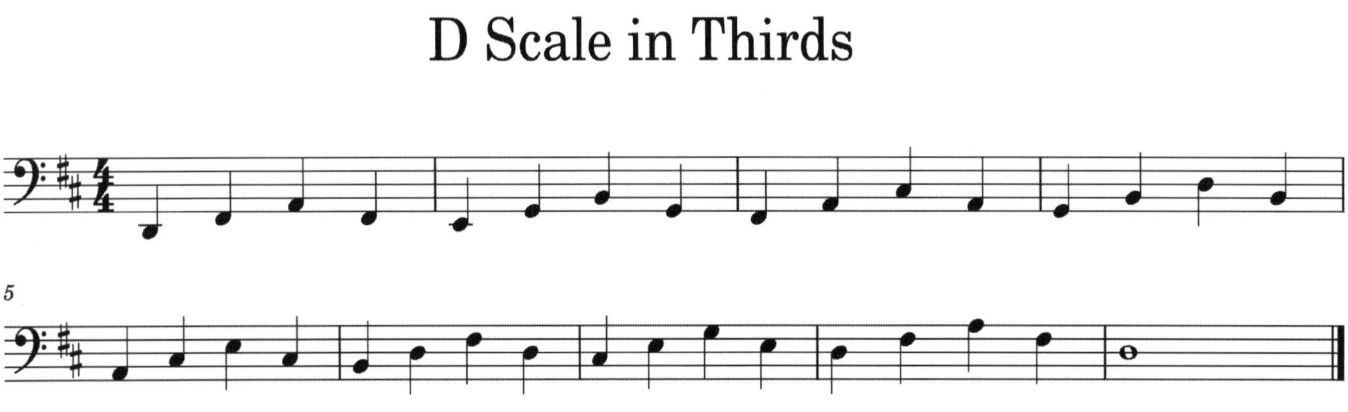

Figure 97: D Scale in Thirds

The exercise above is a unique pattern of thirds. Notice the first measure has four notes, all on "spaces" in the bass clef. Then, the next note of the scale is selected and the pattern of thirds continues, but now all on lines in the bass clef, etc. It is important to "see" the relationship between the notes as being an interval of a third away from each other, with D to F♯ being a leap of a major third in the D scale, and F♯ to A being a minor third. Likewise, in measure 2, E to G is a minor third, and G to B is a major third. Practice this exercise with both the shift and stretch methods.

We suggest the following two-octave etude for daily practice. Play this pattern slowly at first. Try playing without looking at your fingers and trust your ears to "tell" you if you are playing the correct notes. Once the pattern of shifting is committed to memory, try to play it from memory without looking at your left hand.

D Scale - in Thirds - 2 Octaves

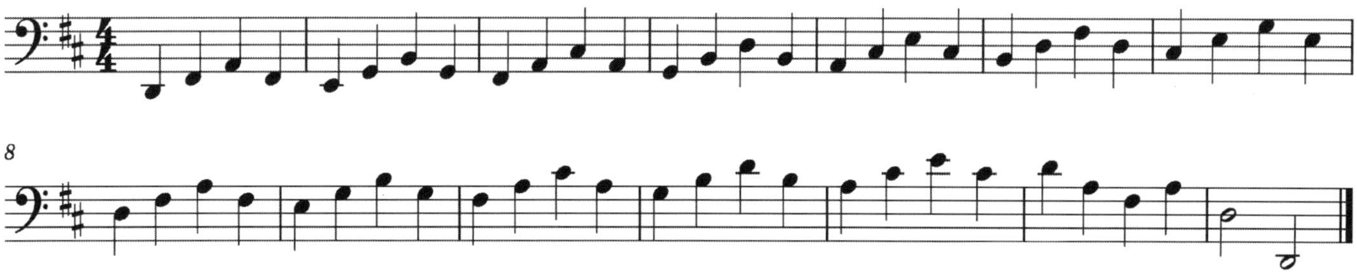

Figure 98: D Scale - in Thirds - 2 Octaves

Depending on how you finger this etude you may notice a consistent pattern that makes it easier to master.

Bickford "Exercise in D"

The next exercise provides an opportunity to "fine tune" your method of playing a tune in the key of D. The fingering placement defined by Bickford is not included. Photocopy this page and write-in your own fingerings. Adjust as needed until it feels comfortable to play and can be played consistently, with no need to watch your hands. Notice that only the first two measures illustrate when to play downstrokes or upstrokes – all eighth notes are downstrokes, all sixteenth notes are played with alternate picking.

For review, the two musical terms are: *Fine* and *D.C. al Fine*. The Italian musical term *"fine"* (pronounced fee'-nay) marks the end of the tune, or movement. *D.C. al fine*, or *da capo al fine*, means "play from the beginning to the end or *fine* marking."

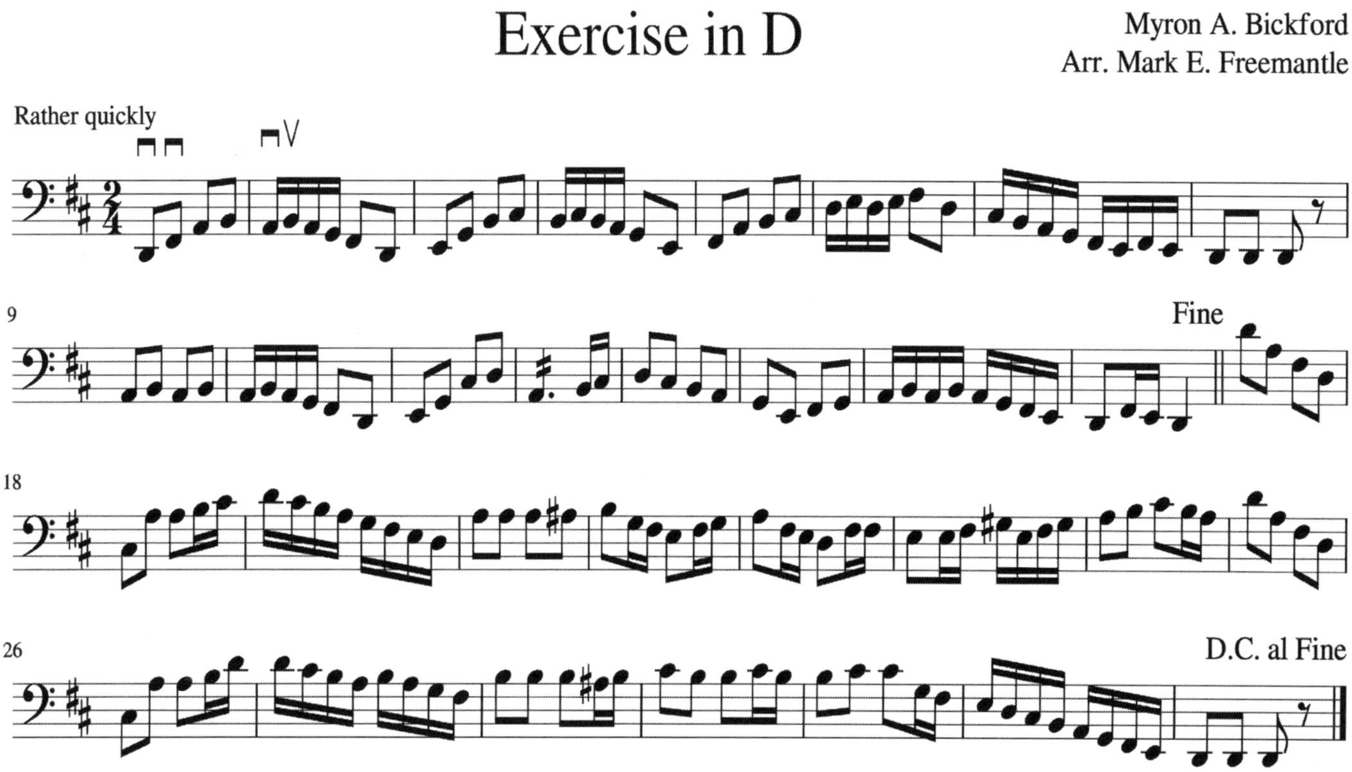

Figure 99: Bickford – Exercise in D

Analysis of "Exercise in D"

Consider the following analysis of the first phrase of the tune, from measure (M) 1 to 8:

M1: D to F♯ – Consider using fingers 1 and 3 or 1 and 4. Shift or Stretch.

A to B: No need to shift, so use fingers 1 and 3.

M2: Play G as an open string to provide time to reach or shift for the F♯.

M3: Start in position IV (P4), using fingers – 1, 4, 1, 3

M4: Start in position IV (P4) and shift to position II (P2), and end on the E in P4.

M5: P4, P2, P4

M6: P2, with open string for D, then shift to P4 at F♯, so the last note (D) can be played with the pinky, which facilitates…

M7: descending the scale, P4, P2, P4

M8: P2.

The important principle, whether shifting or stretching, is that your fingering should be consistent. Your ears will tell you if your fingers are wrong, so try not to look. If your fingers play the wrong note, review both methods for playing tunes in the key of D. Both methods require a commitment to playing more notes with the pinky and fewer notes on open strings. This skill will be essential for playing more complex tunes.

2.6 Tunes in the Key of D or B Minor

Scarborough Fair

This traditional tune provides an opportunity to apply tremolo for a smooth, connected (*legato*) feel. Use tremolo on all half notes and all the notes "connected" by a slur. Notice that the fingering suggests starting in position IV. This is necessary in measure 3, to connect the C♯ and D.

Scarborough Fair

Trad. English Ballad

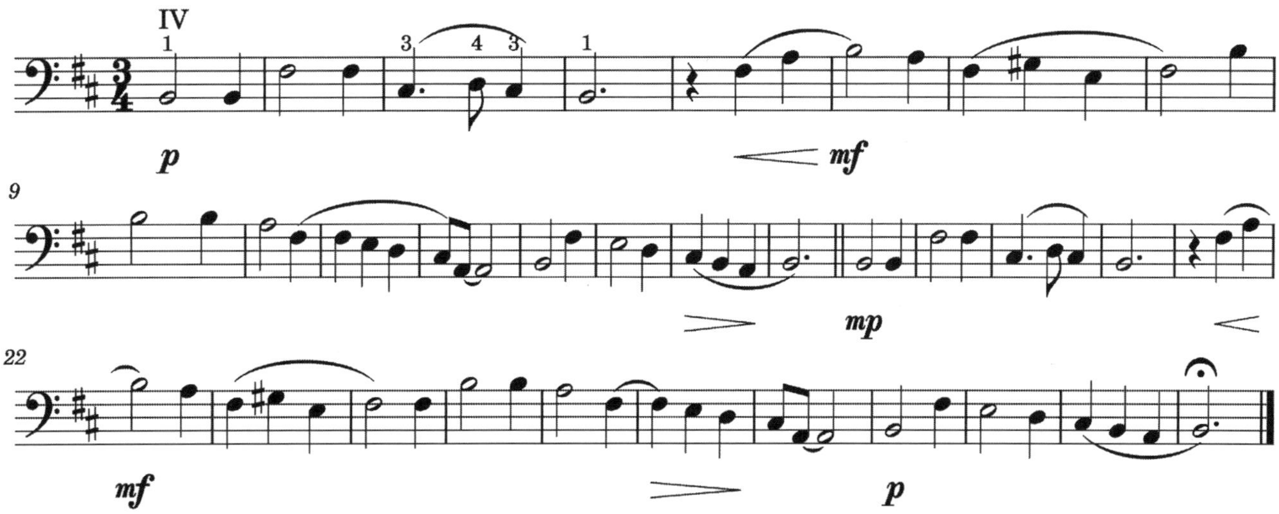

Figure 100: Scarborough Fair

Rondeau – by Mouret

The following tune, "Rondeau," by the French composer Jean-Joseph Mouret, is a tune popularized as the theme to a public television show.

Rondeau

Jean-Joseph Mouret

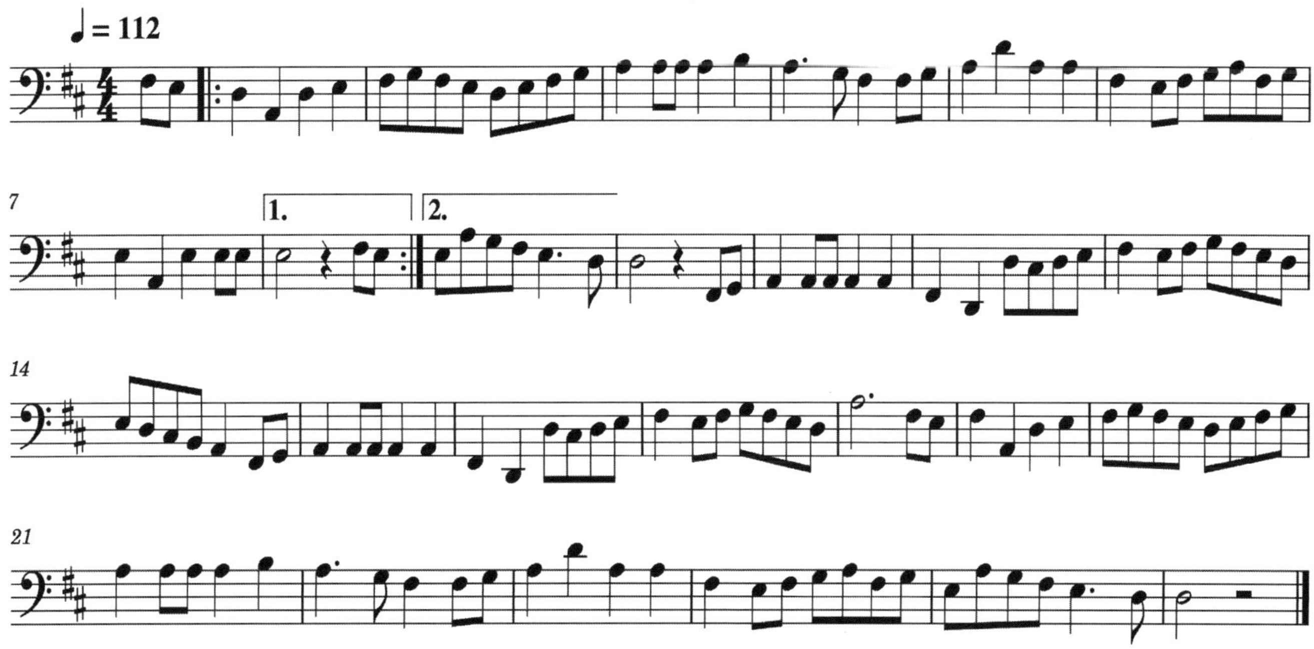

Figure 101: Rondeau – by Mouret

Musette in D Major

The following tune, by J. S. Bach is a fun piece to play and very challenging when played at full tempo. The first eight measures fall into place at the standard second position (finger one on fret 2). The challenge comes in the second section, from measures 9 to 20. I have shown a shift to position VI but have only provided a few fingerings. This section also needs to shift back to position IV, which is not marked as such, but the fingering shows the first finger playing different notes, hence, a shift. Don't forget that all four D-notes in measure 17 are D-sharps.

Musette in D Major

J. S. Bach

(From the *Anna Magdalena Bach Notebook*)

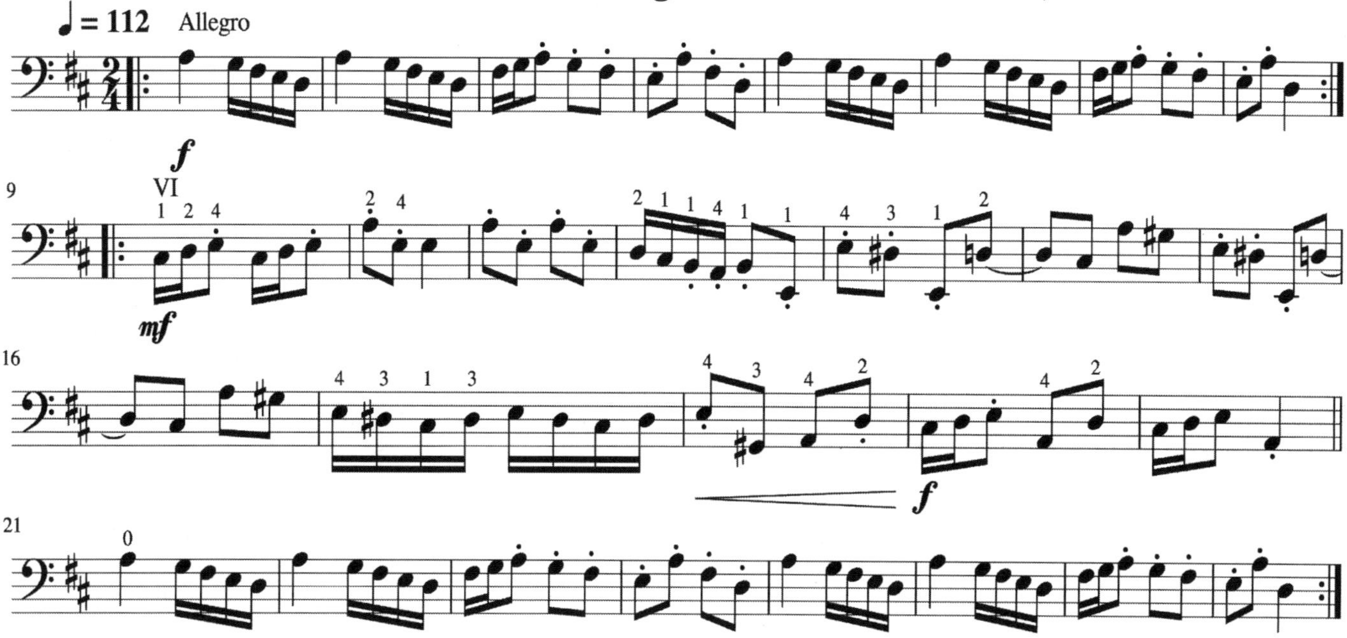

Figure 102: Musette in D Major

Allegro Maestoso – Handel: Water Music

This G. F. Handel tune, "Allegro Maestoso," introduces 3/2 time. It may have three beats per measure, but it is nothing like a waltz. [*Maestoso* means "stately, majestic."] Measure 1 starts with three simple notes, so it is easy to count 1, 2, 3. At measure 2, a simple 1, 2, 3 count won't work. Suggested sub-division counting is included in measures 2 and 3. Note that although there are no C♯'s in this melody, it is in the key of D major, not G major. The last note of a piece is usually the tonic and defines the key.

Allegro Maestoso

From *Water Music*

G. F. Handel

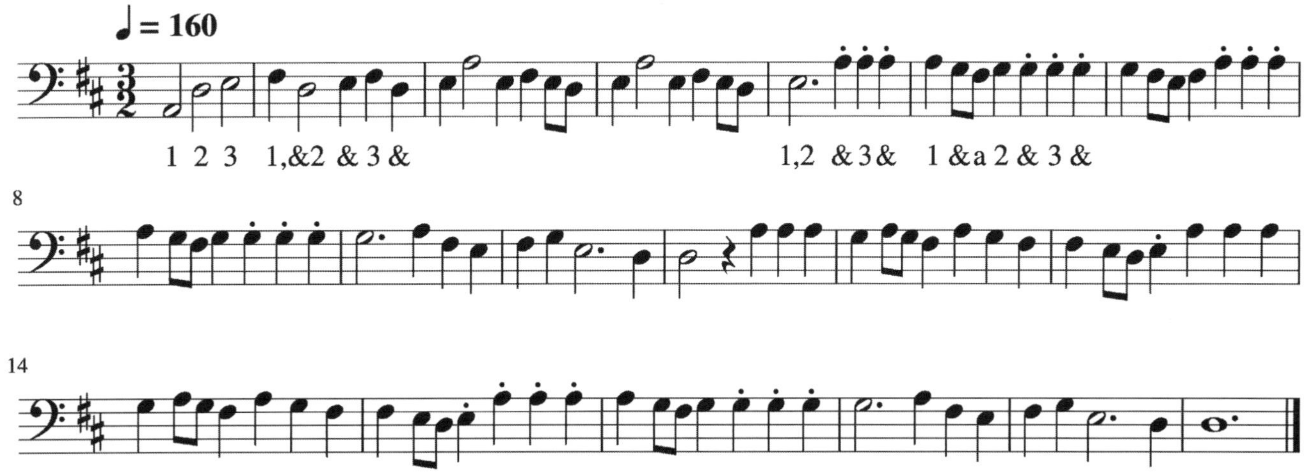

Figure 103: Allegro Maestoso

2.7 Marching in Time

Marches can be a lot of fun to play on the mandocello. They are faster-paced, ranging in tempo from 100 bpm to 120 bpm. The composer rarely identifies the exact tempo, so it is left to the performer or conductor. The time signature can vary as shown below:

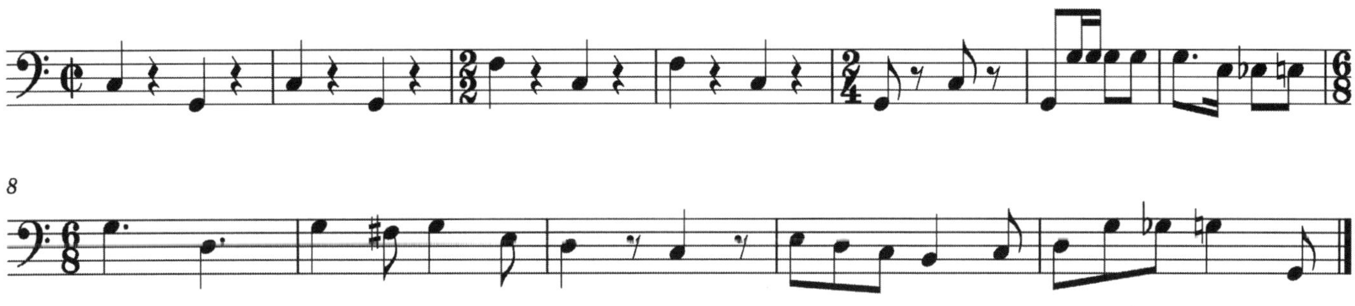

Figure 104: March Etude

In measure 1 above, the time signature symbol is for "cut time". The symbol "cuts" the typical common time symbol in half, so it is easy to identify, provided you remember that common time is another way of saying 4/4 time! In measure 3 the time signature is 2/2 meaning two beats per measure and a half note gets a beat. This is the same as cut time. Notice that in this example we write it with a quarter note followed by a quarter rest. This is very typical for a march because the "feel" of the march has two strong beats; the rest helps bring that out. Measures 5 and 6 are similar, but written in 2/4 time. Measures 1 to 5 would be counted as "One-and-Two-and", etc. Measure 6 introduces 16th notes, so be sure to sub-divide into the four counts normally associated with 16th notes – "one, e, and, ah". The first beat of measure 6 is only an eighth-note, but think of it as two 16th notes even if you count this measure as "One, and, ah; Two, and…". Likewise, in measure 7, the dotted quarter note is three 16ths long. One, dah; two, and. The longest example, from measures 8 to 12, is in 6/8 time. A march in 6/8 time has the feel of two pulses and is normally counted and conducted in two, not in six. Measure 8, with two notes, would be counted as "one, two", not "one, two, three; four, five, six." Measures 9 and 10 is "One, da, two, da." Measures 11 and 12 both start with three notes in the time frame of one beat. Count this as "One, and, ah. Count the second beat as two, dah.

Radetzky March

The marching tune "Radetzky March" will serve as a good example of a march in cut time. Measure 5 has both a rehearsal letter and a repeat symbol; this tells us that a new phrase or theme is being introduced and we will return to this spot. The first ending starts at measure 9 and continues to measure 12. The closing repeat symbol sends us back to the start of the "A" section. Play until measure 8, then jump to the second ending, which starts at measure 13. Measure 16 ends with a double bar, which normally means the end of a theme; the symbol "*Fine*," as a reminder, means *the end*. We continue by playing the "B" section. Section "C" starts at measure 25 with a change in dynamics. Be aware that it is possible to change to a new key signature when a new section is introduced, but that does not occur in this arrangement. The *D.C. al Fine* at the end tells us to return to measure 1 and play to the *fine*. The *D.C.* also means we only play the second endings of any repeated sections, so play measures 1 to 8, then 13 to 16.

Radetzky March

Johann Strauss I (1804-1849)
Arr. Mark E. Freemantle

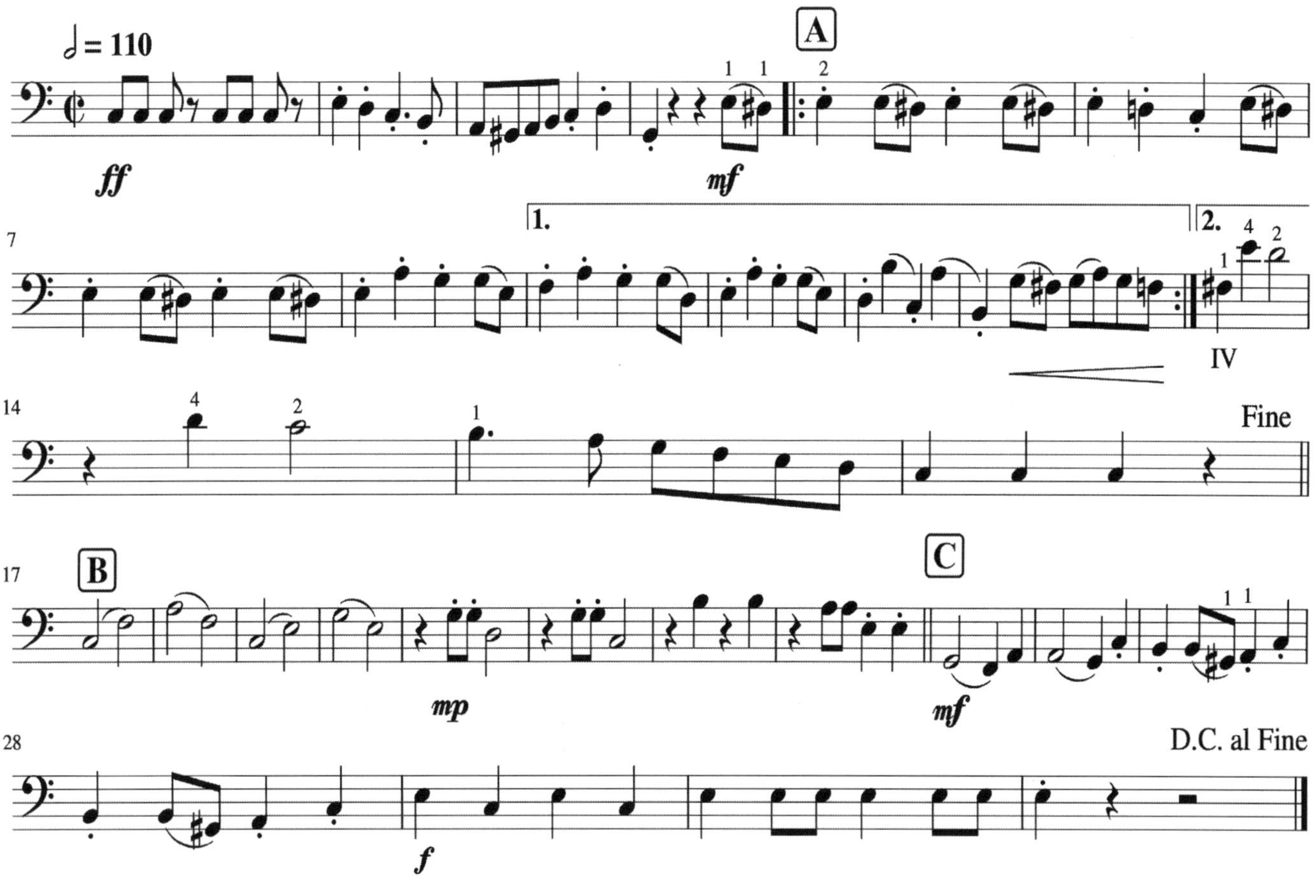

Figure 105: Radetzky March

Let's evaluate the rhythm to get the sense of counting in cut time. Cut time is sometimes written in 2/2 but we don't even see a half note until measure 17, so remember to subdivide. Two half notes or four quarter notes, or, as in measure 1, eighth notes would be counted: 1, e, and, ah; 2, e, and, ah. Remember, this is a march, so start by thinking just 1, 2; 1, 2, then add the divisions. Notice that the tempo is set to a half note equal to 110 beats per minute. Work up to this speed. Notice the dots over the quarter notes in measure 2. These are *staccato* marks, which means to play the notes short and detached from one another. This helps to emphasize the beat in march time.

Roadmaps in Music

Before we discuss specific measures in the next march, we need to explain the concept of "roadmaps" in sheet music. In the early 1900s, major music publishers produced a monthly magazine with a new tune provided each month for mandolin orchestras. To save space, they wrote each part on one page. Deciphering how to play the tune is often a challenge since it typically includes repeats of major sections, then skips to an ending section. "Colonel Bogey" is a popular march tune in cut time that provides us the opportunity to understand the roadmap, or flow of the piece.

"Colonel Bogey" starts with an introduction from measure 1 to 4. Notice the accent marks > over several notes; play them forcibly. Section [1] introduces the main theme and is 16 measures in length. Section [2] is also 16 measures long. Section [3] introduces the repeat symbol, so play this part twice, with the two different endings as shown by the bracket that extends over measures 50 to 52. Play to the repeat measure, then return to measure 37, or Section [3].

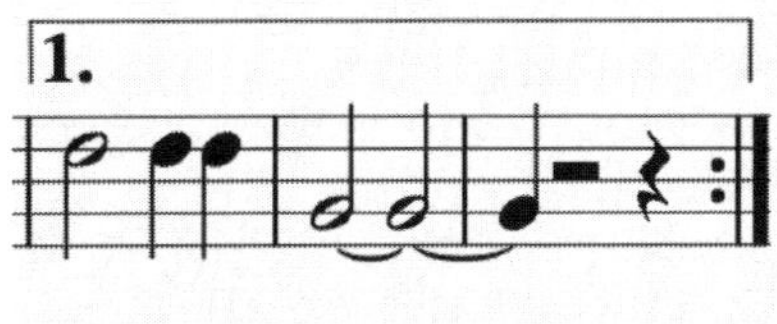

Figure 106: First Ending

Now play from measure 37 to 49 and advance to the second ending, which starts at measure 53.

Just after the bracket for the second ending is a new symbol, the *segno*:

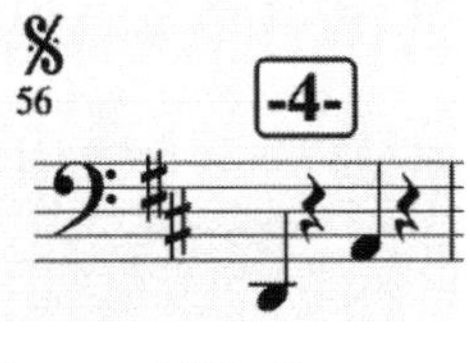

Figure 107: Segno

It resembles the letter "S" placed at an angle and has a slash through it. It is the sign, or place marker, to which we will return later in the piece. At measure 87 we see the text phrase "*To Coda*", with the additional reference, "Last Time." So, the first time playing through Section [5] you ignore that reference and continue to Section [6], also referenced as the **Trio**. At the end of Section [9], at measure 119, we see the phrase "*D.S. al Coda*". The "*D.S.*" is an abbreviation for "*Dal Segno*", which means to return to the *Segno* (sign) that appears at the start of Section [4]. The "*al Coda*" references the "exit" from the repeated section and tells the musician to play measure 87, then jump to the measure that begins with the new symbol, the *Coda*:

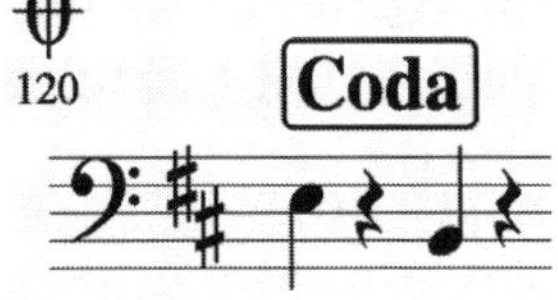

Figure 108: Coda

It is common to add the word "*Coda,*" just to make it obvious.

A final thought on playing "Colonel Bogey": Due to its tempo, it is not common to play it with tremolo. Some exceptions to this rule might be: If the measure consists of only a whole note, or if the tie connects the same note across measures. Measure 35 is an example of a tie that would sound best with tremolo.

Mandocello Part

Colonel Bogey

arr. Mark E. Freemantle

K. J. Alford

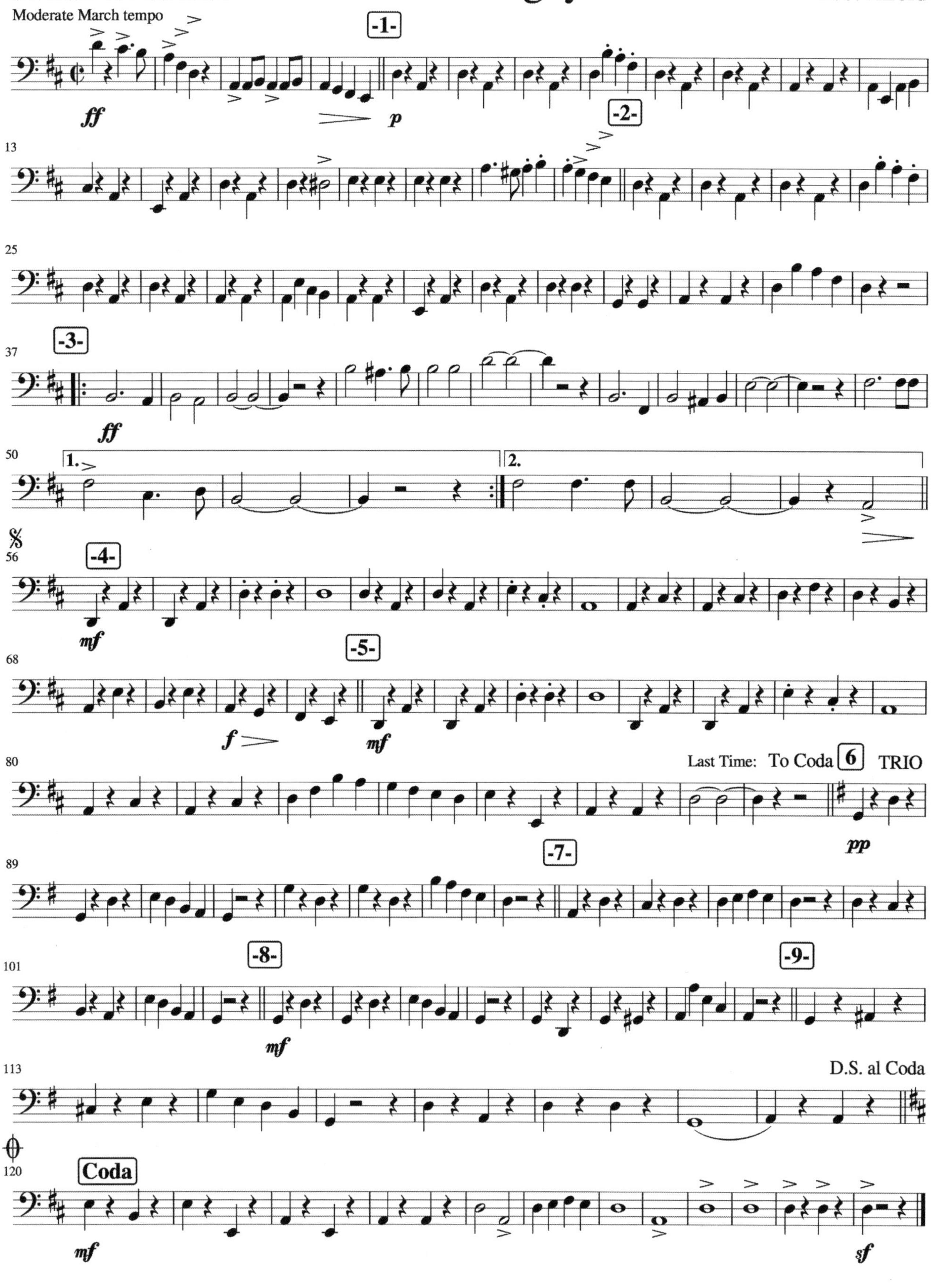

Figure 109: Colonel Bogey

El Capitan

Our next march, “El Capitan,” is written in 6/8 time. Review the section “Marching in Time” above. Both measures 2 and 3 contain a note that must be played on the sixth fret – a G♯ on string ② and a C♯ on string ③; shifting will most likely be required to reach those notes with your pinky. Measure 13 requires a shift to position IV as marked in the score.

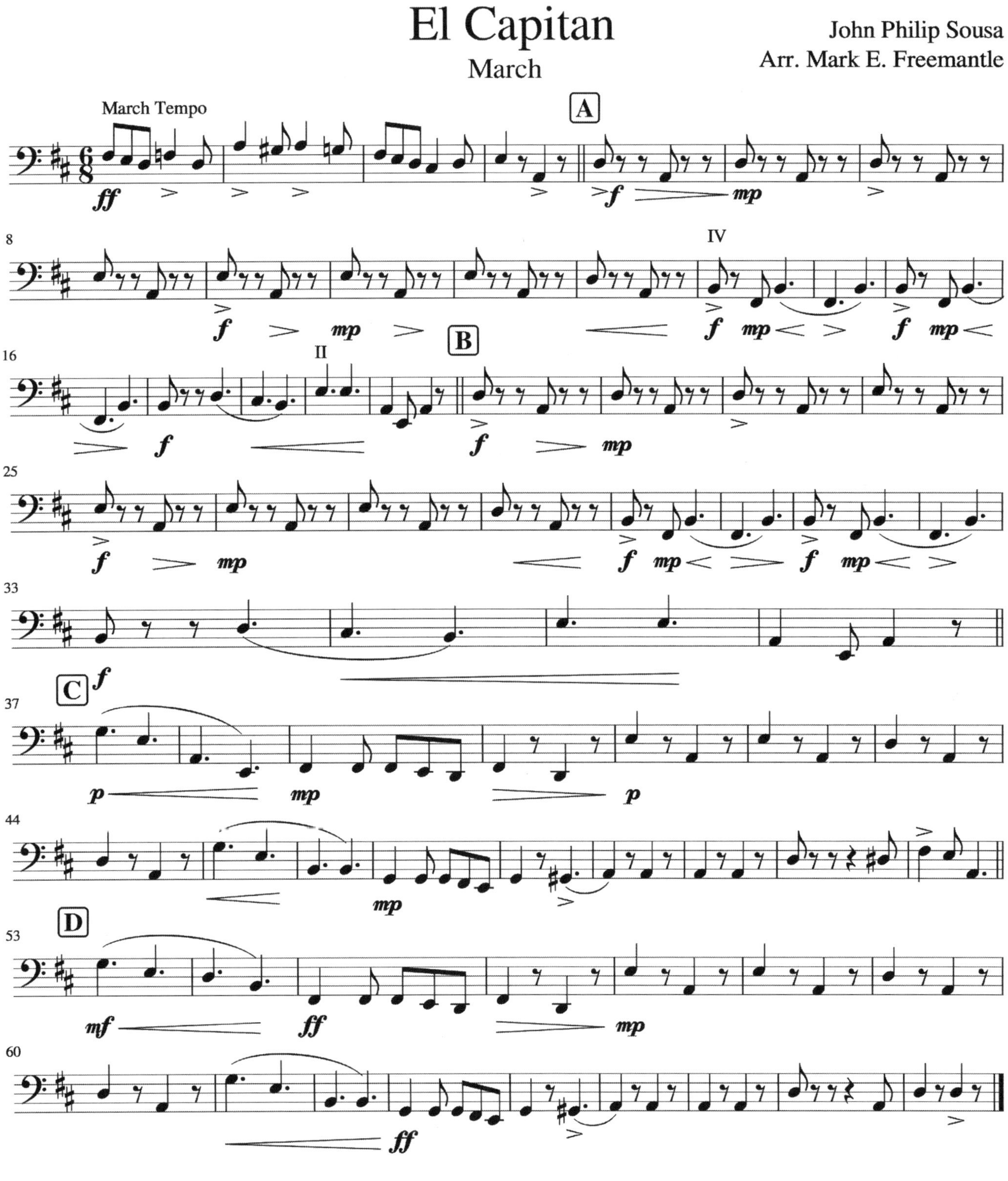

Figure 110: El Capitan

Chromatic Study

With any pitched instrument we usually play the notes that occur within the scale identified by the key signature. When a specific note is not in that key signature, we identify it as an **accidental**. If we played twelve notes in a row, starting with an open string and playing by half tones up to the twelfth fret, we would be playing a chromatic scale. Because we have four pairs of strings, it is easy to conceive how to play the chromatic scales for C, G, D, and A. Most people would play with fingers 1 to 4, then shift, and continue the pattern. When playing a tune, however, we may only be playing a small set of chromatic notes, making this process more difficult. Study the example below and notice the specific suggestions for fingering.

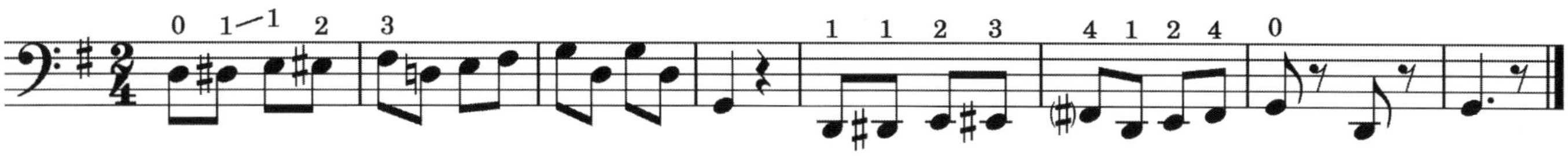

Figure 111: Chromatic Etude

To play the second note of measure 1 (D♯), it is necessary to slide both the thumb and first finger back one fret, then slide them both up one fret [home position] to play the rest of the measure, followed by measures 2, 3 and 4, all played normally. [Notice that the last note of measure 1 is an E♯, which we fret the same as an F, but because the key signature has already identified all F's as normally sharp, it is the convention to call it an E♯.] The same pattern of notes occurs again, but one octave lower. The shifting process varies from the previous measures.
To play the second note of measure 5, again a D♯, the thumb and first finger are again shifted up the fretboard. Fingers 2, 3, and 4 fall comfortably into place. But then we have the D, E, and F♯, which we play with no chromatic notes in between. While this movement of fingers 1, 2 and 4 seems fast, notice that your hand position and shifting are exactly the same. That is, we play the D, E and F♯ with the same fingers. It is important to master shifting to play chromatic notes. It is often impossible to read the music and watch the fingers without getting lost. With practice, you will "see" the chromatic movements coming and shift consistently, without looking at your fingers. The next tune applies this process, using the pattern we have just learned.

Fieldston March

"Fieldston March," includes some challenging chromatic shifting. Measure 5 introduces the term "Con spirito," with mean "with spirit". Measure 5 and 6 and 13 and 14 consist of two tied notes, and should be played with tremolo. Measure 38 ends with a ♮ symbol not associated with a specific note; it is an indication that the key signature has changed. Whereas the orignal key included an F♯ (for the key of G) now the F is a natural, so the key signature is C. Also notice in measure 39 that the dynamics change during the repeat.

Fieldston March

W. J. Kitchener
Arr. Mark E. Freemantle

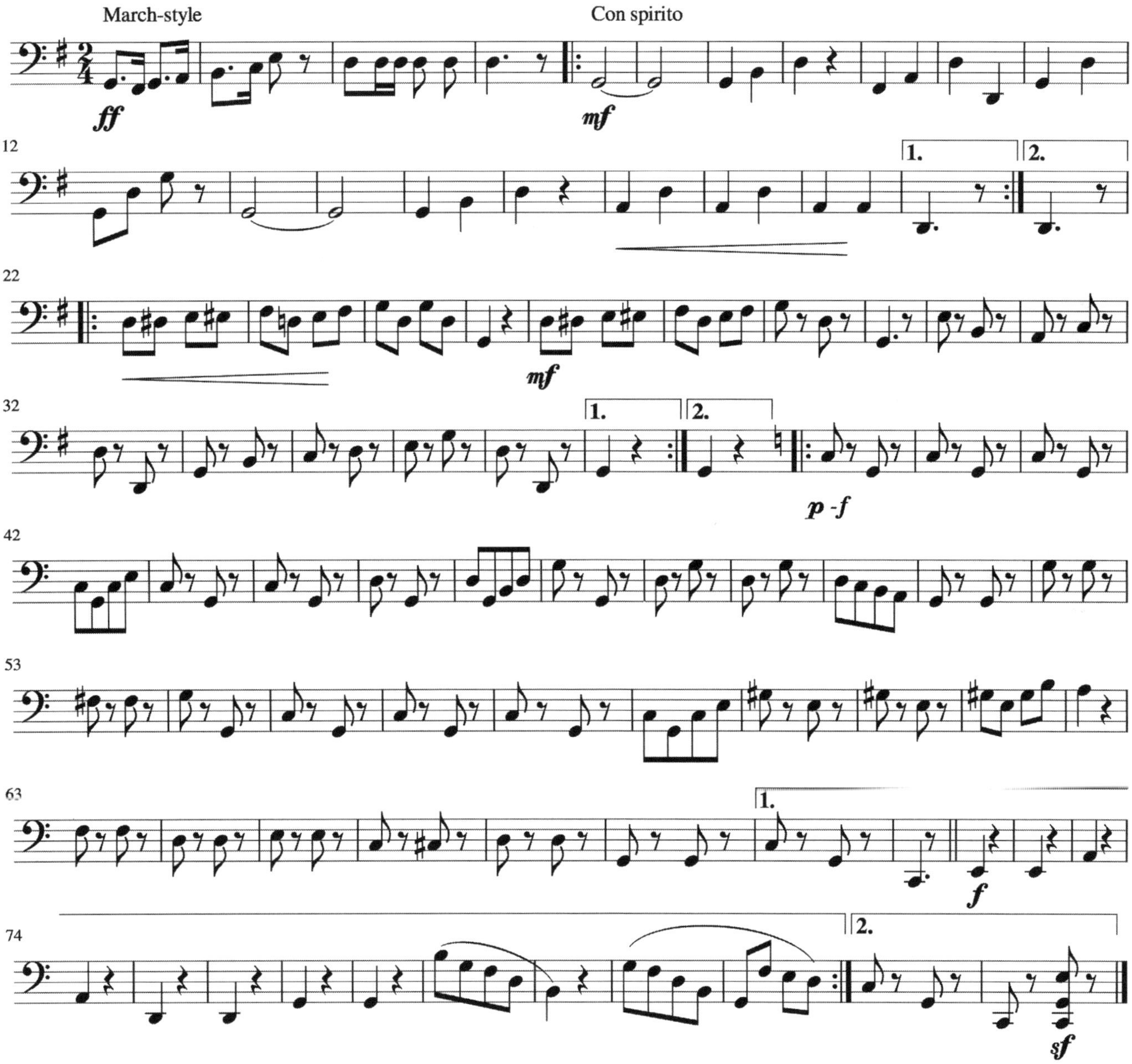

Figure 112: Fieldston March

2.8 Shifting and Stretching – Playing in Higher Positions

Occasionally it is necessary to play notes that are beyond the reach of our normal or home position. Consider the following etude:

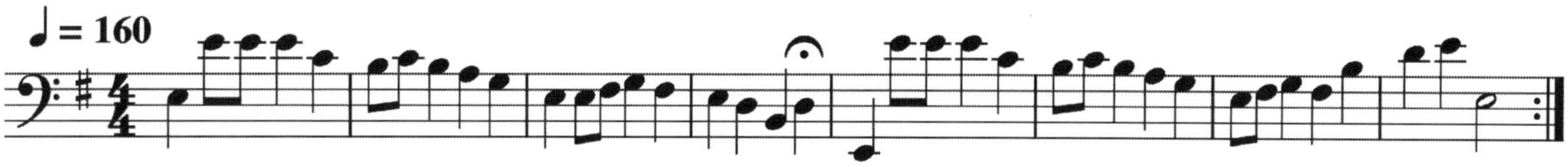

Figure 113: Higher Position Etude

Notice that the second, third, and fourth notes are all an octave above the opening E note. This requires a shift to the seventh fret on the A string. Beat four of measure 1 goes back to the third fret, if you stay in position II, which most people would prefer.

Try playing this etude in position VII, with the first note played on string ③, 9th fret. The G (beat 4) of measure 2 requires a stretch to the 12th fret or a shift to play it on the second string, fret 5. Most people prefer to stay in position II and only shift for the one high E note. We will consider alternate approaches to playing higher notes in a later section.

Stretch and Shift Etude

It is important to review all new music to identify where the high (or low) notes occur. A shift to a new position is not always necessary. The following etude starts in position V. The first three notes extend over five frets, which is a stretch for most people. **A stretch always involves a separation between fingers one and two**. This is a common method for cellists, so play this pattern with fingers 1, 2, and 4. Measure 7 has an F♯ which requires a reach-back finger stretch; keep the thumb in place and simply reach back to play this one note.

Section B starts a new melody at measure 8 and requires a shift to a new position. Apply the finger-stretch principle consistently; play this opening phrase with fingers 3, 2 and 1. Measure 10 presents a challenge. Can you play the D-E-D without shifting your thumb? Try it! You have two options: Reach back to the 5th fret on the A string, or the 12th fret on the D string. Measure 12 returns to the opening theme and requires a shift back to position V, either immediately or at the very end to play the F♯ in measure 15.

Stretch and Shift Etude

Mark E. Freemantle

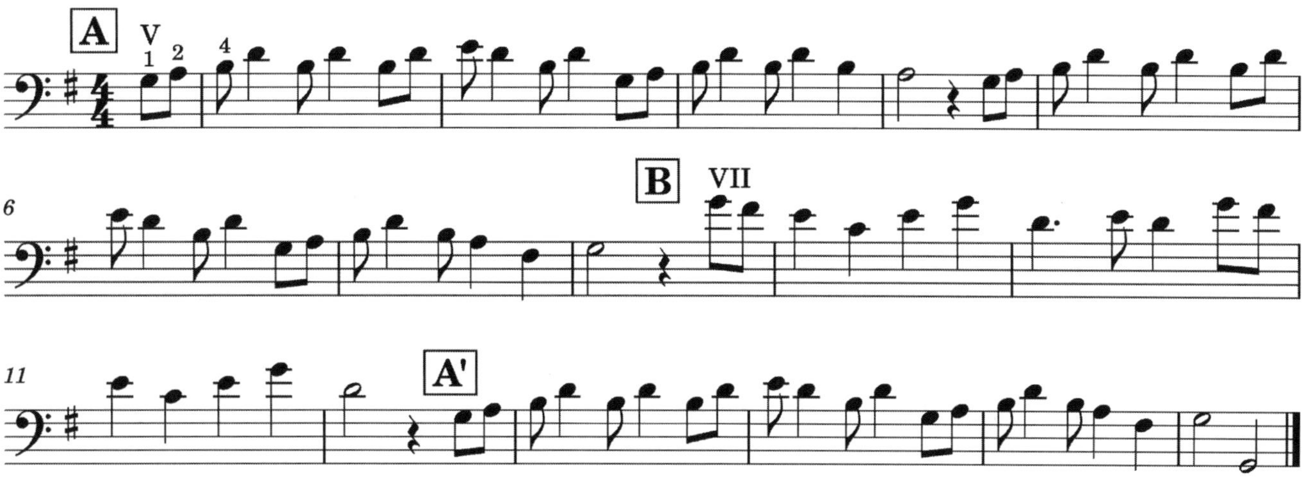

Figure 114: Stretch and Shift Etude

The following illustration demonstrates the application of the **stretch principle**. In the image on the left, you can see the space between fingers one and two. The angle of the wrist must change to accommodate this stretch. The image on the right shows that fingers 2, 3, or 4 are spaced appropriately to fret as needed. Finger 1 is relaxed; it may not be possible to keep it in its original position. With practice and proper finger and hand warmup, it is possible to maintain that stretch, but remember – if it hurts, stop!

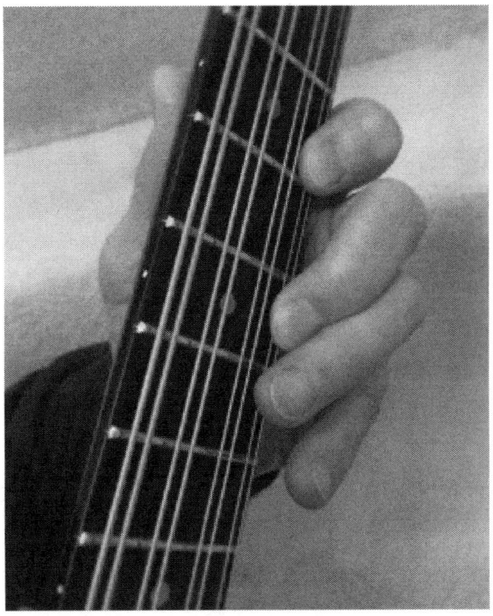

Figure 116: Finger Stretch - Example 1

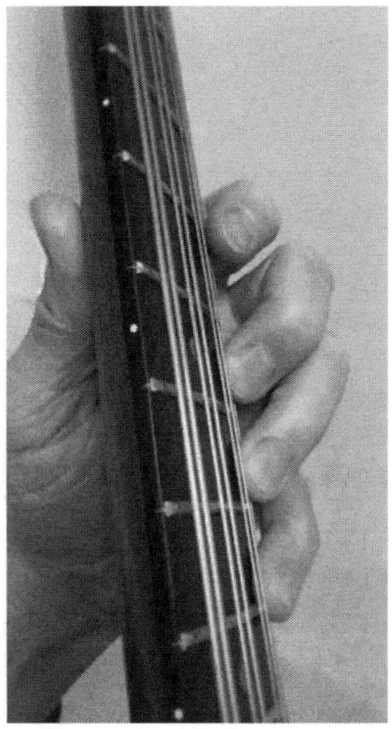

Figure 115: Finger Stretch - Example 2

Zacatecas March

"Zacatecas" is a march that incorporates all the principles we have covered to this point. It includes some chromatic notes that require a shift of the index finger. There is a recurring pattern (see measure 14) that works best if played in fourth position, with all fretted notes and no open strings.

Most marches move along quickly and the bass instruments normally play simple downstrokes; this tune includes a lot of half-notes and dotted quarter notes that tie to the next measure. Try playing these with tremolo for dramatic effect. The dynamics vary from very soft (*pp -pianissimo*) to very loud (*ff- fortissimo*). Study the "roadmap" for this tune before beginning to play. Section A, in C major, is repeated and ends with a change of key to G with one sharp. Section B is repeated and ends with a change of key back to C major.

Section D includes a first and second ending, with the last measure of the second ending showing a *fermatta* (hold) symbol and the word *Fine*. Many composers include both the *fermatta* and the *Fine* reference. The *Fine* means "end" but we are not yet at the end of the tune, so continue to the next measure, again noticing a change of key to F with one flat. The third measure of Section E includes a double bar || which indicates a change, in this case the term *Dolce* which means to play "sweetly," that is, with a light touch and mellow tone.

Section E ends with a *D.C. al Fine* which means to *Da Capo* (go back to the top, or measure 1), and play to the *Fine* (end). One thing that is not indicated in the music, and is simply understood by all orchestra players—when you *Da Capo* and start playing again from the beginning, you do not play the repeat(ed) sections; i.e., if there are alternate endings, always take the second ending.

Zacatecas

Don Fernando Villalpando
Arr. Mark E. Freemantle

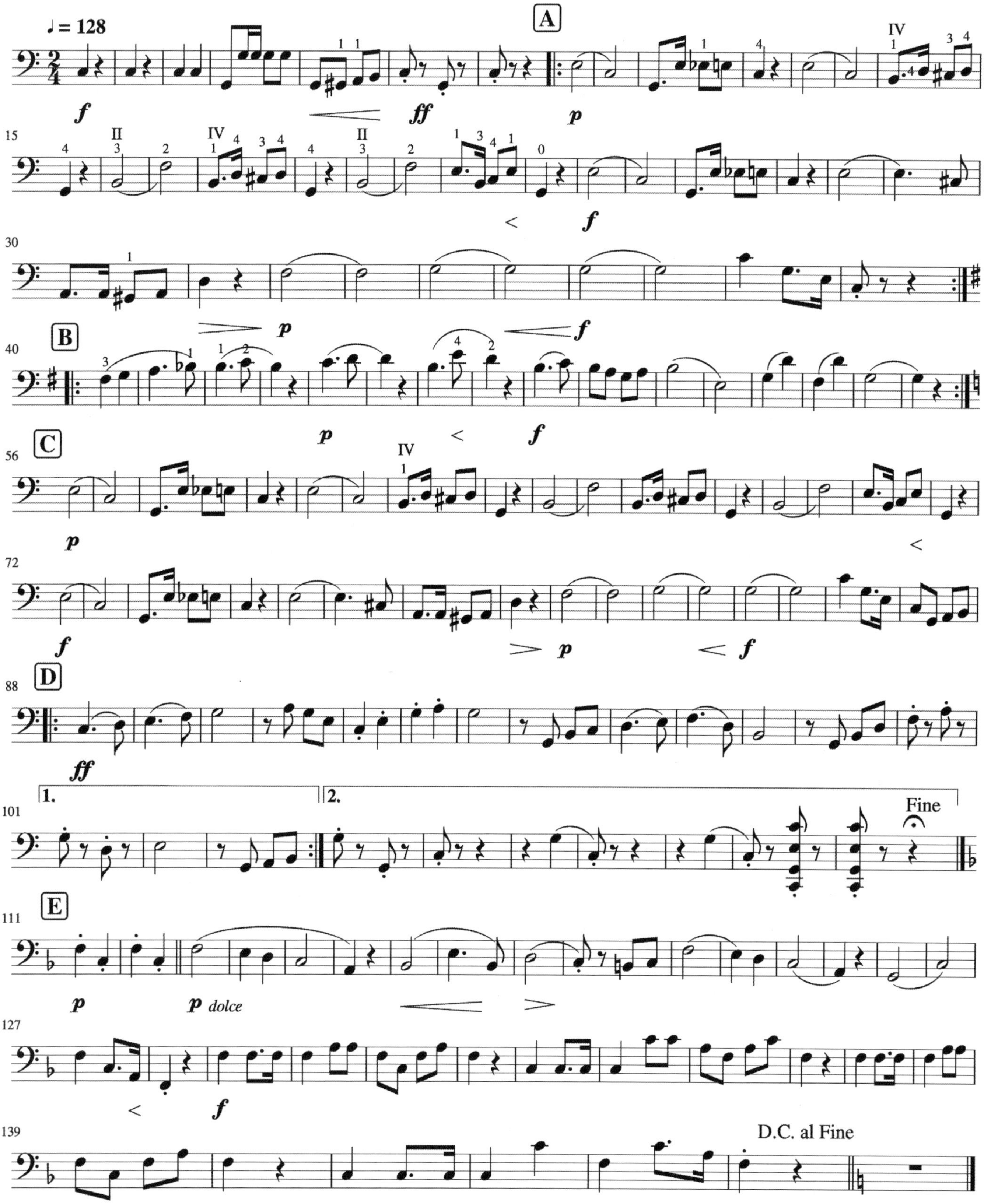

Figure 117: Zacatecas

2.9 Triplets

"*A Triplet is a group of three notes which are to be played in the time of two notes of the same value, or, as it is usually easier to grasp mentally, in the time of one of the next larger denomination.*" [Bickford, page 28] In the example below the time signature is 4/4, so measure 1 has four quarter notes, measure 2 has eight eighth notes, while measure 3 has two, 3-note triplets, taking the place of two eighth-notes each. Two ways to count triplets are shown. Notice that measure 4 has a precise down-up-down picking pattern and does not simply alternate. Practice this exercise with a metronome that provides a sounding beat for the quarter notes.

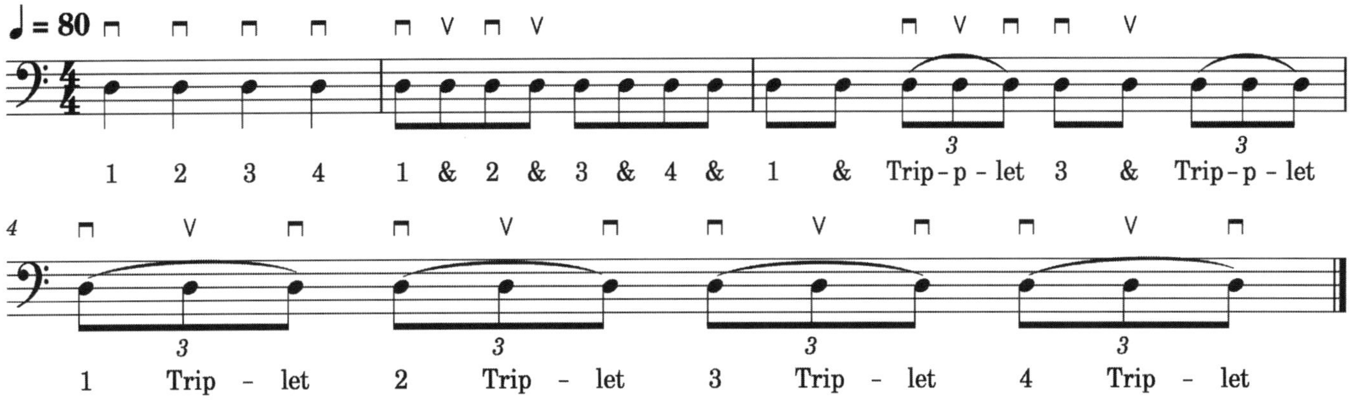

Figure 118: Triplets

Triplet Etude

This following etude is written without the slur marking over the triplets; this is common practice in modern music notation programs. Without the slur, the triplet is not as obvious but shows the importance of reviewing the music before playing to ensure the number of notes per measure matches the "musical math" required. Continue with the picking pattern suggested in measure 1. Be sure to practice with a metronome and repeat the etude. The timing in measure 3 will probably feel "too slow" at first. Don't rush the second half-note of measure 3; let the metronome reinforce the counting that you are already applying while you play.

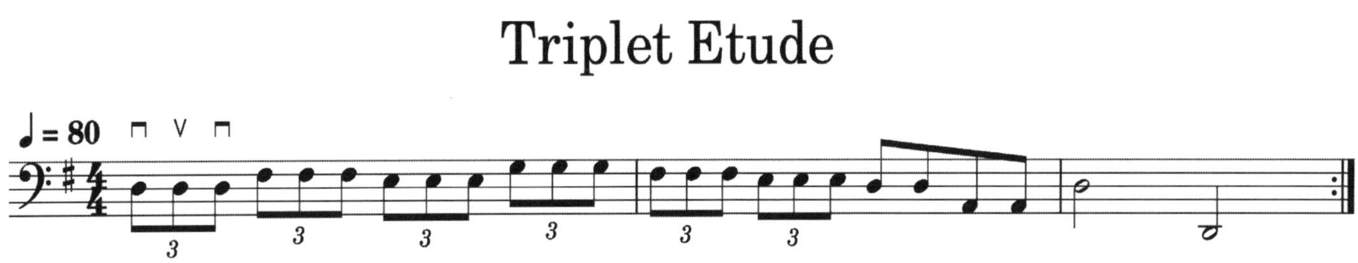

Figure 119: Triplet Etude

The Old Monaghan Twig

This tune includes several triplets. A reel is a dance tune, so the tempo could be as fast as 160 bpm.

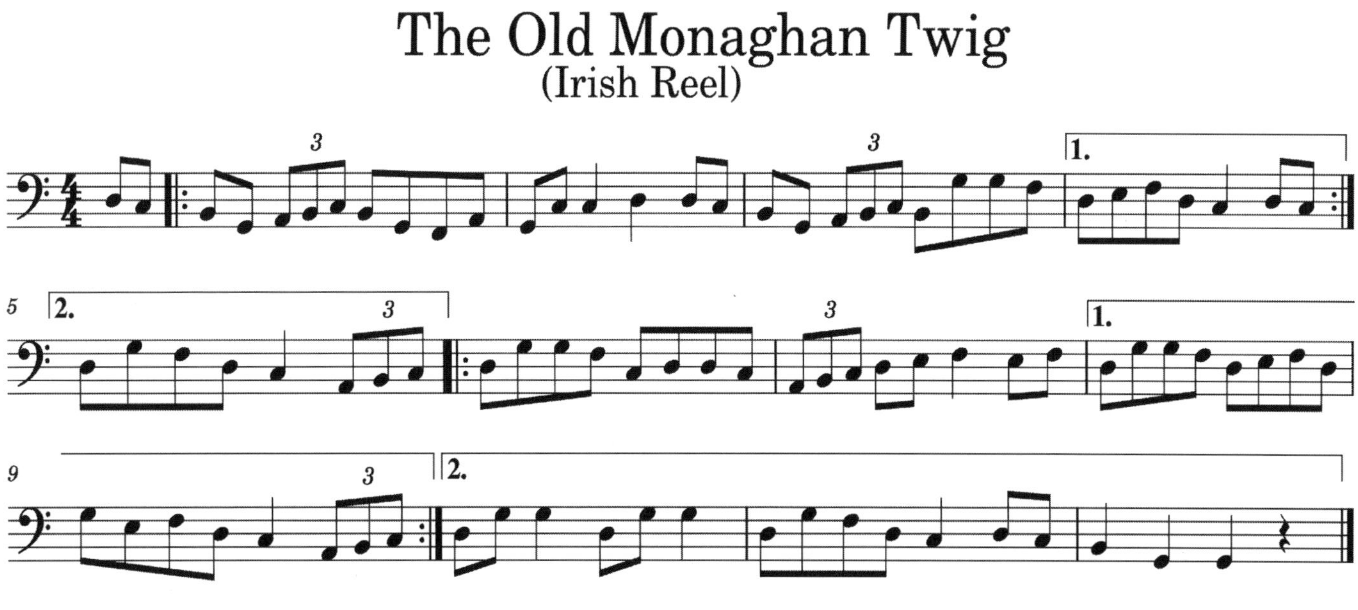

Figure 120: The Old Monaghan Twig

Carolan's Welcome

Another Irish tune featuring triplets, originally composed for the harp.

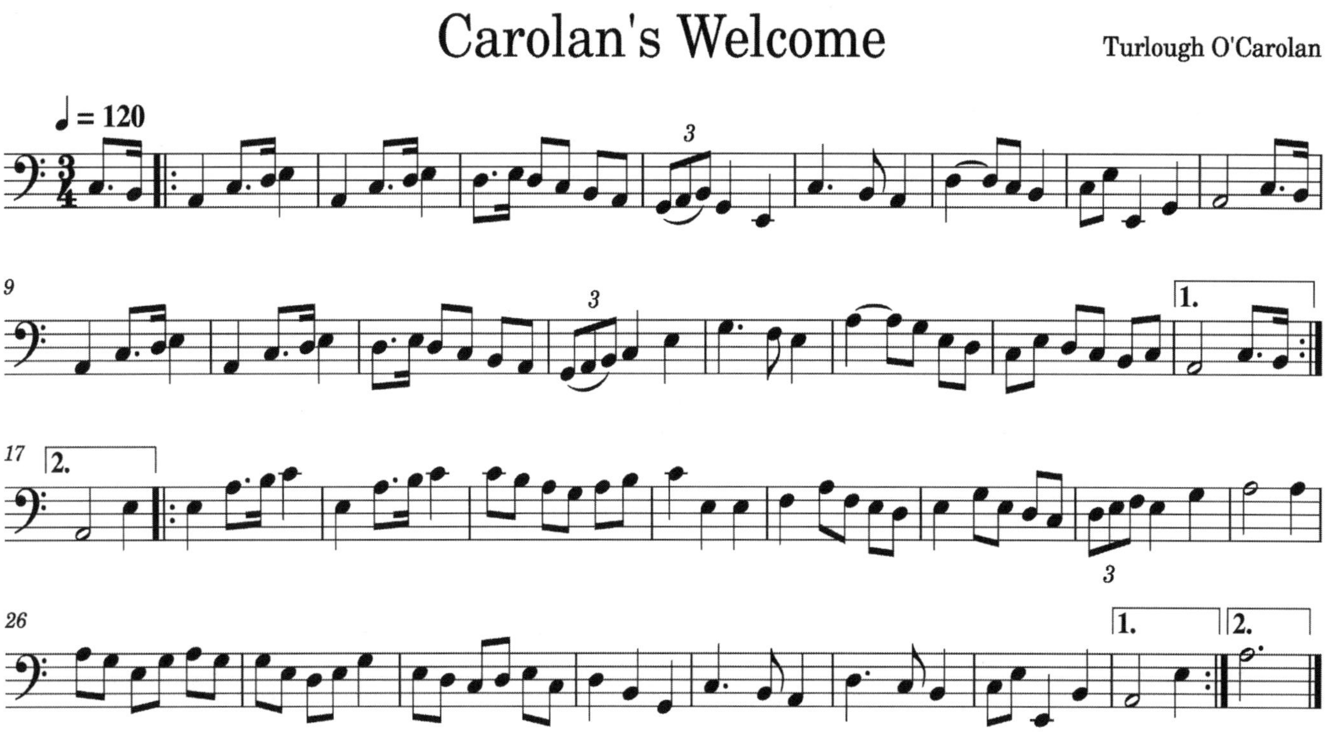

Figure 121: Carolan's Welcome

2.10 Introducing the Key of A Major with Three Sharps

The key of A major includes three sharps: F♯, C♯ and G♯. Depending on the tune, the challenge of playing the range of notes from fret 1 to 6 can be daunting. It is essential to learn how to shift to a new position or stretch within the same position. Let's examine a few simple etudes:

The A Major Scale – with Open Strings

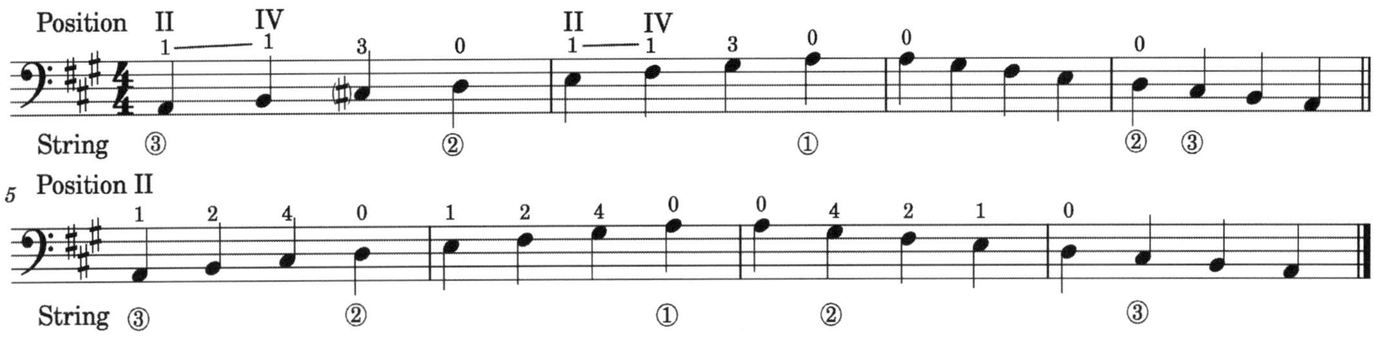

Figure 122: The A Major Scale – with Open Strings

The fingering for these four measures follows the pattern we have been using – start in position II and shift the thumb and fingers to position IV. Use open strings going up and down the scale. The next approach requires finger extension while keeping the thumb in place.

The A Major Scale with Open Strings and Extensions

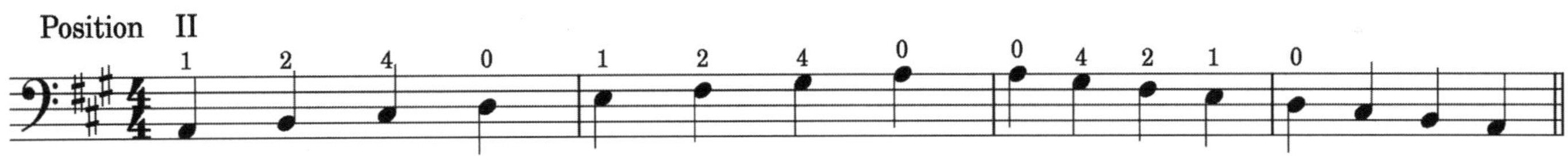

Figure 123: The A Major Scale with Open Strings and Extensions

The second approach has the advantage of keeping the thumb and first finger in place, which facilitates both sight reading of the music and speed of performance. This requires significant extension of the left-hand fingers, so be sure to warm up the left hand before using the stretch approach.

Both methods of playing scales (and tunes) in the key of A use open strings. There is one disadvantage to this method: If you play any notes that descend lower than the open string you just played, the open string will continue to sound unless you mute it. For example, when going from the open A string to a G♯ (on the second string), you must mute the A string to prevent a dissonance.

Neither of the two previous etudes extended the scale below the first A note on string ③, fret 2. For an additional challenge, try the next etude.

The A Scale in Thirds

The following etude does not provide any fingering for open strings and moves between positions II and IV from measure 1 to measure 9. Measures 10 to the end adds positions I and III. This is a great pattern to practice for warming up and should be easy to memorize and play without looking at your fretting hand. The fact that there are no open strings makes it easy to play the same pattern both up and down the scale.

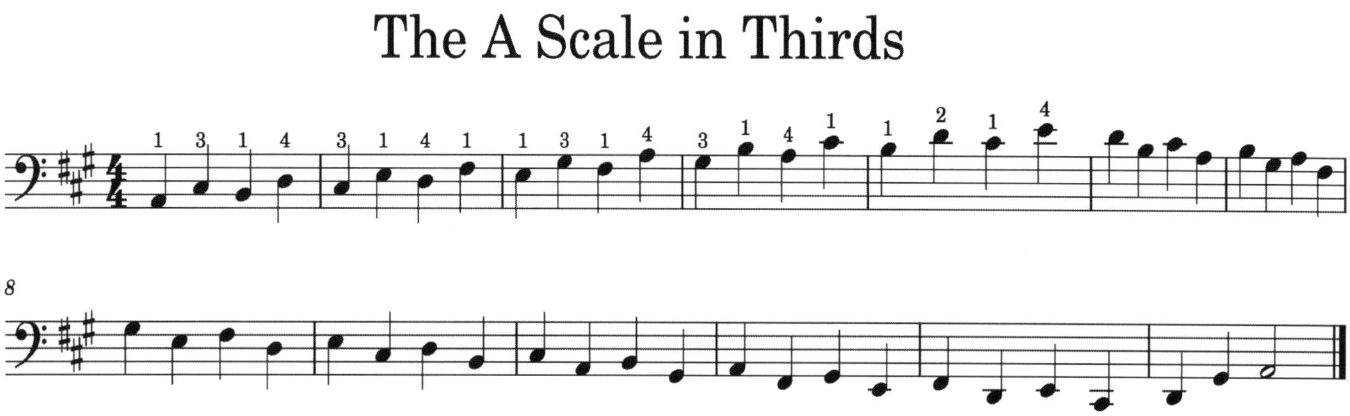

Figure 124: The A Scale in Thirds

When to Play Open Strings

Because of the challenges in reaching notes on the sixth and seventh frets, it is common to play open strings whenever possible. There is a specific reason for playing a note in closed position (seventh fret) rather than the open string: When moving up the scale, you can play an open string, if the note that follows remains on that same string; for example – Open D followed by E on the second fret. If you are moving down the scale, however, say from D to C♯, if you play an open D you must prevent it from continuing to sound when you move to the C♯ on string ③. Of course, if you play all closed-position notes, there aren't any open strings to worry about, but in practice, it is often necessary to keep one's eyes on the music and the open strings aid in maintaining control as to your exact position on the fretboard. There are no specific exercises for practicing how to mute open strings.

There are two options for muting an open string. The first approach is to rest the heel of the palm of the right hand on the open string. This can work in most circumstances, but may present a challenge in picking the next note. The second approach only works if the next note played is a lower-pitched note. In this case, the finger playing the next note (on the lower string) can be relaxed and, rather than playing directly on the finger-tip, you play closer to the center of the finger. (Near the swirl of the finger-print.) The remainder of the first joint touches the open string and prevents it from sounding. Try using both methods, and listen carefully to the open strings to make sure they are not sounding past their actual note duration.

2.11 Tunes in the Key of A and F♯ Minor

Carolan's Welcome – Redux

Let's re-visit "Carolan's Welcome" with an arrangement in the key of A. Measure 4 requires a shift to position I, whereas measures 7 to 8 work well with a simple reach. Cellists would call this a **backward extension**. We see another new musical term, *D.C. con rep.* which is short for *Da Capo with replica*. This means to go back to the beginning and this time play **both** repeated sections. There is an important distinction between a simple *D.C.* versus *D.C. con rep*. Without the *con rep* we would return to the beginning and play only the second endings. This seems counterintuitive, but it is the convention in all modern music. So with *con rep* we play both the first and second endings when we repeat.

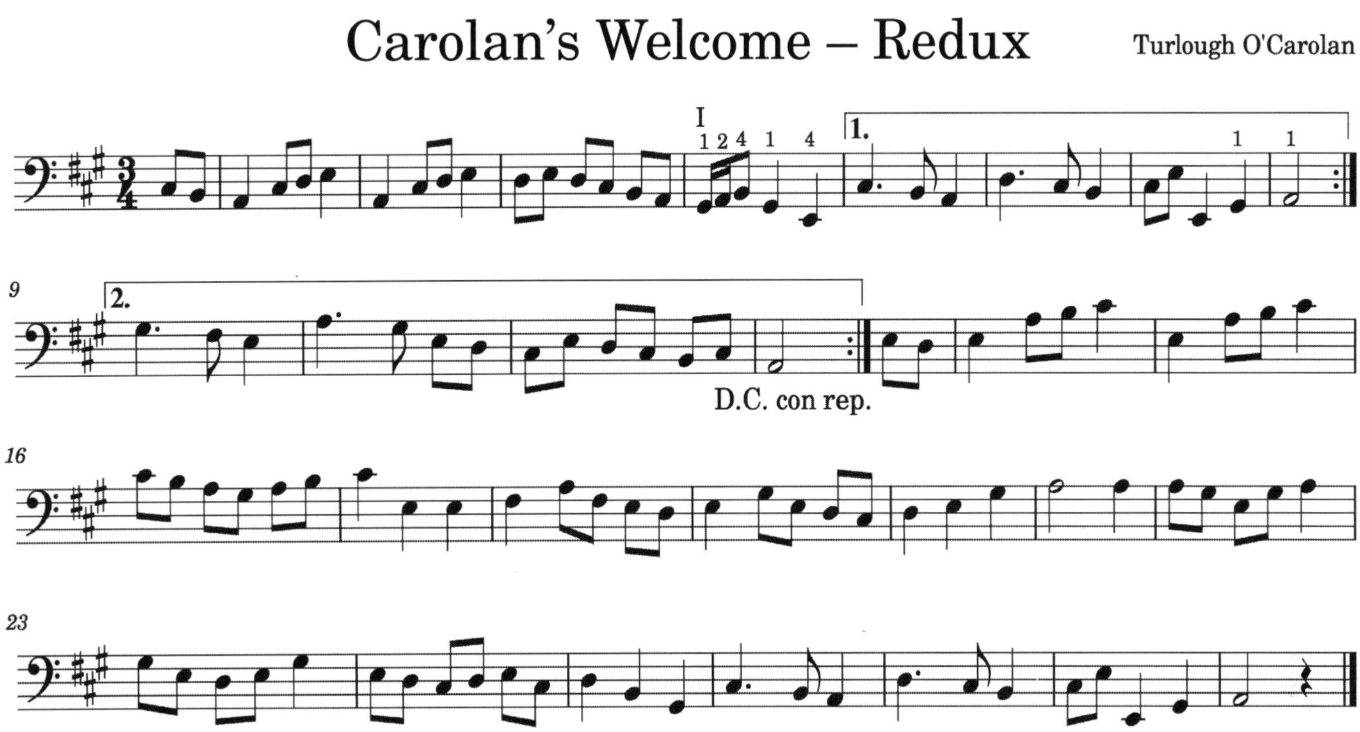

Figure 125: Carolan's Welcome – Redux

Tzur Chassidi

The tune "Tzur Chassidi" is a traditional Israeli dance tune. Notice that it has three sharps but is in the key of F♯m, the relative minor to A major. [Look at the last note in measure 13 and you'll see the tune ends on the F♯.] The tune consists of three sections. All three sections are four measures long, with two, 2-bar phrases. Sections 1 and 3 have the same rhythm with an eighth note starting each phrase. In the second section, each phrase starts with a dotted quarter note. Section 1 can be played in position III or IV. Section 2 requires a first-finger extension to play the B. [Position II works for measures 6, 7 and 8, but not for measure 9.] Alternate picking, with string crossing, seems to work well.

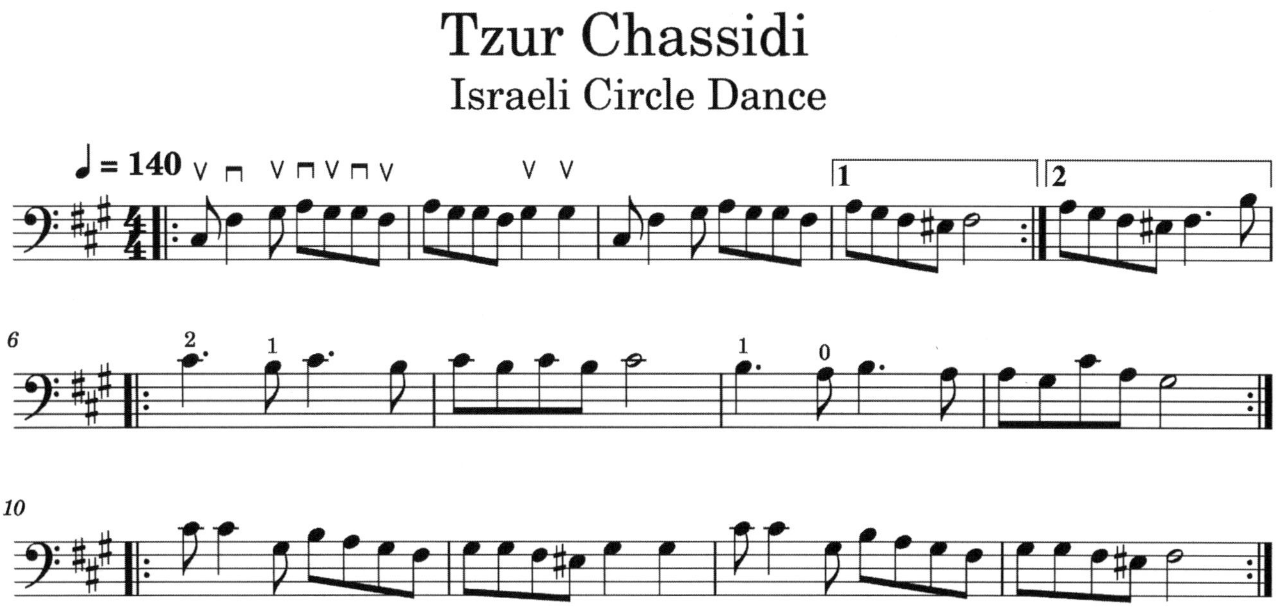

Figure 126: Tzur Chassidi

2.12 Reconsidering the Tremolo

Many players cannot gain sufficient speed when attempting to play the tremolo. As mentioned in Section 1.24, the tremolo may require changing the way we play the alternating pattern. The following exercise should help if you still struggle with the tremolo. It is called "Tremolo Train Wreck" because the aim is to play as if you are a train leaving the station (slowly, at first) until the speed is so great the train derails. The notes in this etude are **not** of equal duration. This approach is counterintuitive; the timing of the alternating picking pattern is intentionally changed. Play it with a dotted eighth note followed by a sixteenth note. Apply the downstroke with the pick resting on the string below it. The upstroke, applied at the time of the sixteenth note, is a quick upstroke, followed immediately by the downstroke. The method forces the right hand to drop-and-stop and facilitates the muscle memory needed to play a faster tremolo.

Each measure is marked with a repeat. While you determine the number of repetitions for each measure, increase the speed of the tremolo as you transition to the next tempo marking. No dynamics are indicated. Try to play at a medium volume (*mf* – for *mezzo-forte*, moderately loud). Do not grip the pick too hard as this adds tension to the right hand. Start on the D string as indicated, so you have a string below it (the A string) to perform the Stop action. Continue to increase the tempo until your tremolo "fails", viz. the train falls off the tracks. Stop. Take a "Tension Releasing Break" and start again. There is no perfect tempo. The last measure changes to the "ideal" tremolo of equal duration notes for both up and down strokes. The aim is to generate a consistent alternating stroke, before "falling off the rails." Try experimenting with a thinner pick if necessary. This can reduce tension in the right hand, but sacrifices tone.

Tremolo Train Wreck

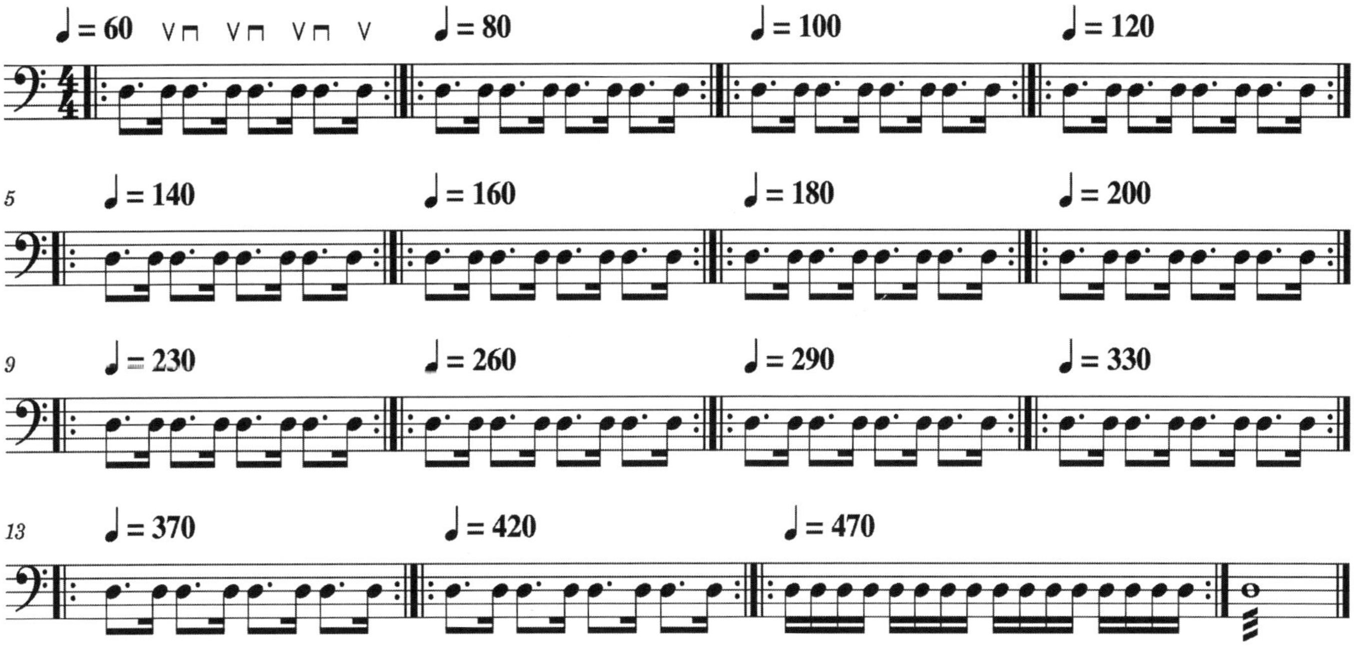

Figure 127: Tremolo Train Wreck

2.13 Left-Hand Finger Extensions

The next simple etude is included to provide the opportunity to practice the extension of the pinky of the left hand. Position II is assumed, which makes reaching the C♯ and high E out of range for most people. Often, it's only one note that requires a quick shift with the pinky. Practice this tune with the goal of shifting without looking at the left hand.

D Shifty Etude

Mark E. Freemantle

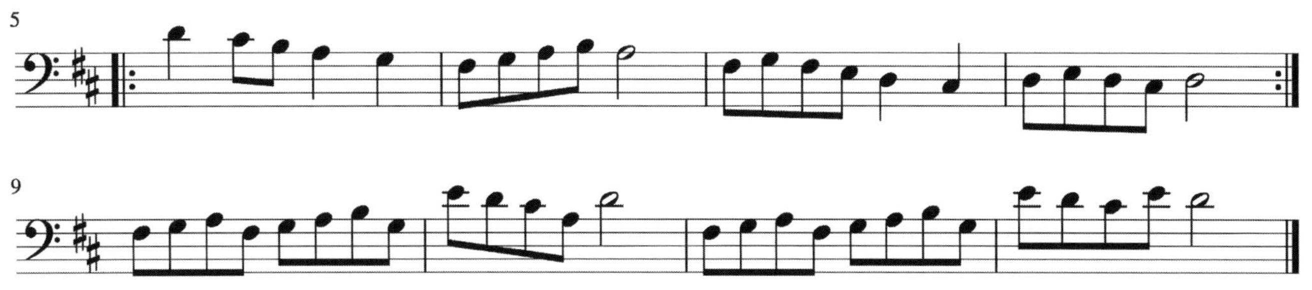

Figure 128: D Shifty Etude

The next etude focuses on the extension of the first finger. Again, position II will feel most comfortable except for the extension required to play the E♭ and B♭. [Notice the key signature contains 3 flats; the tune is in C minor, the relative major of E♭.] This etude should be played with a swing feel, as identified. No references to shifting or fingerings are provided; you should be comfortable identifying where and when to shift.

First-Finger Shift Etude

Mark E. Freemantle

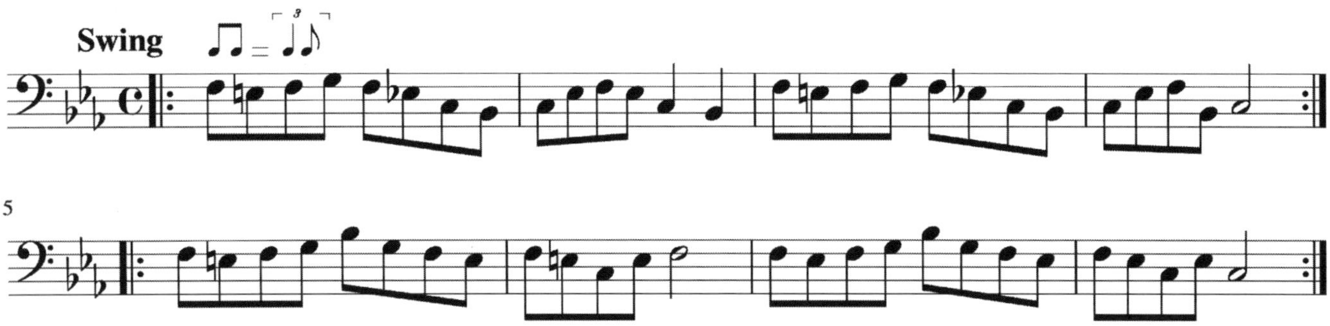

Figure 129: First-Finger Shift Etude

2.14 Duet Studies

The only reason we have deferred the introduction of duets up to this point is the assumption that you do not have an instructor or fellow mandocellist with whom to play. The repertoire for duets is considerable, because the mandocello can play any cello part of a classical duet as well as substitute for almost any bass clef instrument.

Playing with a duet partner presents new challenges. First, there is the music selection process. This may require some give and take with the obvious need for each player to be sufficiently skilled to perform their part. After selecting the music, there is the challenge of simultaneous sight-reading of the score. If the music identifies a performance tempo, agree to a significantly slower tempo to start. Allow time for each player to mark the position and fingering on the music if needed. If the score has both a duet page and a set of separate parts, start on the duet page, so you can easily identify where you both are during the rehearsal. Afterwards, having separate pages might encourage you to practice your part alone. Be sure to use a metronome when practicing your part. While the metronome can act as the conductor of the duet it can also be a cause for distraction during the "find-the-fret" efforts during initial rehearsals. After your rehearsals have achieved a level of comfort, consider using an electronic metronome in "flash mode" only.

Bourrée Duet

This arrangement takes the melody we played previously, moves it to the key of D minor (relative of F major, so it has the same key signature), and assigns it to a treble-clef instrument. The challenge of playing with a duet partner is initially setting a comfortable tempo at which you both can play. As always, use a metronome to keep the tempo steady.

Bourrée Duet

J. S. Bach
Arr. Mark E. Freemantle

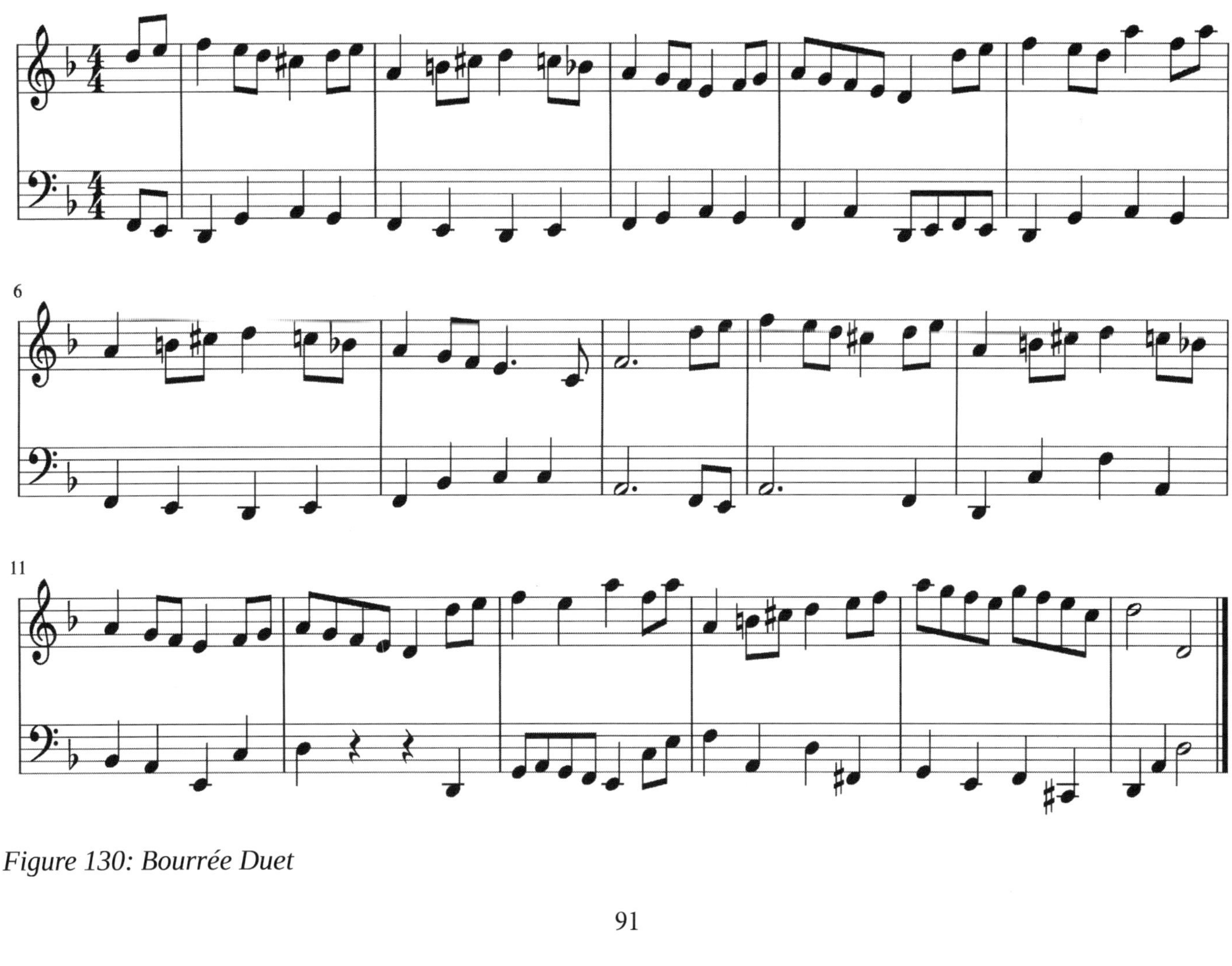

Figure 130: Bourrée Duet

Bickford's "Duet in G"

Bickford's "Duet in G" (abbreviated) is written for the mandocello and a mandolin or other treble clef instrument. The mandocello part is played as tremolo, with emphasis on proper phrasing. Tremolo all the notes under the phrase markings. In measures 6, 7, and 8, use tremolo on the half notes with a separation between them and play the two quarter notes with downstrokes. Be sure to select a tempo that is comfortable for both instrumentalists.

Duet in G

Myron A. Bickford

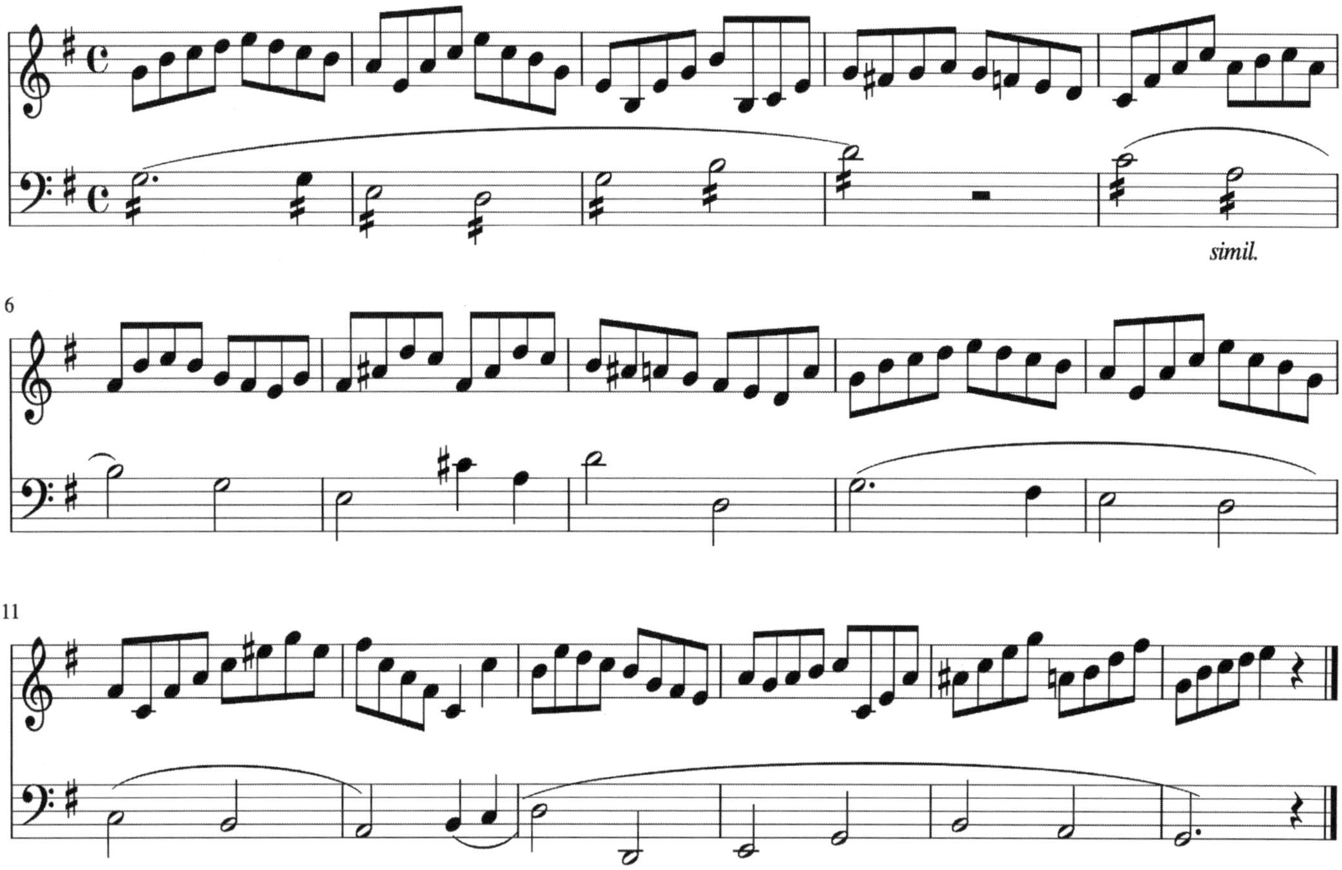

Figure 131: Duet in G

Work It Out (Shuffle) – Duet

The following duet, "Work It Out (Shuffle)" is written for mandocello and guitar. It is an uptempo shuffle and demonstrates that the mandocello can "set the groove" in the context of a duet. The guitarist may choose to merely play the provided "comping chords" until the melody is learned. Alternately, it can become a trio with one guitar playing the melody and another playing backup chords. Be sure to honor the ties, to establish the proper "groove."

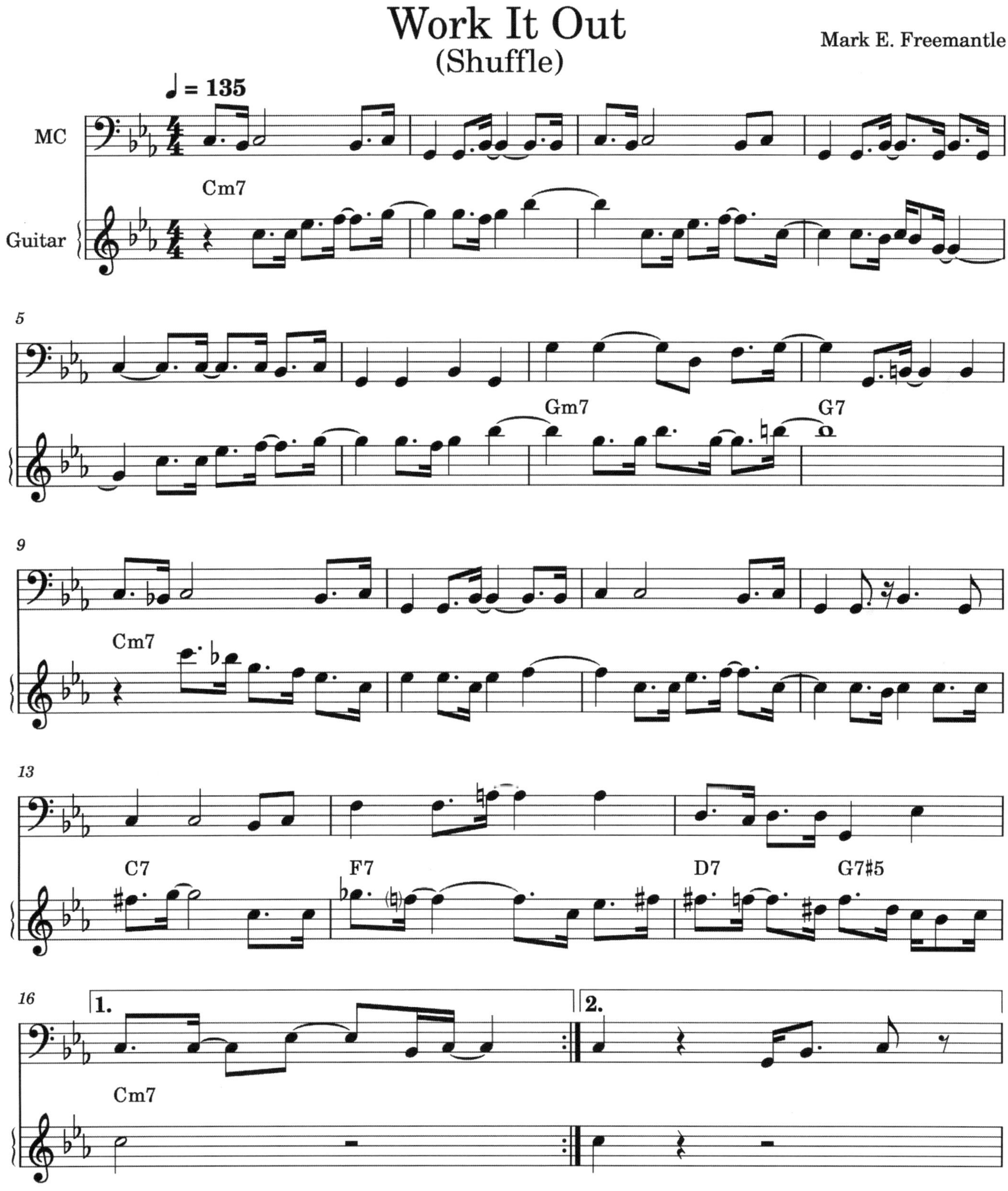

Figure 132: Work It Out (Shuffle) – Duet

2.15 Double-Stops – Providing Your Own Accompaniment

A double-stop is nothing more than the fingering and playing of two notes at the same time. If you play guitar or any other chord-capable instrument, you know how to create a chord. In music theory, a chord comprises at least three harmonically related notes sounding at the same time. If we only have two notes, we are playing a **dyad** or interval. While not technically a chord, a dyad can function as a chord and provide harmony to the melody.

Double-stops are always played on two separate strings, normally adjacent. There are two general methods to play a double-stop: The first option is to play both strings with the pick using a simple downstroke. The second option is to hybrid-pick, which requires the combination of thumb-pick-first-finger and middle finger. Guitarists trained in the classical technique might even choose to play with only their fingers.

Oh Shenandoah

This arrangement of "Oh Shenandoah" contains many examples of double-stops. Notice the phrasing and allow time for each phrase to "sing" on its own. No fingering is provided, but it should be easy to decipher. Let the melody notes dominate the harmony and be sure to honor the phrasing and slurs. The melody moves (mostly) between strings 1 and 2. Be sure the melody dominates while playing a double-stop. If the melody seems to be over-powered by the harmony try changing to an upstroke, which applies more force to the melody note.

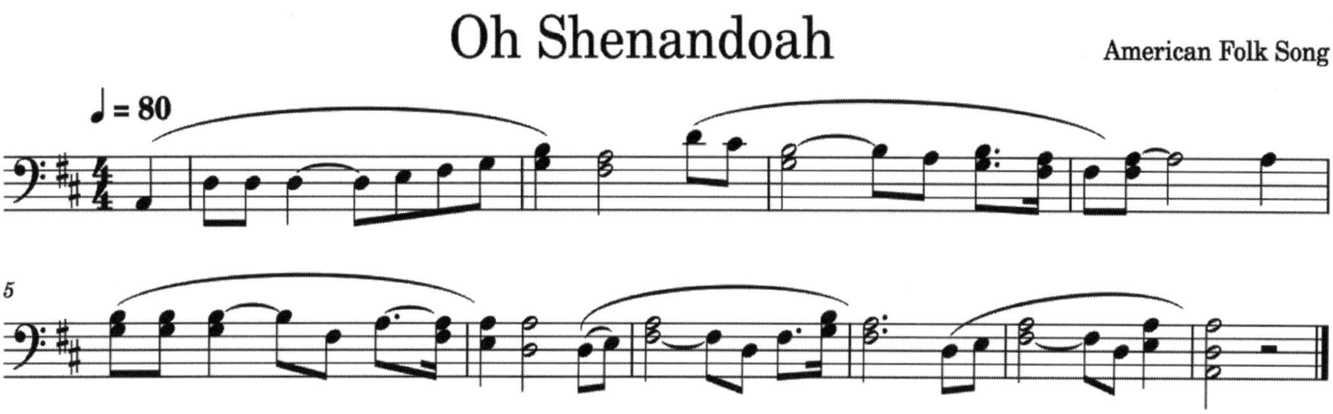

Figure 133: Oh Shenandoah

Jesu, Joy of Man's Desiring

Another Bach favorite. This shortened version of the tune should challenge you with its numerous double-stops.

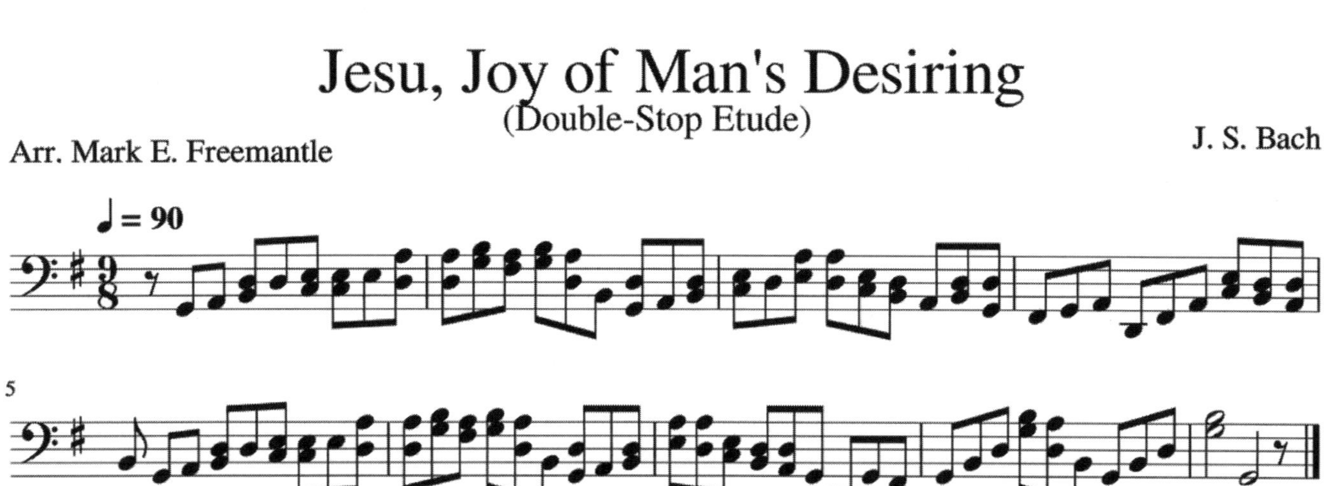

Figure 134: Jesu, Joy of Man's Desiring

Section 3 Becoming an Advanced Mandocellist

This section will explore many areas and opportunities for advancing your mandocello skills.

3.1 Learning New Tunes

Let's address the question – "How do you learn to play a new tune?" To those with musical training, the answer is obvious – Read the sheet music! This sounds so obvious, but what does it mean precisely?

To determine the key of a piece, you must check the key signature plus the last note of the melody, which is usually the tonic. It's the tonic note that identifies the major or relative minor key. The sharps and flats in the key signature are not accidentals. Accidentals are the variants that occur in the music outside of the key signature.

The best method for reviewing a new piece of music is to use a simple mnemonic – STARS:

S – for Key Signature

T – for Time Signature

A – for Accidentals

R – for Rhythm

S – Signs

S for KEY SIGNATURE: as addressed above.

T for Time Signature: a time signature expresses the meter, or pulse, of the music. Be sure to identify the smallest note duration, which facilitates counting.

A for Accidentals: It is important to look for these notes prior to playing the music because you might need to change your fingering to reach a note.

R for Rhythm: Rhythm is the element of music pertaining to the time value of the notes played. When we evaluate a new piece of music for rhythm, we are looking at the way the composer groups the notes in a measure or within a phrase. We also want to identify which notes are accented or unaccented on the beat. The rhythm varies with the duration of the notes played. The **meter** of the tune remains the same and is another way of expressing the beats per measure.

S for Signs: Sort of a "catch-all" topic. Think of them as road signs that reflect changes in tempo, dynamics, timbre, repeat symbols, soloists, etc., and include: *D.S., D.C., fine, Coda, f, ff, p, pp, rit., accel.*, etc.

Review the new piece of music for all of these elements before picking up the mandocello. Think before you begin to play. Even before playing the tune, practice the appropriate scale, major or relative minor, to "tune your ear" as well as identify potential playing positions. Then, start the tune at a slow tempo and determine the best position, fingerings, shift-or-stretch, etc.

For more information on music theory, see: *Theory and Harmony for Everyone* (93790) by L. Dean Bye, or *Music Theory 101* (99393) by Larry McCabe.

3.2 Two and Three-Octave Scales

Most of the tunes in Sections 1 and 2 cover the range of notes from the low C string to the E note on the seventh fret of the A string. It is important to learn how to play notes that occur higher up the fretboard. While it is possible to play all the high notes only on the A string, it is often not practical. The best way to get comfortable playing higher up the fretboard is to learn scales in three octaves. We will introduce the three-octave C scale to illustrate this learning process. The two most common positions that we have played in this book are position II and position IV. The 3-octave C scale also uses positions V, VII, X, and XII.

Pay special attention to the positions and fingerings. Here, the C notes are intentionally repeated to facilitate the transition to a new position.

The C Major Scale in 3 Octaves

Shifting Exercise

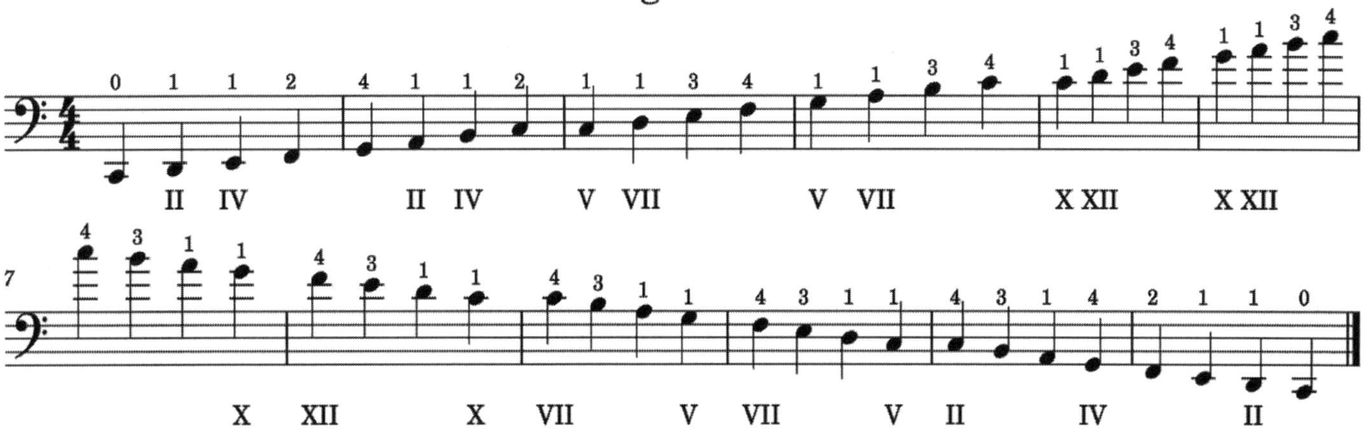

Figure 135: The C Major Scale in 3 Octaves

3.3 Tenor Clef

The next exercise is a three-octave C scale but uses the tenor clef, starting at the end of the second octave. The tenor clef has an advantage over the four ledger lines in the exercise above. The ending C in measure 4 is repeated at measure 5 in the tenor clef. Notice that the upper C (string ②, 10th fret) is in the middle of the tenor clef, not the middle of the staff.

C Major Scale in 3 Octaves

Shifting Exercise with Tenor Clef

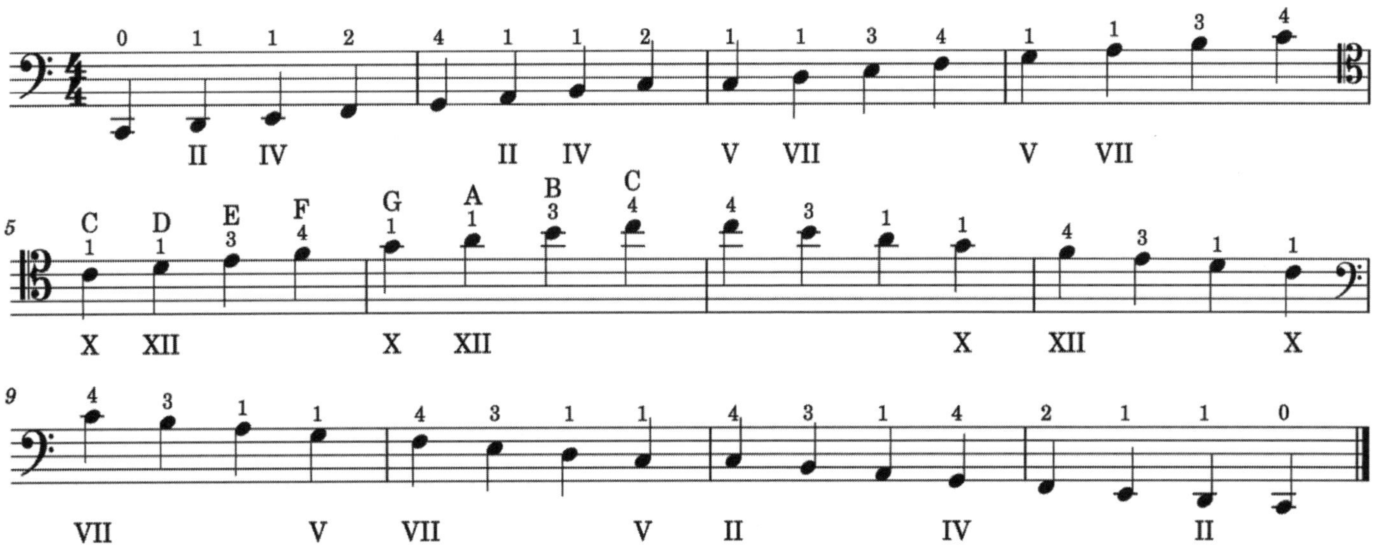

Figure 136: C Major Scale in 3 Octaves with Tenor Clef

Suggested fingerings and positions are provided. If you apply finger extensions instead, try to be consistent when playing both up the scale as well as down. Note that the tenor clef places middle C at the 4th line of the staff, reducing the number of ledger lines needed above the staff. Compare this scale to the same scale written on the previous page in bass clef only.

3.4 Chords

The mandocello rarely serves the role of a rhythm instrument in an ensemble setting. That said, nothing prevents the mandocellist from playing many common chords used in folk, Irish and bluegrass music. Playing the same chord shapes used on the mandolin is of limited value because of the huge stretch required to play four separate notes on four strings, sometimes covering six frets! The following are some common chord shapes, presented in two common keys.

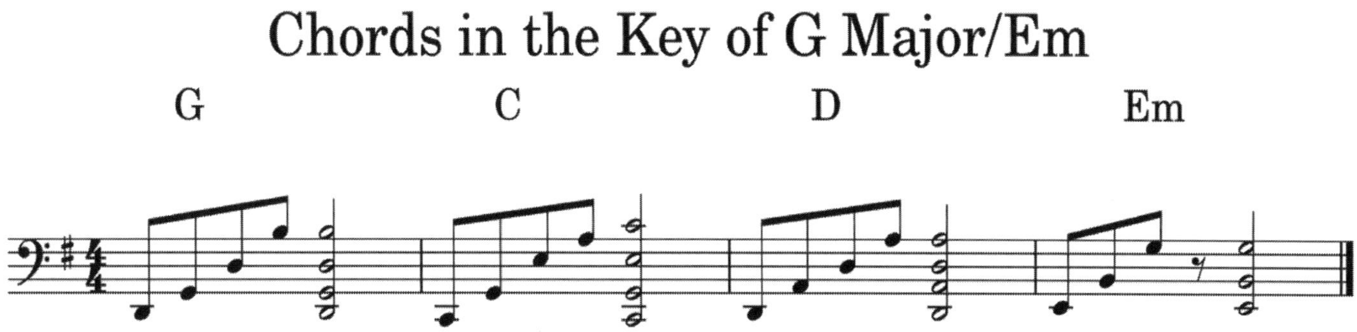

Figure 137: Chords in the Key of G Major/Em

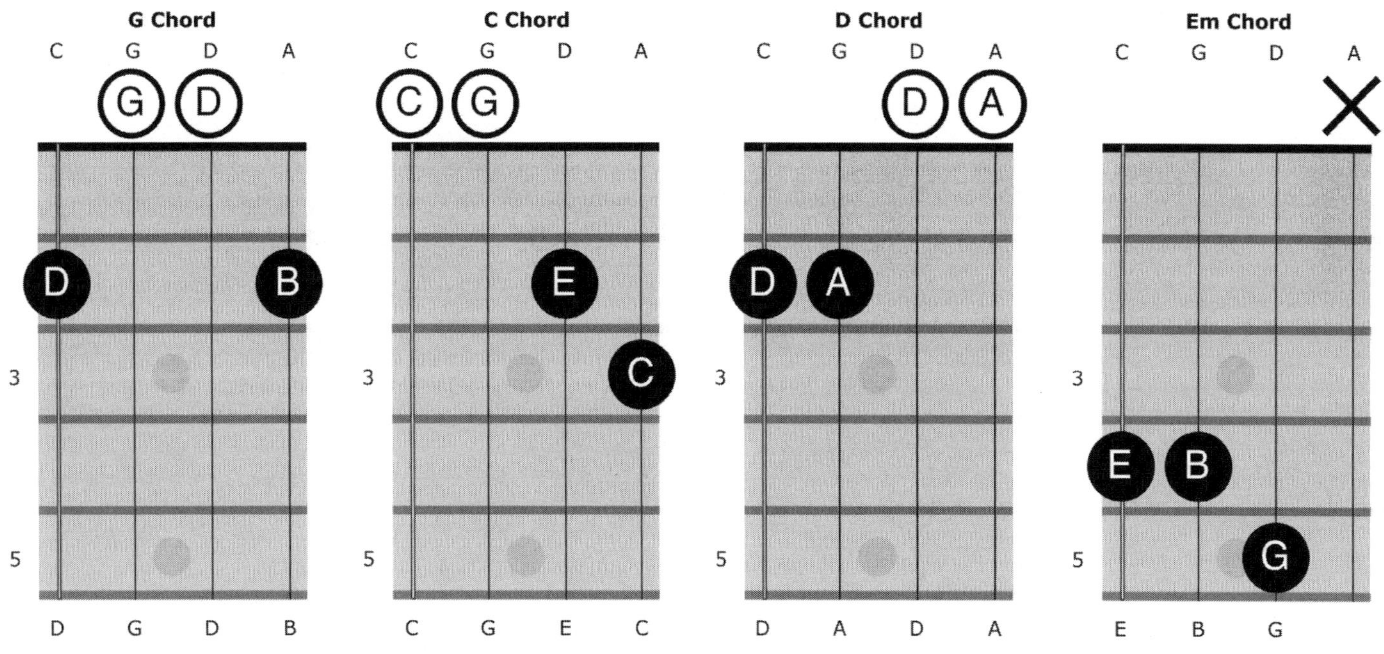

Figure 138: Chords in the Key of G Major/Em – Fretboard View

Chords in the Key of A Major/F♯m

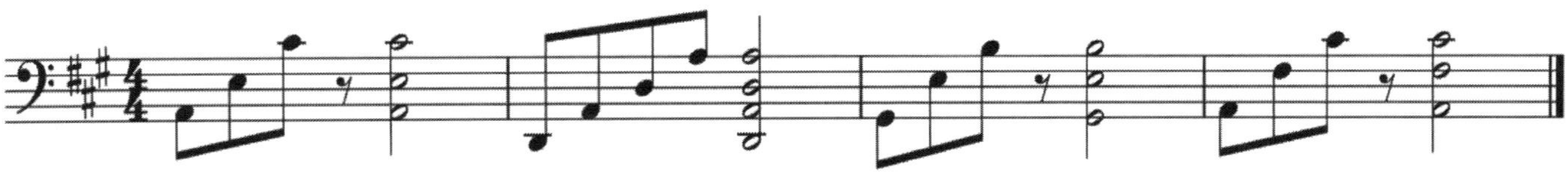

Figure 139: Chords in the Key of A Major/F♯m

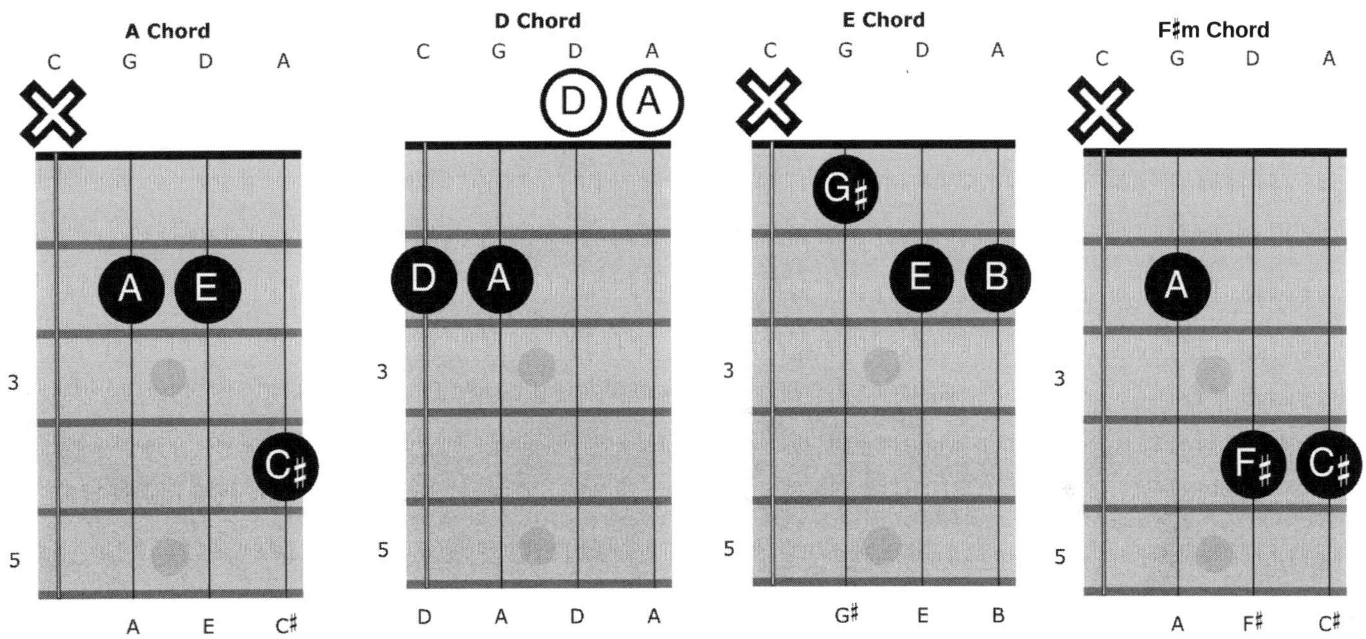

Figure 140: Chords in the Key of A Major/F♯m – Fretboard View

Those with an extensive background in music theory will notice that the D chord is actually just two pairs of perfect 5th intervals. In theory, a chord must have three distinct notes. Because the D and A notes are a fifth apart, this is technically a D5 or **power chord**. It functions either as a D major or a Dm chord. As the power chord is missing the major or minor 3rd interval, it can function as <u>either</u> a major or minor chord, particularly in the presence of other chord-capable instruments. Can you see how easy it would be to make it a Dm chord? Just play the F natural on the third fret of string ②. The index finger can barre the D and A.

There is limited value in purchasing a "Mandocello Chord Book" because so many chord shapes would be unplayable for those with an average-sized hand. So, how do you "create" the additional chords you might need? By applying simple chord theory. To do this you will have to know the scales in the mandocello-friendly keys.

3.5 Chord Theory as Applied to the Mandocello

Any chord, regardless of the instrument that plays it, requires at least three harmonically related notes, defined in a specific interval relationship. If we assign the number 1 to the root note, then we add the third and fifth notes in that key to create a major chord. We have already introduced the common chords in the key of G and A in the previous section. Let's analyze how to play the major chords in the key of C.

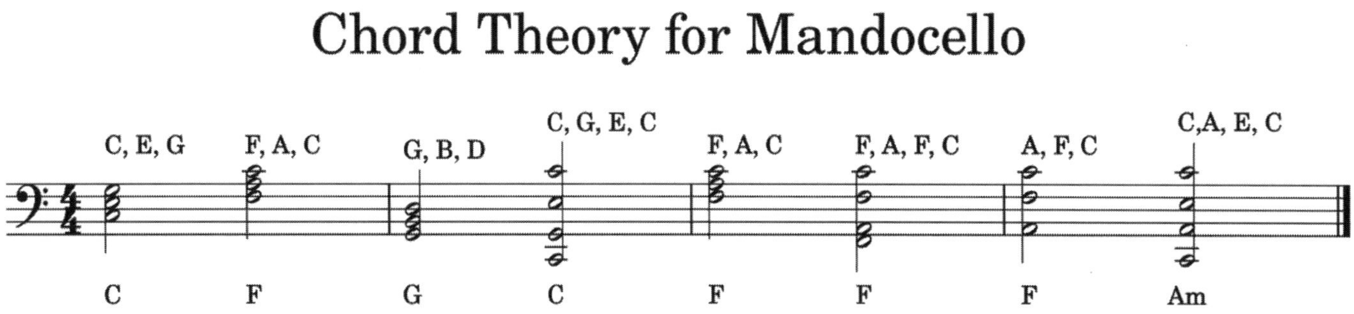

Figure 141: Chord Theory for Mandocello

To create a major chord in root position, the first, third and fifth notes in a given key would be required; in C major, that's C – E – G. In measure 1 above we see the first C chord with the C, E, and G notes "stacked" on top of each other in intervals of a third. Now, grab your mandocello and try to play the first chord in measure 1; you won't be able to because the E and G both occur on the D string. [It is possible to arpeggiate this chord, but we are speaking with reference to strumming the chord.] The F and G chords in measures 1 and 2 likewise cannot be strummed. In order to play a three-note chord on three separate strings, we need to rearrange the notes to create some combination or **inversion** of at least three notes and possibly four; furthermore, the notes must lie in sufficient proximity so our fingers can reach them.

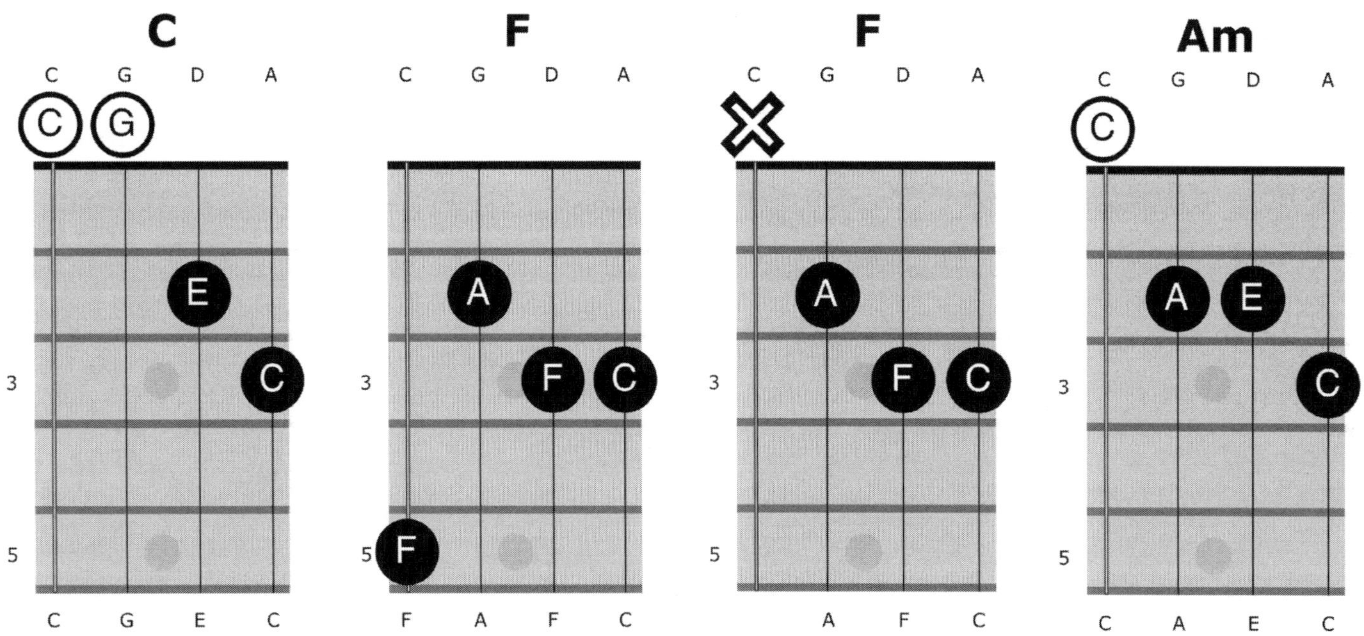

Figure 142: Common Chords in the Key of C Major

The chord diagrams shown above repeat the C chord from the previous section and show two forms of the F chord. You may find it impossible to play the first F chord. The simple solution is to avoid playing the fourth string and just strum strings ③, ②, and ①.

Minor Chords: To create a minor chord, lower the 3rd degree of the major scale (the 3rd of the chord) by one half-step. The primary chords in the key of C major are C, F, G, and A minor (Am). The A minor chord consists of A, C, and E. The diagram above shows the Am chord starting with the C on the fourth string. Alternatively, do not play the C and just play a 3-note version of the chord.

Dominant Seventh Chords: The dominant seventh chord (V7), based on the 5th degree of the major scale, is popular in folk and blues tunes. It consists of a major triad (1, 3, 5) with a flat seventh (♭7) note added. So, in principle, we should be able to create a Dom7/V7 chord on the mandocello with the 1, 3, 5, and ♭7 on four separate strings. The following chord diagram shows some common V7 chords.

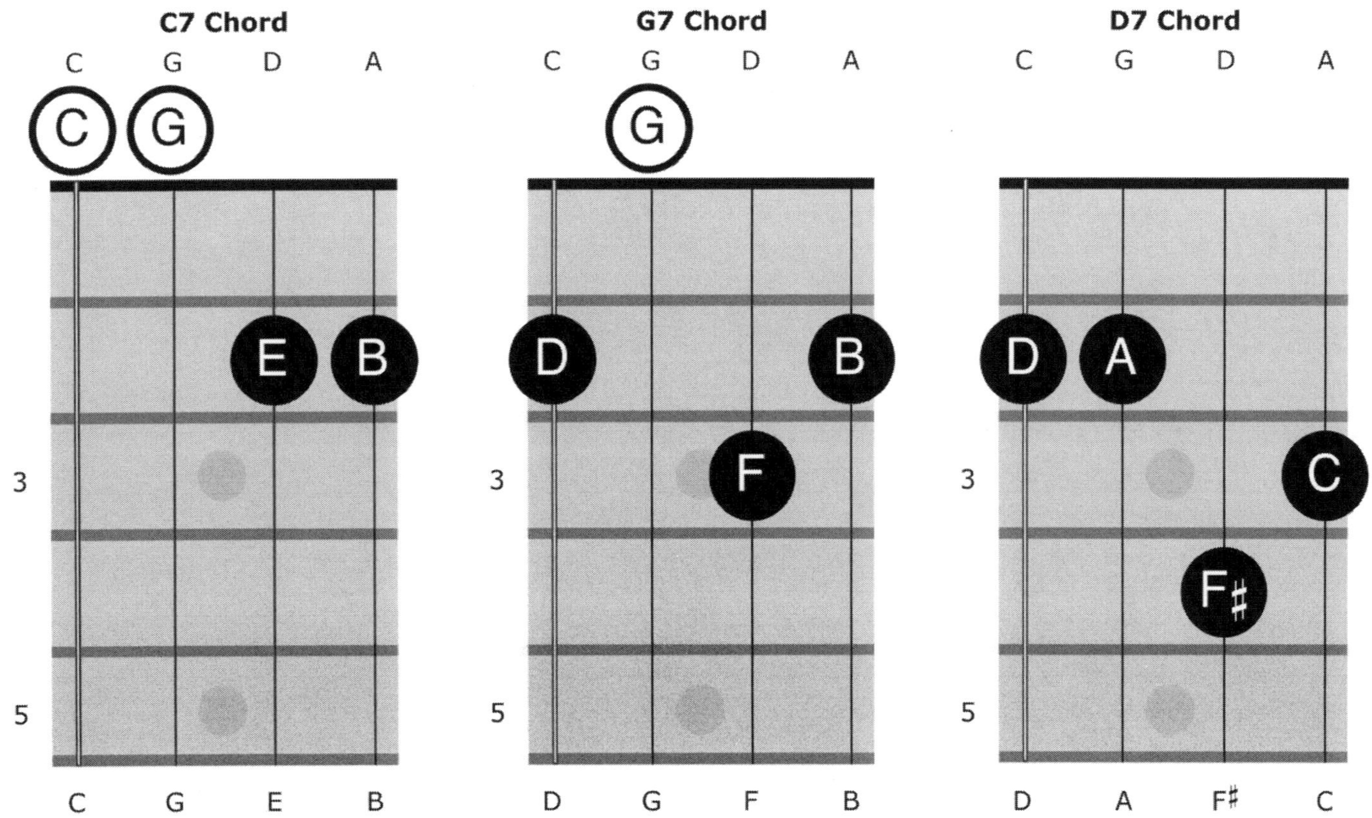

Figure 143: Dominant/V7 Chords

Whenever it becomes impossible to play all four notes on four separate strings, consider the following guidelines:

1. If another instrument is already playing the root note, the mandocellist can skip it.

2. The flatted-seventh note is obviously the note that should not be dropped.

3. The third degree note is more important than the fifth degree note because it gives the chord its major or minor quality.

3.6 Sight-Reading Sessions

The ability to sight-read music is a skill essential to advancing as a mandocellist. In ensemble playing, the mandocellist is often called upon to play in almost every type of ensemble, since it is the only bass clef instrument within the mandolin family. The mandocello can play the double-bass part whenever a mandocello part does not exist.

The opportunity to sight-read specific music for the mandocello may seem limited; sight-reading workshops or sessions are common at mandolin conventions, but where else can you find that opportunity? There is nothing to prevent the mandocellist to advocate for the instrument while volunteering to join guitar ensembles or more eclectic music groups, including bluegrass, jazz jams and Irish music sessions. Take the initiative by researching potential scores and creating separate 3-ring binders for the other instruments that might come to a sight-reading session. The classical music repertoire is immense, with Vivaldi and Bach being two favorite composers at mandolin conventions. Prepare by practicing the cello or bass parts for at least one popular tune for each session. You will probably hear the question “What’s next?”

That’s up to you. Have fun playing the mandocello!

About the Author

Mark E. Freemantle has been playing fretted instruments since the age of six when his father showed him how to play his first 3 guitar chords, then handed him a *Mel Bay* guitar method book. As a teenager he spent a brief period attempting to play in a rock band, but abandoned that effort when he acquired a 12-string acoustic guitar. His family obtained a 1912 Gibson F2 mandolin upon purchasing a home from a retiree who no longer planned to play the instrument. During his college days he was able to take both a 12-string guitar and a mandolin with him on a ten-week tour of Germany for the U.S. Army Chaplin Corps while performing with a contemporary Christian music group. He continues to play 12-string guitar in his church's praise band and is also a neophyte jazz guitarist.

In March of 1995 he had the opportunity to hear Marilyn Mair perform and immediately joined the local mandolin and guitar orchestra in Arlington, Virginia [www.mandoleers.org]. He switched from mandolin to mandocello a few years later. He has served as the orchestra's webmaster, mandolin and mandocello instructor, digital librarian and is a former president of the organization.